The Day
Before
Doomsday

Previous Books

THE LABOR WARS
THE PROMISE AND PITFALLS OF REVOLUTION
POVERTY, YESTERDAY AND TODAY
THE FORGING OF THE AMERICAN EMPIRE
THE MILITARY INDUSTRIAL COMPLEX
POVERTY—AMERICA'S ENDURING PARADOX
WHAT UNIONS DO
RADICALISM IN AMERICA
A COUNTRY IS BORN
THE FUTILE CRUSADE—ANTI-COMMUNISM AS AMERICAN CREDO
AFRICA, AWAKENING GIANT
WORKING MEN
THE CRISIS OF AMERICAN LABOR
A WORLD IN REVOLUTION
THE COUNTERFEIT REVOLUTION
LEFT, RIGHT AND CENTER

The Day Before Doomsday

AN ANATOMY OF THE NUCLEAR ARMS RACE

Sidney Lens

BEACON PRESS *BOSTON*

To
Shirley

First published as a Beacon Paperback in 1978
by arrangement with Doubleday & Company, Inc.

Beacon Press books are published under the auspices
of the Unitarian Universalist Association

Published simultaneously in Canada by
Fitzhenry & Whiteside Limited, Toronto

Library of Congress Cataloging in Publication Data

Lens, Sidney.
   The day before doomsday.
   Includes index.
   1.   Atomic weapons and disarmament.   2. United
States—Military policy.   I. Title.

JX1974.4.L348   327 .174   78-53086
ISBN 0-8070-0491-X

Acknowledgments

I'd like to thank Erwin Knoll, editor of the *Progressive* magazine, who has been editing articles of mine for years and who spent a considerable amount of time on this manuscript giving me expert advice and suggestions. I'd also like to thank Samuel H. Day, Jr., editor of the *Bulletin of the Atomic Scientists,* for similar help and most especially for checking scientific facts and figures. Professor Milton Leitenberg of the Center for International Studies at Cornell University generously made available to me his voluminous library on military affairs, and Harry Zubkoff of the Office of the Secretary of the Air Force was kind enough to give me access to a massive file of newspaper clippings. I'd also like to express my gratitude to Howard Bray and the Fund for Investigative Journalism, which subsidized part of the research, and to scores of people who graciously submitted to interviews and questioning.

Contents

Foreword

The thirty-ninth President of the United States, Jimmy Carter, inherits a nuclear arms race that started during the administration of the thirty-third President, Harry S. Truman.

Addressing himself to that problem at a press conference two months before his inauguration, Carter expressed the hope that the United States and the Soviet Union would be able "to freeze present developments and then to lower, step by step, the quantity, at least the quantity, of atomic weapons on which we presently depend, with an ultimate goal of reducing dependence on atomic weapons to zero."

Encouraging as this may sound to those who seek a termination of the nuclear race, the fact is that every President since World War II has made similar statements, and usually more forcefully.

The Baruch Plan, presented to the United Nations in 1946 under the sponsorship of President Truman, provided that:

"1. Manufacture of atomic bombs shall stop.

"2. Existing bombs shall be disposed of . . ."

President Eisenhower, in his address to the United Nations (December 8, 1953) on "atomic power for peace," called on the superpowers to "begin to diminish the potential destructive power of the world's atomic stockpiles."

President Kennedy, in the course of proposing a "Program for General and Complete Disarmament" to the United Nations in the fall of 1961, pictured the horror of "a nuclear disaster, spread by wind and water and fear," and asserted that "mankind must put an end to war—or war will put an end to mankind." "The risks inherent in disarmament," he continued, "pale in comparison to the risks inherent in an unlimited arms race."

President Johnson, during his first year in office, proposed the

same kind of verified freeze on nuclear weapons as Mr. Carter—
twelve years earlier. When he signed the Non-Proliferation Treaty
in 1968, Johnson hailed it as "the most important international
agreement in the field of disarmament since the Nuclear Age
began," and promised "to make this but a first step toward ending
the peril of nuclear war." The treaty itself pledged that Washington and Moscow would "pursue negotiations in good faith" for
"cessation of the nuclear arms race."

President Nixon, in an address to Congress (February 18,
1970), observed that "The nuclear era places on the two prepon-
derant powers a unique responsibility to explore means of limiting
military competition. . . . Agreement to limit strategic nuclear
weapons would be an unprecedented achievement not only in the
field of arms control, but also in the evolution of political relations."

President Ford's Secretary of State, Henry Kissinger, expressed
the view in 1975 that an impending SALT II treaty based on
the principles agreed to at Vladivostok between Ford and Soviet
leader, Leonid Brezhnev, "will mean a cap has been put on the
arms race for at least ten years."

There has been no end of rhetoric for peace, disarmament, and
arms limitation. Yet despite six thousand negotiation sessions on
disarmament under the auspices of the United Nations, not a single nuclear warhead has been destroyed as a result of agreement
between the superpowers. On the contrary, the stockpiles are
growing, new weapons are being engineered, and perhaps most
alarming of all, the world stands at the threshold of a *second* nuclear age in which membership in the nuclear club will be almost
universal. By 1985, according to President Ford, forty nations will
have the nuclear material and the capability to produce nuclear
weapons. By 1995 the figure is expected to be a hundred nations.

Clearly, rhetoric and reality are not in accord. The question is
why?

Are the men in power insincere, or do we face an impersonal
process, generated by deeply entrenched bureaucracies, which
forges ahead on its own thrust? Does President Carter really want
to contain and reverse that process; assuming he does, can he?

And what of "we, the people"? Are we really safe under a "balance of terror" and a policy of MAD ("mutual assured destruc-

tion"); or are we in fact an "endangered species," facing actual extinction unless we take matters into our own hands?

I have surveyed in these pages the background of what, to me, seems to be the greatest crisis in humankind's existence. I have tried to be realistic rather than diplomatic, and if the recitation is often somber, so is the situation we find ourselves in. I hope I have compensated for it in the last chapter by offering a program to meet the challenge. Even more, I hope this book will help initiate a broad discussion.

Sidney Lens

1

Spoon-fed Myths

The first nuclear age—we are now in the second one—dates from three events in mid-1945: the testing of an atomic device at Alamogordo and the atomic bombardment of Hiroshima and Nagasaki.

Harry Truman was returning home aboard the cruiser *Augusta* from a seventeen-day conference with Churchill and Stalin at Potsdam when the second of these events took place. As he paced the deck he was handed a note he had been anxiously waiting for: the first atom bomb ever used in warfare had been "successfully" dropped by a B-29, the *Enola Gay,* on the Japanese city of Hiroshima. The President, in office less than four months, was exuberant. Turning to a group of sailors he exclaimed: "This is the greatest thing in history."

In a message to the American people that day, read from Washington by Secretary of War Stimson, the President radiated the pride of a nation touched by the wand of destiny: "What has been done is the greatest achievement of organized science in history." Lauding "the capacity of industry to design, and of labor to operate, the machines and methods to do things never done before," he boasted that there was no other country where such a "combination could be got together." Truman also flexed the American muscle. Addressing the enemy, he warned that the United States was "now prepared to obliterate more rapidly and completely every productive enterprise the Japanese have above ground in any city. We shall destroy their docks, their factories, and their communications."

With these remarks Harry Truman in effect christened the nuclear age and set the stage for America's role in it. That role in 1945 seemed awesome and unassailable, but looking back a generation later, "the greatest thing in history" does not appear quite so lustrous. It was certainly "the greatest" in terms of military technology; it represented a quantum jump in the art of warfare that was indescribable. Until then the most devastating bomb dropped from the air had been the "grand slam," or blockbuster, about ten tons of TNT. But by applying the principle of fission to uranium an explosion had been produced equal to 13,000 tons of TNT. Human ingenuity had devised a means of killing human beings far beyond anything known before, and it seemed to Truman and most of his inner circle that the nation which had a monopoly of this instrument—even a head start—had the wherewithal to impose its will on world affairs for a long time to come. The peaceful potential of fission, moreover, offered prospects in the near future of cheap and limitless supplies of electricity, again giving the nation with a head start an impressive advantage. This was the day, it may be said, when American ambitions knew no bounds.

None of it came to pass. The Bomb did not bring the United States a single significant victory, military or diplomatic—as Henry Kissinger, an early and eager fan of The Bomb, was to concede years later. Even the victory over Japan, in the view of many generals (Eisenhower, for instance) and historians, could have been achieved without it, and probably at about the same time. As for the peaceful reactor that was supposed to solve the energy problem, not only has it worked below technical expectations and created problems relative to radioactive waste and security that put its utility to question, but it is the means by which nuclear arms are about to proliferate to dozens of countries that would not have had them otherwise. The upbeat tenor of Truman's remarks has not been confirmed by subsequent events. On the contrary, the legacy of "the greatest thing in history" has been an arms race more ominous than any in the past—one that is self-propelled by a

rampant technology, and a constituency many times more powerful than the old "merchants of death." Like a plane flying on instruments, it proceeds on its own.

A second feature of the nuclear age, the tendency to sail into
uncharted waters without due regard to the dangers ahead, similarly belies the "greatness" of the "greatest thing in history."
The Bomb came on the scene unexpectedly, a creature of wartime,
with no one outside a select number of top government officials
and a few hundred scientists really knowing what it could do or
what its portent was for the future. It would be years before the
veil would be partly lifted, much too late for temperate discussion,
evaluation, or vote. It is evident in retrospect, however, that no
one at the decision-making level really weighed the full implications of the atom. Here for the first time since homo sapiens had
made his appearance on planet Earth, he was about to draw energy from a source that did not originate with the sun. It was the
kind of technological development that, like the domestication of
animals, the discovery of agriculture, and the industrial revolution,
was bound to change humankind's social structure. Few people,
however, weighed these implications.

At a meeting of an elite "Interim Committee" called together on
May 31, 1945, the ailing but alert seventy-seven-year-old Henry
L. Stimson, Secretary of War, urged the members not to think
of the fission bomb "as a new weapon merely but as *a revolutionary
change in the relations of man and the universe.*" It was not as
if the scientists were tinkering with an advanced type of chemical
explosive that might destroy, say, ten buildings instead of five. It
was a discovery of a new dimension, with far more unknown than
known. Yet as Martin J. Sherwin asserts in his book *A World Destroyed,* there never was any question in the minds of those who
approved the atomic program that if The Bomb could be made,
it would be used.

The scientists who conducted the first atomic test at Alamogordo Air Base, New Mexico, on July 16, 1945, were confident
the device would work and confident that the chain reaction had
finite limits. But they weren't *sure.* Arthur H. Compton, director
of the atomic energy program at the University of Chicago and a
member of President Roosevelt's Top Policy Group of scientific
administrators, told novelist Pearl Buck of a discussion he had

with J. Robert Oppenheimer, the scientific chief of the project, during The Bomb's development period. The two men asked themselves, Compton recalls, how the chain reaction would affect "the hydrogen in seawater. Might not the explosion of the atomic bomb set off an explosion of the ocean itself? Nor was this all that Oppenheimer feared. The nitrogen in the air is also unstable, though less in degree. Might not it, too, be set off by an atomic explosion in the atmosphere?" The planet, in other words, could be "vaporized." Such a result obviously "would be the ultimate catastrophe. Better to accept the slavery of the Nazis," Compton concluded, "than to run the chance of drawing the final curtain on mankind!"

On the Monday morning that the test was made, according to Stephane Groueff in a book on the Manhattan Project (published in 1967), Enrico Fermi, the physicist who had effected the first chain reaction under the Alonzo Stagg Stadium of the University of Chicago, "was making bets with his colleagues on whether The Bomb would ignite the atmosphere, and, if so, whether it would destroy only New Mexico—or the entire world." Tortured by such questions Compton ordered a mathematical recalculation of the possibility of these kinds of accidents. "If it were proved," he reminisced to Ms. Buck, "that the chances were more than approximately three to one million" he intended to scrap the test. With one or two exceptions all scientists today discount the idea that a chain reaction can be so continuous as to destroy the planet —Hans Bethe calls it "absurd," "utter absolute nonsense"—but in 1945 they weren't so sanguine. One can only speculate whether, if the American citizenry had known these odds, it would have given its sanction to proceed with atomic experiments. Odds of 999,997 to 3 that an automobile won't crash on the freeway may be acceptable to the average driver, but similar odds that the planet won't blow up might make at least the timid hesitate. Nor has the American citizenry ever been given the odds or been consulted on a single major facet of nuclear development since then.

To a considerable extent science was shooting in the dark. The scientists on the Interim Committee, which selected four possible targets for The Bomb (Hiroshima, Nagasaki, Kokura, Niigata), had calculated that 20,000 people would die from each incident. But they so underestimated the effects of fire and radiation that the number who did perish in Hiroshima was four times as great, 78,000 (plus 84,000 injured and 62,000 buildings and homes pulverized). The number of deaths at Nagasaki was somewhat less, 27,000 killed (and 41,000 wounded), but only because the drop was a mile off target. (Incidentally, had it been three miles off target in the other direction it would have killed 1,000 American prisoners of war whom American intelligence knew nothing about.) From Nagasaki to the present, there has been uncertainty and room for argument on every important atomic event. The Arms Control and Disarmament Agency today concedes that "many of the important discoveries about nuclear weapons effects have been made not through deliberate scientific inquiry but by accident." Such has been the mesmerizing impact of The Bomb, however, that American leaders—then and now—continue to plunge mindlessly into the hazards of the unknown.

Most disquieting of all, perhaps, has been the penchant for manipulating public attitudes—through concealment, misinformation, and skillful deflection of attention from the true intent of national policy. A listener on August 6, 1945, hearing Truman's paeans of national self-congratulations on radio, could not have guessed that scores of scientists who had produced The Bomb had pleaded with their government not to use it; that such generals as Dwight D. Eisenhower and Henry H. (Hap) Arnold had had grave misgivings about it; that the man most responsible for initiating the atomic program in 1939, Leo Szilard, and others who had made decisive contributions to fission science, most notably Niels Bohr, had warned—correctly, as it turned out—of an impending nuclear arms race. Admittedly wartime is not an ideal moment for discussion and balloting on whether to use a certain weapon. But a democratic dialogue could hardly have done any harm: everyone is agreed that there was nothing the Japanese could have done on or after August 6, 1945, which could have saved them from defeat. And in any event, a technological innovation which changed the relations "between man and the universe" should have warranted debate in any kind of circumstance.

Popular acceptance of The Bomb was achieved in 1945 by playing on pride; subsequently manipulation was accomplished by a curious admixture of reassurance and fear. Before the Soviets had acquired or even tested their first atomic device, for instance,

Lieutenant General Leslie R. Groves, who had headed the Manhattan Project to develop nuclear weaponry, warned that in the first five hours of a nuclear attack 40 million Americans would be killed; and General Carl A. Spaatz cautioned that it would be too late for defense after the atomic bombs started falling. By drawing this ominous picture the military was able to win approval for a $12-billion budget in fiscal 1948. Simultaneously, however—then and every year since—the Administration has resolutely insisted that if "we are strong" there is nothing to worry about. If so, at what point—if ever—are we "strong" enough?

II

The consequence of all this is a disquieting dichotomy between the perceptions of the American public and the objectives of the American government.

Napoleon once said that you can do anything with bayonets but sit on them. In our times the popular notion seems to be that "you can do anything with nuclear bombs but use them." They are indispensable for something called "deterrence," they are essential for maintaining world "stability," and their core material, enriched uranium or plutonium, is capable of generating enough low-cost electricity to solve the world's energy problems. But—and this is the conventional wisdom—they are too frightening for any world leader (unless, of course, he is a madman) ever to set them off.

This general conviction is buttressed by the statements of national heroes such as Eisenhower that "war has become not just tragic but preposterous. With modern weapons there can be no victory for anyone." Or the even more explicit remarks of General Douglas MacArthur, that "war has become a Frankenstein to destroy both sides. . . . No longer does it possess the chance of the winner of the duel—it contains, rather, the germs of double suicide." So too the picturesque comment by John F. Kennedy after the 1962 Cuban missile crisis—that "the fruits of victory would be ashes in our mouth"—appears to indicate that while the young President was willing to brandish his nuclear stick he would not have plunged us into atomic terror because he understood its consequences.

Every President and every Secretary of Defense during the nuclear age has asserted with what seems to be genuine conviction, that "our" bombs are for "peace" not war, for "defense" not "aggression," for "readiness" not for use. "The primary purpose of our arms," President Kennedy told Congress in 1961, "is peace, not war—to make certain that they will never have to be used—to deter all wars, general or limited, nuclear or conventional, large or small—to convince all aggressors that any attack will be futile." The essence of this message, though in less florid prose, has been oft repeated. "The primary U.S. objective," said Secretary Donald H. Rumsfeld in presenting his fiscal 1977 report to Congress, "is, of course, deterrence and international stability. . . . We are not the world's policeman and we do not pretend to be." Among the goals he set for himself was "to reduce the perils of nuclear war. . . . To build a rational relationship with potential adversaries. . . . To help resolve regional conflicts that imperil global peace."

The American people, by and large, either accept such assertions as coin of the realm, or tune out their fears; and they have conjured in their minds—based on what they have heard that the word "deterrence" means—an image of how peace will be maintained. The United States aims its nuclear missiles against Soviet cities, the Soviets aim their missiles at American cities, and in this "balance of terror"—*stalemate*—lies the miracle of peace, or at least non-war. Because the United States has enough weapons in its arsenal to totally devastate the enemy even if it strikes first, the enemy is deterred. The Bomb, in sufficient number, thereby guarantees safety, security, survival.

But what does "sufficiency" mean? Here begins the divergence between conventional wisdom and reality. Early in the Cold War the military informed Truman that it needed 400 atomic bombs to keep the Soviets from becoming belligerent. Some years later, in May 1956, General Earle Partridge told a congressional subcommittee that fifty nuclear devices would destroy or bring under fire 40 per cent of the Soviet population and 60 per cent of its industry; one weapon per target, he said, was enough. The National Planning Association, in a 1958 study, concluded that 200 warheads would be adequate to demolish "a large nation-state." In the early 1960's, members of Kennedy's national security staff were saying privately—according to one such member—that the Russians could be deterred with 100 missiles. That would suffice to knock out or render inoperative the nine Soviet cities with a million or more population—plus many of the lesser ones. Robert McNamara, Defense Secretary under both Kennedy and Johnson, in the latter days of his career put the figure somewhat higher: 400 one-megaton bombs (equal to a million tons of TNT each) would deter a general war. This would assure destruction of 76 per cent of the Soviet industrial plant and 74 million of its people. McGeorge Bundy, who was in charge of the White House "War Room" from 1961 to 1966, wrote in *Foreign Affairs* (October 1969) that "ten bombs on ten cities would be a disaster beyond history; and a hundred bombs on a hundred cities are unthinkable." In his opinion ten to a hundred missiles, if "deliverable," would deter an enemy.

These are modest figures—offered by men with an intimate knowledge of militarism. They raise the question as to why the nuclear race could not have been stopped a long time ago. Whether computed in firepower, delivery vehicles, or warheads, the Pentagon obviously has many times what is required for simple "deterrence." In firepower, by the calculations of Ruth Leger Sivard, former chief economist of the Arms Control and Disarmament Agency, the United States possessed as of 1975 "a nuclear stockpile of 8,000 megatons"—equal to eight billion tons of TNT; or, to put it another way, firepower the equivalent of 615,385 Hiroshima-type bombs. "Using the Hiroshima analogy," says Ms. Sivard, "the nuclear stockpile of the United States alone translates into a potential kill-power 12 times the present world population." In terms of delivery vehicles the United States had at its disposal 1,054 land-based Minutemen and Titan missiles, 656 Polaris/Poseidon missiles on 41 submarines, and approximately 500 strategic bombers; most of these capable of carrying two, three, or more warheads, each targeted at a different city or silo. In terms of warheads the U.S. in 1975 held 8,500 strategic weapons (those designed for a long-distance exchange with the Soviet Union) and 22,000 tactical bombs (equal in power in many instances to strategic weapons, but designed for use in a "limited" war). In addition the factories were assembling three nuclear weapons a day, as they had been doing each day for the previous four years. These are, it should be noted, conservative figures; Milton Leitenberg of the Cornell Center for International Studies, a long-time observer of nuclear affairs, puts the arsenal at almost double that figure, "at least 50,000."

A supply so large cannot be reconciled with the thesis that Washington is trying to preserve a stalemate, a balance of terror. The standard rebuttal by militarists, of course, is that we need this enormous stock as a reserve, if the Russians knock out many or most of our missiles in a surprise assault, a "first strike." But this argument has two ineradicable flaws: (1) that at every stage of the arms race it has been the United States which set the pace—the United States which first acquired the A-bomb, the H-bomb, the intercontinental ballistics missile (ICBM), the nuclear submarine, the MIRV, the MARV, the cruise missile, the miniaturized nuclear bomb, the guided weapons for an automated war; and (2) even if the Russians did demolish all the U.S. land-based missiles—an unlikely possibility—any single one of the 41 nuclear submarines, each with up to 160 warheads, could level Soviet cities and industries beyond hope of viability. In any case, no less an authority than former Defense Secretary James R. Schlesinger denigrates the notion that Moscow was prepared to or capable of a "first strike" in the 1950's, when the nuclear race gained its head of steam. "In the 50's," writes Schlesinger, the Strategic Air Command (SAC) "began to fear that the Soviets . . . would launch a war by attacking our strategic forces—and possibly our cities as well. There was, of course, every reason to protect ourselves . . . by strengthening our second-strike posture. Nonetheless, all too many Americans deceived themselves into regarding a Soviet 'bolt from the blue' as a relatively probable event." Evidently it wasn't; yet the mountain continued to grow—upwards and sideways. According to former Senator Stuart Symington, the arsenal—like a grocery warehouse—carries twenty-six distinct types of weapons (each with dozens of variations for different purposes) such as free-fall bombs, glide bombs, air-to-surface missiles, surface-to-surface, surface-to-air, tube artillery, and so forth and so on. New guidance mechanisms based on the computer can now bring missiles so close to target they multiply their effectiveness many fold. Why then 30,000 warheads—to threaten the 218 Soviet cities with a population of 100,000 or more? There is no rational explanation for this immense arsenal on the theory of simple deterrence; some other explanation must be sought.

The conventional wisdom runs aground on other shoals as well. Allegedly the American posture is defensive, to *retaliate* against aggression. But periodically strong hints emanate from Washington of *aggressive* intent. "Our arms," said President Kennedy in 1961, "will never be used to strike the first blow . . ." Kennedy's Defense Secretary McNamara, however, was soon propounding a military strategy which promised to do just that: strike the first blow. In a commencement address at Ann Arbor, Michigan, on June 16, 1962, the Secretary outlined a strategy for "counterforce" which belied a defensive posture. America's "principal military objectives," he said, "should be the destruction of the enemy's military forces, not his civilian population." Instead of a "counter-city" or "counter-value" strategy, which would kill tens of millions of people, the Pentagon would focus on destroying the enemy's bombers and missiles, hidden away in isolated areas.

To the uninitiate, "counter-force" seemed loftily humane. Instead of aiming at people, it would aim at missile silos, reducing the death toll—what the militarists in their exquisite language call "collateral damage"—to a minimum. This was, many felt, in the American tradition, confining the war to destruction of property, not people. The counter-force doctrine, however, was not quite so well intentioned; it was a synonym in fact for aggression, a surprise attack. The reason is obvious. It makes no sense to hit the enemy's missile silos if the missiles themselves are no longer there —if they have been dispatched simultaneously with, or before, the American missiles were set off. In that case the Pentagon's hardware would hit empty holes. The essential requirement of counterforce, therefore, was that U.S. missiles and bombers must be aloft and near target before the enemy knows what is happening. Thus, while Kennedy was denying that America would ever strike first, his Secretary of Defense was elaborating a plan—and retargeting his missiles—to give the United States exactly that capability.

Both McNamara and Kennedy, of course, denied an offensive purpose. In their scenario the counter-force strategy would be put in play only if Western Europe "was being overrun [by Russia] with *conventional* forces"; America's action would be a *response* to the other side's aggression. Be that as it may, it is evident that the former Ford Motor Company executive and the President were thinking beyond an uncomplicated stalemate. What they seemed to be saying, in fact, was that deterrence may not be workable, and that we must therefore plan other options, including first use of nuclear weapons.

McNamara himself understood there was an inconsistency in the McNamara Doctrine. American officials for years had been saying that they had more than enough warheads to take the bluster out of the Soviets. The United States—despite Kennedy's rash, and false, claim during the 1960 election campaign, that there was a "missile gap"—held unquestioned superiority in the instruments of megadeath. By the time the ex-Senator from Massachusetts was installed as President the storehouse contained many times the 400 that the Pentagon itself had told Truman was enough—and far, far more powerful weapons at that. In that arsenal were now 2,000 10-megaton hydrogen bombs, each with almost 800 times the firepower of the Hiroshima bombs, and 1,600 24-megaton bombs, each almost 2,000 times as powerful—as well as warheads of lesser capacity. As of 1963, according to a Pentagon strategist and writer, Colonel G. W. Casey, the United States was armed with 7,000 strategic warheads (slightly less than today) and 25,000 tactical warheads (slightly more). Presumably the Russians should have been terrified into immobility, especially since the estimate at the National Security Council at the time—according to one of its former staff members—was that the Kremlin had only 60 intercontinental ballistic missiles (and few bombers) capable of reaching the American mainland. Raymond Aron, in his book *The Great Debate,* puts the estimate by "United States sources" at "50 to 100." How, then, was it possible that the Russians were not "deterred"? How could they be so misguided as to contemplate attack on the United States in face of these odds?

McNamara's explanation was a classic example of obfuscation. Yes, he said, deterrence is a sound policy that safeguards our nation from attack—but it is not an *absolute* safeguard. "The mere fact that no nation could *rationally* take steps leading to a nuclear war does not *guarantee* that a nuclear war cannot take place. Not only do nations sometimes act in ways that are hard to explain on a rational basis, but even when acting in a 'rational' way they sometimes, indeed disturbingly often, act on the basis of *misun-*

derstandings of the true facts of a situation" (emphasis added). If the Russians, even when rational, can misunderstand American motives and plans, it is just as conceivable that the United States can misunderstand their motives and plans—and launch a surprise attack on them. "Disturbingly often," then, deterrence would not deter; and if that is the case, what difference does it make whether the United States has 100 or 100,000 warheads? The explanation clearly does not explain.

McNamara, in the latter years of the Johnson administration, revised his attitude toward "counter-force." He retreated to a softer position, called in Pentagonese "Mutual Assured Destruction," or MAD. Each side would feel secure, he said, if it knew it could inflict "unacceptable" destruction on the other. "I would judge that a capability on our part to destroy, say, one-fifth to one-fourth of the Soviet population and one-half of her industrial capability would serve as an effective deterrent."

But the counter-force doctrine, like the chime of old clocks, keeps ringing. It is sometimes expressed negatively, sometimes in circumlocutious rhetoric, but it is there. "No President," said Richard Nixon in his 1972 foreign policy statement, "should be left with only one strategic course of action, particularly that of ordering the mass destruction of enemy civilians and facilities. . . . Our strategic policy should not be based solely on a capability of inflicting urban and industrial damage presumed to be beyond the level an adversary would accept." Oblique as is this language, its meaning is clear: the President must also have the option of ordering the destruction of the enemy's force—his silos, military bases, airfields—the option, in other words, of a surprise "first strike."

The most fervid advocate of counter-force in our times has been the brilliant ex-University of Virginia professor and former RAND journeyman James Schlesinger. "We have no desire," Schlesinger told a Senate Foreign Relations subcommittee during the Ford administration, "to develop a counter-force capability against the Soviet Union." That seems encouraging, but it is a denial followed by what sounds suspiciously like an affirmation: "What we wish to avoid is the Soviet Union having a counter-force capability against the United States *without our being able to have a comparable capability*" (emphasis added). Note the way in which this is put: "we" don't want to have the capability of striking first, but if "they" have that capability, "we" must have it too. The question, then, is do they have that capability? Of course, and the Secretary was quite aware of it.

In a 1975 report to five congressional committees on "The Theater Nuclear Force Posture in Europe," Schlesinger contends that "the Soviets apparently see escalation of war in Europe to nuclear conflict as likely," and they intend in that case to depend on the element of surprise. "Soviet declarations indicate that if the Warsaw Pact believes NATO is about to launch a major nuclear attack, it will seek to preempt with nuclear strikes on military targets"— counter-force in other words. And since *they* plan for it and have sufficient missiles at this point, both in their silos and submarines, to implement it, the inescapable conclusion from Schlesinger's convoluted words is that we too must have a counter-force capability.

Probing further behind the circumspect verbiage, it is evident that "first use" of nuclear weapons is high on the list of Washington's contemplated options. The President, said Schlesinger, must not be limited to a single strategy; he must have the capacity for "flexible response." That of course encompasses everything from a CIA operation to a counter-force nuclear war. Reporters repeatedly asked the former CIA director and RAND theorist whether there was anything new in his policy. No, not really, they were told; we have only made "a change in *targeting* strategy as it were" (emphasis added). Targeting, however, is the name of the game. If you target against the enemy's cities you are pursuing a policy of "counter-city" or "counter-value," as it is sometimes called. If you target against his silos and airfields you are pursuing the policy of "counter-force."

The United States, surfeited with missiles and warheads, is capable of and actually is targeting both—and in fact has been doing so for many years. The Air Force Chief of Staff, on March 25, 1974, told a Houston audience, "of course we did not in the past exclude military installations in our targeting. But now we have made this a statement of national policy." The 25,000 targets in the vast computer complex of the Single Integrated Operations Plan (SIOP)—so estimated by two New York *Times* writers— clearly must be much more inclusive than the few hundred Soviet cities. Anyway, it no longer matters. As Schlesinger told Congress in 1974, with the "Command Data Buffer system in all Minutemen III wings" the Air Force can "change target sets in the missile computer in 36 minutes" (it used to take between sixteen and twenty-four hours), and do it "remotely from the launch control center" rather than inside the missile silo. Even if there had been no change in "targeting strategy as it were," the Strategic Air Command can now redirect U.S. weapons against the Soviet Union's "force" in a mere half hour. "Deterrence," which implies that American strategists are thinking merely in terms of retaliating after the Russians strike first, takes on the character of myth when there are 150 times more bombs available than the Soviet Union has cities. Inevitably SIOP targeting will include the other side's "force," and if perchance it hasn't already been done—an assumption hard to believe—the change can be made almost immediately. The concept of "counter-force," "first strike," "pre-emptive strike," is thus inherent in the saturation of weaponry itself.

Presidents come and Presidents go but the logic of a massive stockpile impels in a single direction, not towards "defense" or "retaliation" but towards the "pre-emptive strike," when and if conditions are ripe, when and if American leaders feel they can reduce "damage" to their own industry and people, should nuclear war break out, to a tolerable level. Even as they try to play down the nuclear option they refuse to exclude it. Presidential candidate Jimmy Carter, in an interview with the New York *Times* June 24, 1976, seemed to rule out the "possibility of a limited nuclear war" because, he said, "once you start using these weapons you are likely to get into an all-out war." There being only two types of nuclear conflict, limited and total, that would appear to place Carter foursquare in opposition to the employment of super-weapons in any type of engagement.

Yet, when a team of interrogators from the Hearst newspapers asked Carter a month later whether he foresees "any circumstances in which we would be justified in resorting to a first strike with nuclear weapons," he replied that he would order a surprise, pre-emptive attack "if I was convinced that the existence or the security of our nation was threatened." Since he also included "our commitments to the security of Western Europe and Japan" as "inseparable from our own security" he opened the door to nuclear adventure much the same as other Presidents and presidential candidates have done. Each one, since 1945, has introduced changes in strategical emphasis, but in fact the formulations have always been determined not so much by the man as by the circumstances of a rampant technology and a mounting stockpile.

While denying that the United States is thinking of surprise attacks on the enemy, moreover, the Pentagon continues to develop weapons systems whose only purpose is to make surprise attack feasible. It has been concentrating, for instance, on improvements in the *accuracy* of ICBM's and the projected Trident submarine missiles, through the "stellar inertial guidance system" (SIG). This is of little advantage in a "second strike" against urban areas, but of immense import in penetrating the enemy's hardened missile silos. Concomitantly, the engineers and scientists have been put to work on a project to make land-based missiles *mobile*. By placing them on moving trucks, trains, and the big C-5A airplane, the Soviets will have difficulty keeping a "fix" on them.

Two new weapons in particular cater to the hit-them-first strategy—the maneuvering re-entry vehicle (MARV) and the cruise missile, both of which stress dead-center accuracy. You don't need an on-target bomb to wreck a city; even if it lands a mile or two from the center of town it will make a shambles of it. The 1945 Hiroshima warhead destroyed brick buildings and severely damaged steel construction 1.2 miles from where it exploded (Ground Zero). A 20-megaton bomb, which both sides can produce in abundance, would cause similar devastation up to 10.5 miles from Ground Zero—and that does not include the incendiary effects which would inflict first-degree burns 27 miles away, and radiation injuries and deaths that might occur much further from Ground Zero. Missile silos, however, are encased in concrete so thick that an attacking missile must come fairly close to knock it out of commission. In the absence of pinpoint accuracy, McNamara estimated years ago that six missiles would have to be launched against each enemy silo—"it takes a lot of missiles to destroy a fully hardened site," he said. Accuracy has improved since then, but it still requires three or four missiles, according to Dr. Leonard Rodberg, a military specialist at the Institute for Policy•Studies. If this ratio could be reduced to one on one the Pentagon would have an ideal counter-force weapon.

That is precisely what the researchers have on the drawing boards and what they expect to deploy within a decade. The

MARV—not to be confused with the MIRV, or MRV—is described by the *Bulletin of the Atomic Scientists* as "a new type of missile warhead that would be capable of changing direction in flight to evade defensive missiles fired on it." MARV has a homing device that guides it directly toward its objective during re-entry into the atmosphere.

The other wonder weapon, again magnificently suited for counter-force strategy, is the cruise missile, a delivery vehicle supported by small wings, and propelled by jet engines, which can be fired from an airplane or a submarine. The advantage of the cruise missile—an offspring of the World War II "buzz bomb"—is that it has been combined with a precision guidance system and is expected, in the not too distant future, to come within yards of its objective thousands of miles away.

According to MIT physicist Kosta Tsipis, the Pentagon is working on a Global Positioning System (GPS) "that would allow a missile to determine its position while in flight with an accuracy of 7 to 10 meters anywhere on the surface of the Earth . . ." This is a very marked "improvement" over present accuracy standards, which for U.S. missiles ranges from a fifth of a mile to a mile, and for Russian missiles from a half mile to two miles. GPS will be ready for deployment, says Tsipis, by 1980. The missile will be fitted with "terminal guidance" able to match the terrain and recognize the target through its computer; then zero in no further than 15 yards from its assigned destination. Only 246 inches long and 21 inches in diameter the long-range cruise missile will "fit a standard torpedo tube." A Polaris submarine can be equipped to carry a few dozen of them; a commercial 747 jet, 100 of them.

There are problems with the counter-force strategy, most notably that neither the United States nor the Soviet Union has as yet found a way to "kill" nuclear submarines. It is generally conceded that land-based missiles, even in hardened silos, are vulnerable to enemy missiles, but for the time being—and probably for quite a few more years—the nuclear submarine is relatively invulnerable. Though billions have been spent on anti-submarine warfare (ASW) research no one as yet has found a foolproof technique for tracking it down and destroying it—at least not in sufficient number. Since most of the Navy's forty-one subs, and many of the Kremlin's, can single-handedly devastate any nation on earth beyond recognition, counter-force is not yet a viable strategy. SAC may be able to annihilate most of Russia's "force" on land, but not on sea; and vice versa.

Nevertheless, though the Pentagon's preparations may be hobbled by the inability to score a breakthrough in anti-submarine warfare, they are quite evidently not geared to so limited an objective as achieving a stalemate with the Soviet Union. They are not designed, as the public has been led to believe, for "defense" or "deterrence"—at least not in the usual meaning of those words.

There are oddities in the behavior of the government which clearly belie its stated goals. Despite a vast stock of arms, for instance, Washington seldom speaks any more of "disarmament" but of "arms *control*"; and when it negotiates "arms control" agreements, they invariably provide for further increases in weaponry rather than decreases. The 1974 Vladivostok "agreement in principle" between Gerald Ford and Leonid Brezhnev, for instance, would permit both sides to double and triple the number of deliverable warheads each has today.

Political leaders repeat by rote the phrase "superiority"—not "equality" or "parity" or "less"—and they do it even while admitting that the Pentagon has the wherewithal to wipe the enemy off the map. "We have the full and complete ability," said Representative Gerald R. Ford, Jr., early in 1963, "to destroy the Soviet Union and win any war today. But I am still worried about the situation five years from now." Ford insisted that we must "push ahead with new programs which promise to maintain U.S. *superiority*," a theme he continued to emphasize from the White House—especially during the 1976 primaries, when he was challenged by Ronald Reagan. Everyone in Washington is aware of the military's "overkill" capacity, but nothing is done to reduce it. Senator John Sparkman, chairman of the Foreign Relations Committee, suggested in 1975 that we "stop this dangerous, ruinous rivalry," that we "simply recognize that overkill is overkill, and superfluous weapons are superfluous." The military budget for nuclear weapons in the next budget, however, was not pared.

Far too much is unexplained—or, if you will, deliberately deceptive—for anyone to rest easy with administration avowals. The nation, by way of example, has been told for many years that the President must have exclusive power to determine when and if the nuclear "button" will be pressed. The reason—so it is said—is that when the bombs and missiles start flying there will be no time to consult Congress or the public. Yet, when Secretary Schlesinger in 1974–75 propounded a new civil defense program, he argued that there would be *plenty of time* to remove tens of millions of citizens to rural areas, mines and caves. True, a missile could land here from Russia within thirty minutes, but according to the Secretary and his aides there would be at least a few days and probably weeks, while the diplomats were arguing, to ship most people from the cities. If that is so, there would also seem to be time to debate the subject of war and peace in Congress, even to take a popular referendum.

Such contradictions raise grave doubts, not so much about the integrity of leaders who say they want to avoid Doomsday, as about whether they are still masters of unfolding events, or impersonal vehicles for a self-fulfilling lunacy.

2

The Military Ladder

It is difficult to "make a fix" on the nuclear arms race because it is a moving target. The technology, the strategy, even the level of hostility between the two superpowers keep changing, like electrons jumping out of orbit, without preconceived pattern. There is, in addition, the feeling that it is a drama on another planet—no nuclear bomb has been dropped on people for more than three decades. In the distance, scientists and engineers work on fission bombs, fusion bombs, miniaturized bombs, nuclear submarines, missiles, MIRV's; strategists in Pentagon-sponsored research institutions—"think-tanks"—debate the virtues or vices of "counter-value" versus "counter-force," "unconditional" versus "conditional" deterrence, "second strike" versus "first strike," "mutual assured destruction" versus "damage-limitation," and speak in the strange, indigestible phrases that flow out of RAND and its sister think-tanks in endless torrents. But apart from the enduring conflict between the United States and the Soviet Union, there seem to be no threads that bind the nuclear arms race to the everyday world. It does not even seem to relate to normal military affairs; like the magician's wand it hangs in mid-air.

If we begin at the lower end of the spectrum of violence, however, the place of The Bomb in the calculus of modern war comes into focus. Though the general impression is that the nuclear era has been a "peaceful" one, in fact it has been marked by a spate of fierce "little" wars—each one a potential spark for bigger ones. According to a study by the Army War College Strategic Studies Institute in October 1975, the United States has been confronted with twenty-eight international crises since 1945, in which it had to make the choice of whether or not to employ military force; on twenty-three occasions it did act, ranging from what is called a military "presence" to direct intervention. Lincoln P. Bloomfield and Amelia C. Leiss, in their book on *Controlling Small Wars,* list fifty-three "local conflicts" in the quarter of a century from V-E Day to 1969, most of them involving the United States and the Soviet Union as off-stage participants—the Chinese civil war, the Algerian and Indochinese wars against France, the guerrilla wars in the Philippines, the internecine war in the Congo, the Middle East wars, Korea, Vietnam, and others. According to a report by Barry M. Blechman and Steven S. Kaplan of the Brookings Institution, issued in January 1977, the United States deployed its ships, aircraft, and troops in a "show of force" on 215 occasions since the end of World War II, while the Soviet Union did so on "at least" 115 occasions.

The fact that the world has not erupted in total war and that no bombs have fallen on American territory tends to obscure the reality that warfare has become more prevalent on the planet Earth than at any time in known history. Professor Istvan Kende, a Hungarian specialist on militarism, has made a study showing that from 1945 to 1969 there have been ninety-seven international and civil wars as against twenty-four from 1900 to 1941. The total period of warfare, says Kende, was nearly 300 years, an average of three years for each conflict. "On every single day since September 9, 1945," adds Frank Barnaby, director of the Stockholm International Peace Research Institute, "at least one war was being fought somewhere in the world. The number of people killed in these conflicts amounts to tens of millions [more than the number killed in World War II]. And the territories of about 60 countries (in Europe, Asia, Africa and Latin America) were the theaters of war. Shocking though these statistics are, there is as yet no sign of any decrease in the frequency of armed conflicts. On the contrary. In 1974, as many as 14 wars were under way."

That none of these "small wars" graduated to nuclear confrontation, is due less to forbearance than other considerations. Either the stakes were not high enough or nuclear weapons were unnecessary for the limited objectives involved. It would have been both wasteful and unrealistic to use atomic arms, for instance, in the CIA-sponsored overthrow of the Arbenz government in Guatemala (1954), when planes and artillery pieces were more than adequate. On the other hand, in Korea and Vietnam Generals MacArthur and Westmoreland contemplated nuclear action but were overruled by their superiors on the ground that the benefits were outweighed by the risks.

The science of warfare, today as always, is a continuum of options beginning with low levels of violence and pyramiding to the highest levels, the latter always being an implicit and direct extension of the former. During the Korean War, writes Joseph C. Harsch, *Christian Science Monitor* analyst, "Washington was divided between those who . . . thought all hope was gone and that the only recourse was to be a 'preventive war' with the Soviet Union, and those who counseled, and won, the policy of redressing the military balance of power . . . Their abiding purpose was to handle the Korean crisis when it broke, and the Korean War as it developed, without taking the United States beyond 'the point of no return,'" i.e., a nuclear war. In fact, "they considered a localized war like the one waged in Korea as a lesser evil to a general war engulfing the whole world and even then carrying the ultimate threat of atomic reprisal upon the United States. They assumed in all their calculations that if ever either Moscow or Washington accepted the inevitability of a general war, then the very assumption would make it inevitable."

The lines between lower and higher martial forms are arbitrary conveniences for the purpose of study, but in real life they blend. Thus, while nuclear warfare seems to be out of bounds, it is seldom far removed as a practical consideration. It is thought about, and seriously, more often than is generally realized. If there is any confusion on that score it peels away if you pinpoint the position of nuclear war on a hypothetical ladder of military options.

Leaving aside nonviolent forms of conflict between nations, such as diplomatic, trade, and currency disputes, there is a range of *violent* conflict today more varied than in pre-World War II days. To put it differently, the two contending sides are in or near violent war all the time, but at the bottom of the ladder the violence is more subdued than the violence, say, of World Wars I and II, and at the top of the ladder it is hundreds of times more destructive.

The first rung in this hypothetical ladder is occupied today by covert warfare, as practiced by the Central Intelligence Agency. It is a form of warfare that the United States resorted to on an episodic scale hitherto (e.g., the attempt to overthrow Pasha Yusuf Karamanli during the naval war with Tripoli at the beginning of the nineteenth century), but has expanded vastly during the period following World War II. By arranging the violent deposition of governments friendly to, or potentially friendly to, the Soviet Union (such as Allende's Chile, Arbenz's Guatemala, Mossadegh's Iran) the CIA narrows the Soviet sphere of influence, weakening it to that extent in the overall conflict.

For the most part such wars are fought by proxies, with the CIA (and KGB) supplying funds, recruiting mercenaries, handling logistics, sometimes giving aircover, gathering intelligence, and training the host country's forces, but avoiding direct intervention. The reason for a low profile is that intervention in another nation's internal affairs is an affront to world public opinion and, if revealed, would give adequate justification for reprisals against the United States itself. In addition, covert war is a clear violation of innumerable treaties, as well as Article 2 Section 4 of the United Nations Charter, which prohibits actions against the "political independence of any state."

Covert or no, however, CIA warfare is a logical starting point for military action, because changes in the international balance of power today are more likely to take place through revolution and counter-revolution *within* nations than by invasions from the outside. Six dozen national and social revolutions have occurred since World War II, and not a few have drawn the superpowers into covert support for one or the other faction—as in Indonesia, Zaire, Chile, Brazil, Angola, to name a few. CIA warfare may seem a mild nibbling around the edges of the worldwide contest between two social systems, but it is a means of softening up the enemy for more decisive action.

The next rung on the ladder is direct intervention, but of a limited nature—as practiced by the United States in Lebanon (1958) and the Dominican Republic (1965). In a sense this is an extension of covert warfare, a back-up, so to speak, when CIA-supported allies fail in their mission. In May 1965, President Lyndon Johnson dispatched 22,000 marines to the Dominican Republic when the junta favored by the American Embassy failed to suppress rebels intent on restoring President Juan Bosch to his elected post. Had Colonel Pedro Bartolome Benoit and General Elias Wessin y Wessin been able to hold off the revolutionaries, direct intervention would have been unnecessary; when they failed and were beaten, Johnson came to their rescue.

The Pentagon understands full well the linkage between the lower and higher rungs of the military ladder, as is evidenced by the four "U.S. options in insurgency situations" outlined at one of its national security seminars:

1. Military advice and assistance to the allied government.
2. Training of its troops by American officers.
3. Adequate material aid for conducting hostilities.
4. "If necessary, direct support by U.S. forces of combat missions launched by government troops, and *unilateral U.S. operations against the insurgents*" (emphasis added).

"Direct support" of combat missions may mean transporting the ally's soldiers in American planes (as the United States did in Ethiopia), spotting the enemy's positions (as the United States did in Angola) and like activities. "Unilateral U.S. operations" of course are self-explanatory.

Admittedly, intervention of this type has been infrequent, in part because victory is usually won or lost at the covert war level— the first rung—and in part because a military "presence" sometimes gets the message across without landing troops. On November 25, 1974, for instance, the aircraft carrier *Constellation* sailed into the Persian Gulf, the first U.S. warship to appear there in twenty-six years, to emphasize, as the *Christian Science Monitor* noted, that the United States "will not accept any threat to, or interruption of the supply of oil from the Persian Gulf states." This "familiarization" mission, as the Navy euphemistically called it, also reinforced the words of Secretary of State Kissinger some weeks later, that the United States would not rule out military action against the oil-producing countries if they threatened "strangulation of the industrialized world." American battleships were similarly present offshore when Brazilian colonels overthrew the Goulart regime, and when Chilean militarists overthrew Salvador Allende.

How important "military presence" is in the calculus of war may be gleaned from testimony given the Joint Armed Services Committees of Congress by Chief of Naval Operations Admiral T. H. Moorer in April 1970. The admiral called his list of seventy-three instances of "presence" a "summary of wars/near wars," and in fact a few came close. Thus in the second case cited, "Trieste (7/46)," Moorer's comment is: "U.S. and British Naval units dispatched to scene with open warfare imminent. Commenced Adriatic Patrol which lasted until Trieste [ownership] issue resolved in 1954." Case 15 is "Kinmen Island (7/57) . . . Naval units dispatched to defend Taiwan." In some instances "presence" evolved into "combat operations," for example, "Vietnam Guerrilla War (9/55-Present)," or "support operations," for example, "Lebanon Civil War (5/58)." Eighteen instances were so sensitive Moorer refused to have them made public, but it is clear from the other fifty-five that the Navy was instructed to make its "presence" felt on dozens of occasions that could have ignited from "presence" to "combat" with a small spark—in Turkey, Greece, Israel, Tachens, Jordan, the Red Sea, the Suez, Haiti, Syria, Lebanon, Cuba, Germany (during the 1959 Berlin crisis), Laos, Panama, the Congo, Guatemala, Thailand, Yemen, the Caribbean, Indonesia, Malaysia, North Korea (after the 1968 seizure of the *Pueblo* and after the killing of two Americans in the truce zone in 1976).

The step above limited intervention on the hypothetical ladder is conventional war, usually taking one of two forms: hostilities between surrogates of the two superpowers (as in the Middle East or the first Indochina War between France and the Viet Minh), or hostilities between one superpower and an ally of the other's (as in Korea or Vietnam). In theory the two superpowers themselves might fight a conventional war, with conventional rifles, artillery, tanks, planes, as in World War II, but that is so unlikely it is next to impossible. If the United States and the Soviet Union were poised for battle they would have to give immediate consideration to the other side's nuclear capability: the United States, for instance, has a Quick Reaction Alert (QRA) system which can put nuclear-armed bombers and missiles in the air over Europe within minutes. "Hundreds of NATO pilots, including Greeks and Turks," we are told by Walter Pincus, who directed an inquiry on tactical nuclear arms for a Senate subcommittee in 1970, "stand 24-hour alerts alongside fighter-bombers, each poised at the end of the runway prepared for a 15-minute take-off, each loaded with a U.S. nuclear weapon that, when armed, could deliver explosive power ten times that of the bomb that leveled Hiroshima." The pressures for a nuclear response, before the other side could put its wings and warheads to use, therefore, would be irresistible. In any case both Washington and Moscow have designed their strategies, in case of confrontation, for nuclear—not conventional—war.

So far no nation has ventured beyond the third rung of the ladder. There has been a "firebreak" between traditional arms and nuclear arms; and that "firebreak," fortunately, has held. But the three higher rungs are integral to the ladder, forming a logical unity with the lower ones—and what's more, they are pondered and discussed incessantly by strategists on both sides.

On the rung above conventional war is *tactical* nuclear war. It is called "tactical" because it would involve only one of the superpowers, not both, and would be limited to a single geographic area, say in Asia, Africa, or Latin America—but not likely in Europe. The Pentagon is fabricating a panoply of atomic weapons suitable to tactical war, ranging from fission bombs with only a fraction the explosive power of the Hiroshima bomb, to warheads dozens of times more powerful; and deliverable not only by missile and plane but, in miniaturized form, by artillery, land mine, or other means.

Tactical nuclear war has been projected by American officials as a serious option on many occasions. Three months after the defeat of the American allies in Indochina, for instance, Defense Secretary Schlesinger emphasized on ABC's "Issues and Answers" program (July 6, 1975), that America would respond with nuclear bombs wherever aggression is "likely to result in defeat in any area of very great importance to the United States." Since reporters had already speculated in print about Korea, the Secretary was asked whether that might be one place where a limited nuclear war could be considered. "We cannot exclude Korea," was the reply.

Edward N. Luttwak, a Pentagon consultant and associate director of the Washington Center of Foreign Policy Research, gives this scenario for tactical nuclear war: "North Korea invades South Korea, jeopardizing thousands of American troops stationed there. The U.S. calls in aircraft from bases around the world to wipe out North Korea with conventional bombs. If that doesn't work and our troops are still in danger we unload the nukes. That ends it."

A fifth rung in the ladder, a notch higher, is the *limited strategic* war, this time involving the superpowers directly. As envisioned, it would be a controlled nuclear exchange with the Soviet Union for the "defense"—if you can call it that—of Western Europe. It would begin with an invasion by the Soviet Union, say, of West Germany with conventional weapons. The United States would react by hurtling tactical nuclear warheads against "soft targets" (depots, troop concentrations, storage facilities, etc.) on the Soviet side; Soviet forces would hit "soft targets" on the American side with similar weapons; then both would sit back and await developments, hopefully some form of negotiations in which the Kremlin gives up. At least that is the scenario.

The rationale behind this "selective strike" strategy is that the United States must have more than one option in a crisis. If the only option is total war—which all experts concede would claim 95 million or more lives on each side—Washington might be so fearful of the consequences as to be musclebound, incapable of *any* response. The "national command authorities," according to the Ford administration, must therefore have the requisite "flexibility and options" so that they need not "make a decision that would bring about a degree of devastation that neither the Soviet Union nor the United States, nor our allies around the world, would find palatable." Translated from Pentagonese this means that the American command must try to contain an atomic war, so that it "wounds" rather than "kills"—and so that the devastation is as far from United States shores as possible. Since a "limited" war of this type is not possible unless the Russians play the game by the same rules, Senator Stuart Symington was constrained to tell Secretary Schlesinger when he outlined his scenario to a Senate subcommittee in September 1974: "You talk as if the Joint Chiefs of Staff of the Soviet Union and the Joint Chiefs of Staff of the United States were together in this thing and started to play a game of chess."

But Schlesinger didn't consider limited strategic war bizarre: "We are talking," he said, "about relative likelihood and unlikelihood."

The sixth rung of the ladder, of course, is the all-out strategic war, for which the United States possessed, as of 1975, about 8,500 warheads and the Soviets about a third as many, but in each case many times more than was needed for simple deterrence. Since there is as yet no adequate defense against incoming nuclear missiles and since both sides would lose at least half of their people and three quarters of their industry, there is a genuine desire—under present circumstances—to avoid strategic war. But it is far from excluded as a realistic possibility—through accident, for instance, or as a normal escalation from tactical nuclear war; and what is more to the point, researchers continue to work furiously to find the ultimate weapon that will make even total wars "thinkable" and "winnable." There may have been a "firebreak" between conventional war and nuclear war in practice, but there has been no such "firebreak" in the planning of American policy makers. In at least a half dozen instances, as we shall see, limited nuclear war has been seriously contemplated; and the October 1962 Cuban missile crisis, everyone knows, brought the world "eyeball to eyeball" with a strategic nuclear war—the sixth and final rung of the ladder.

II

If we keep the military ladder in mind, it becomes possible to reconstruct the history of the nuclear age so as to explain the many shifts in strategy and indicate where the arms race is going.

The original reason for developing The Bomb was of course patently obvious, to use on Germany (and later Japan) before Hitler could use it on the Western Allies. Nine months before the outbreak of World War II two Berlin scientists, Otto Hahn and Fritz Strassman, successfully split the uranium nucleus by bombarding it with a stream of neutrons, and thereby paved the way for development of the atomic bomb. Next, in August 1939, as war became imminent, two Hungarian-born physicists working on fission in the United States, Leo Szilard and Eugene Wigner, conveyed their concern to the world-renowned Albert Einstein that the Nazis might unlock the door first, especially since they controlled the uranium mines of Czechoslovakia, and might be able to seize the much richer mines in the Belgian Congo. Szilard drafted a letter to President Roosevelt which Einstein signed, urging that the United States begin work on a nuclear bomb, and a Russian émigré, Alexander Sachs, delivered it to FDR personally a few weeks after World War II began. "I made one great mistake in my life," Einstein told Linus Pauling later, "when I signed the letter to President Roosevelt recommending that atom bombs be made . . ." But in this historic 1939 missive which launched an epoch, they advised the American chief of state of Szilard's and Enrico Fermi's experiments with chain reaction at Columbia University, and suggested the possibility "in the immediate future" of constructing "extremely powerful bombs of a new type." Germany, Einstein implied, might already be at work on such a project because it had "stopped the sale of uranium from the Czechoslovakian mines which she has taken over."

It should be noted parenthetically that, like so much else in the nuclear saga, Einstein's and Szilard's projections were not quite on target, either technically, militarily, or politically. The atom bomb, they said in their letter, would probably "be too heavy for transportation by air" and would therefore have to be "carried by boat and exploded in a port." If that had been the case, The Bomb would have had a much smaller range of utility and consequently a lesser impact on the art of war and international policies. It would have been only of peripheral value against a nation such as the Soviet Union, with ports far removed from American bases and a sizable air force capable of intercepting slow-moving U.S. ships.

It turned out, moreover, that the Nazis did not embark on atomic bomb development—they didn't believe such a weapon could be made in time. Two months before Hiroshima, Vannevar Bush, chairman of the National Defense Research Committee, reported that "evidence just in from Germany revealed that she was far behind us in the technology of this field . . ." The American "advantage over totalitarian states," he noted, "has been tremendous." In fact when Otto Hahn, the German physicist whose 1938 discoveries had played so large a role in the science of fission, learned of the devastation of Hiroshima, he refused to believe, at first, that it resulted from a nuclear explosion.

Half a decade or a decade later American authorities would insist they needed a stockpile of nuclear weapons for "defense," but there was no question at the outset that it was planned for offensive purposes. Both Presidents Roosevelt and Truman treated The Bomb as simply another military tool—albeit a more effective one—for securing victory against the Axis and strengthening America's hand in world affairs generally. Historian Barton J. Bernstein points out that no one had to make the decision to detonate The Bomb over Japan; it was always assumed that if one could be produced it would be used. Truman himself, in an interview with Cabell Phillips for the *New York Times Magazine* (May 3, 1959) confirmed this judgment: "Let there be no mistake about it. I regarded the bomb as a military weapon and never had any doubt that it should be used."

As the moment approached for deploying the technological wonder, divergent attitudes began to develop between the political administration and a large part of the scientific community. Was this, in fact, just "another weapon," or, as Stimson had suggested to the Interim Committee, did it really change humankind's relation to the universe? Could The Bomb serve the political interests of a single nation-state, or did it make the nation-state itself obsolete?

Many of those who had worked on the project had second thoughts about what they had wrought. A committee of seven scientists at the University of Chicago, headed by Nobel laureate James Franck, stated in a report on the "social and political consequences of atomic energy" that science had uncovered something "fraught with infinitely greater dangers than were all the inventions of the past." At other times, the Franck group said, science had been able to provide "new methods of protection against new weapons of aggression," but it "cannot promise such efficient protection against the destructive use of nuclear power. This protection can come only from the political organization of the world." It was foolhardy to expect that the Soviet Union would be unable to produce a fission bomb before long or that it would be unable to find the uranium ore for that purpose. Unless the atom were placed under international control, the Franck report predicted, there would be a desperate and spiraling "race for nuclear armaments." It urged therefore that instead of using The Bomb against Japanese cities and people, "the U.S. conduct a demonstration of the new weapon . . . before the eyes of representatives of all the United Nations, on the desert or a barren island." Washington could then say to the nations of the world: "You see what sort of weapon we had but did not use. We are ready to renounce its use in the future if other nations join us in this renunciation and agree to the establishment of an efficient control." Dr. Franck was unable to get beyond a lieutenant in the office of George Harrison, Secretary of War Stimson's deputy, to present this petition.

Similar arguments and pleas were made to Washington's decision makers throughout the period when The Bomb was being developed. Niels Bohr, an internationally respected atomic scientist who escaped from Nazi-occupied Copenhagen in 1943, was the earliest and most persistent advocate of international control. He received a respectful hearing from Roosevelt (but no action), cold hostility from Churchill, and imperious disregard from Truman's associates. Along the way, too, Einstein wrote another letter, again with the help of Szilard, stating his fears that whatever military advantages The Bomb offered in the short run were outweighed by the certainty that an atomic armaments race would ensue once the weapon was used. Roosevelt died before the message could be delivered, and Truman was too occupied in the transition period to give it attention. But when Szilard met with James Byrnes, soon to be Secretary of State, he was firmly though politely rebuffed: "Are you not worrying too much and quite unnecessarily about all this?" Byrnes asked. "So far as I know there is not even any uranium to be found in Russia."

Subsequently Szilard circulated a petition urging Truman to rule out "resort to use of atomic bombs" on the grounds that it would open "the door to an era of devastation of an unimaginable scale." General Leslie R. Groves decided to withhold this document from Truman, on the arrogant theory that the matter "had already been fully considered and settled by the proper authorities." Similar petitions came from sixty-eight scientists at Oak Ridge and eighteen in Chicago, but they too never reached the President. In the glow of impending victory the men at the helm thought The Bomb conveyed to its owner power close to omnipotence, especially since it was believed that America's only possible rival, the Soviet Union, had no chance of catching up in the nuclear field for a long time. General Groves dismissed the Soviet potential with the contemptuous comment, "Why those people can't even make a jeep!" As late as 1947 Groves was insisting that "the Russians would need 15 to 20 years to develop an atomic bomb . . ."

The Truman administration, caught up in euphoria, veered 180 degrees away from its scientific critics. Stimson might use apocalyptic prose within government counsels about a new relationship of man to the universe, but the Trumanites perceived The Bomb only in pragmatic terms: when would it be ready, what targets suited it best, how would it affect the war with Japan in the short run, and the conflict with Russia over the longer pull? They gave no thought at all to the possible obsolescence of national sovereignty, and their concern about a new arms race was at best minimal. The Bomb was viewed solely as the means for achieving American victory militarily and diplomatically, and from this focus it appeared that the United States was destined to dominate the rest of the twentieth and perhaps the twenty-first century as Britain had dominated the nineteenth.

The first two bombs available that August were not in themselves so awesome. In fact, America's military forces had shown—in March that year, before Truman became President—that similar devastation could be wreaked with "old-fashioned" munitions. Five hundred and twenty U.S. planes had showered eleven square miles of Tokyo with 4,000 tons of explosives and incendiaries, causing 83,793 deaths, many from asphyxiation when the resulting "fire storm" sucked away their air, and 40,000 to 100,000 wounded. But the single device tested at Alamogordo had three times the TNT-equivalent of all those conventional bombs dropped on Tokyo by 520 planes, and on the drawing boards were weapons that within a few years would make the Hiroshima bomb seem almost insignificant.

J. Robert Oppenheimer and Arthur H. Compton, in charge of the Manhattan Project at Los Alamos and Chicago respectively, had already informed the Interim Committee that much bigger weapons were "a scientific certainty." An imminent second stage, they said, would be the production of fission bombs with a yield of 50,000 to 100,000 tons of TNT (50 to 100 kilotons). After that, in a third stage that might be as little as three years away, would come the fusion bomb, in which a fission bomb would act as a trigger for the fusion of light atoms, producing an explosive power measured in millions of tons of TNT-equivalent (megatons)—one, ten, even a hundred megatons. "The atomic bombs at our disposal," Szilard wrote in July 1945, "represent only the first step . . . and there is almost no limit to the destructive power which will become available in the course of their future development."

For the indefinite future, then, it looked as if American military power could not be challenged. The targets were chosen for using The Bomb on Japan, and a consensus formed to brandish it as a "big stick" against the Soviet Union. In both instances no claim was made by anyone that the United States was threatened in any way if it didn't use the new weapon, or that it was needed for self-defense. It was conceived simply as an instrument for extending Washington's worldwide authority.

No historian today argues that atomic bombing was necessary to bring Japan to its knees, only that it relieved General MacArthur of the need to land foot soldiers on the Japanese islands, thereby saving large numbers of American lives (Karl T. Compton put the figure at "hundreds of thousands—perhaps several millions . . ." Stimson claimed an invasion might have cost the United States a million casualties—a figure also used by Truman, though by 1949 he had trimmed it down to 200,000). Japan, however, was already defeated and trying to enlist Russia's aid to surrender with some grace. A Strategic Bombing Survey group of experts sent to Japan in 1946 to assess the impact of the atom bombs on Tokyo's decision, concluded that "the Hiroshima and Nagasaki atomic bombs did not defeat Japan, nor by the testimony of the enemy leaders who ended the war did they persuade Japan to accept unconditional surrender." In the survey's opinion the last Axis power would have surrendered "in all probability prior to 1 November 1945 . . . even if the atomic bombs had not been dropped, even if Russia had not entered the war, and even if no invasion had been planned or contemplated."

Not a few American military leaders were repelled by the nuclear bombardment—some in advance of the event. General Eisenhower recalls that when Stimson informed him at Potsdam the decision had been made to go ahead, he had "a feeling of depression and so I voiced to him [Stimson] my grave misgivings, first on the basis of my belief that Japan was already defeated and that dropping the bomb was completely unnecessary, and secondly because

I thought that our country should avoid shocking world opinion by the use of a weapon whose employment was, I thought, no longer mandatory as a measure to save American lives. . . . It wasn't necessary to hit them with that awful thing." Fleet Admiral William F. Halsey, Jr., based his opposition on more pragmatic grounds but was equally unequivocal: "The first atomic bomb was an unnecessary experiment. It was a mistake to ever drop it. Why reveal a weapon like that to the world when it wasn't necessary?" General Henry H. (Hap) Arnold, chief of the Army Air Force, wrote: "The fact is that the Japanese could not have held out long, because they had lost control of the air." Similar sentiments were expressed by General Curtis E. LeMay, Admirals William D. Leahy and Ernest J. King, as well as Major General Sir Hastings Ismay, chief of the British General Staff.

In time of course the military dissenters became nuclear enthusiasts for even though it might have been unnecessary against Japan it seemed like the right stick to brandish against the Soviet Union. "The bomb," James F. Byrnes told Truman in April 1945, three months before it was tested, "might well put us in a position to dictate our own terms at the end of the war." To Szilard, pleading for a moratorium on the weapon's use, Byrnes said that "our possessing and demonstrating the bomb would make Russia more manageable in Europe." This was the general consensus of the Truman Cabinet. On May 14, 1945, Stimson counseled the President that the United States had two bargaining chips for making Russia pliable: a vastly stronger economy and The Bomb. Using an analogy from poker, these chips were "a royal flush and we mustn't be a fool about the way we play it." The Secretary recorded in his diary that day that the Soviets "can't get along without our help and industries and we have coming into action a weapon which will be unique." At Potsdam, Churchill noted that after Truman had been advised of the successful test at Alamogordo he became cockier: "When he got to the meeting after having read this report he was a changed man. He told the Russians where they got on and off and generally bossed the whole meeting."

This cockiness was much in evidence in 1945. Bernard Baruch, presidential advisor and financier, expressed the mood of near omnipotence that pervaded Washington with penultimate forthrightness: "America can get what she wants if she insists on it. After all we've got it—The Bomb—and they haven't and won't have it for a long time to come." Stimson's diary on June 6, 1945, notes that Truman was certain The Bomb would force Russia to yield ground on the Balkan, Polish, and Manchurian issues. Byrnes was confident the United States could force the Russians to "retire in a very decent manner" from their position in Eastern Europe, and if they proved surly—by refusing to evacuate East Germany, for instance—"we . . . must make it clear to all that we are willing to adopt those measures of last resort if, for the peace of the world, we are forced to do so." In the context of Byrnes's expressed positions there could be no doubt what "measures of last resort" meant. The United States, true, did not use The Bomb, but in the early postwar years the idea of jumping directly to the sixth and top rung of the military ladder was viewed with little trepidation— and by some with equanimity or eagerness.

Quite a few strident voices, especially in the military, counseled accelerated war preparations, and in some cases "preventative" war—a quick atomic attack to reduce the Soviets to docility. In October 1945, just two months after Japan surrendered, General George S. Patton called on the country to remain "armed and prepared" for an *"inevitable"* new war. A month later General "Hap" Arnold proposed a policy of "offensive readiness." "We must use our most brilliant scientists," he said, "to develop better weapons more quickly and more effectively. We must take advantage of the bases we now have to be closer to an enemy's vital points with our weapons than he is to ours. We must use the most modern weapons of all kinds so that we can beat any potential opponent to the draw."

Major General Orvile A. Anderson, Commandant of the Air War College, lectured "on the advisability of launching an A-bomb attack on Russia," and was generally considered the fiercest advocate of preventative war in the military. "Which is the greater immorality," he asked, "preventative war as a means to keep the U.S.S.R. from becoming a nuclear power; or, to allow a totalitarian dictatorial system to develop a means whereby the free world could be intimidated, blackmailed, and possibly destroyed." The question answered itself; Anderson deemed a first strike against Russia the lesser of two immoral evils. He was suspended from his command in September 1950 for airing such views, but other, and even more influential voices were suggesting the same policy.

Secretary of the Navy Francis Matthews echoing the views of Defense Secretary Louis A. Johnson, told an audience of 100,000 in Omaha (August 25, 1950) that he advocated "instituting a war to compel co-operation for peace . . . We would become the *first aggressors for peace*" (emphasis added). As *Christian Science Monitor* columnist Joseph C. Harsch described the planned scenario: Washington would deliver "a disarmament ultimatum to Moscow and then when that ultimatum had been rejected, as it undoubtedly would be rejected, treat the rejection as a casus belli and go to war with all its atomic weapons in a total effort to destroy the military power of the Soviet bloc . . ." Such plans were being promoted, it should be noted, at a time when Soviet ability to hit American soil with nuclear weapons was nonexistent.

The Administration itself, though it officially frowned on being the "first aggressors for peace," nonetheless thought of The Bomb as the undergirding of its power and was quite prepared to use it. Clark M. Clifford, the Washington lawyer and confidant of Presidents who has moved in and out of government for three decades, has a secret report in his files—still classified—which he prepared for Truman in 1946, when he was a White House counsel. Titled "A Summary of American Relations with the Soviet Union" and based on conversations with the Secretaries of State, War, Navy, the Attorney General, the Joint Chiefs of Staff, Fleet Admiral William D. Leahy, and the director of central intelligence, among others—all of whom, observed Clifford, expressed "a remarkable agreement"—the document was further evidence that leading officials were ready to go all the way, up to and including nuclear and biological war.

After listing a compendium of Soviet sins, from espionage and propaganda to violating agreements and seeking control over most of the world, the Clifford report argued that America must maintain whatever military forces are necessary "to confine Soviet influence to its present area." It ought to dangle a carrot before the Russians so that they "can earn their dividends, among other ways, in American trade," but the carrot should go with a nuclear stick. "The U.S.," Clifford wrote, "with a military potential com-

posed primarily of highly effective weapons should entertain no
proposal for disarmament or limitation of armament." It should
reject all efforts for "outlawing atomic warfare and long-range
offensive weapons" because that "would greatly limit United States
strength while only moderately affecting the Soviet Union." Reflecting the hard line throughout the Administration, he counseled that if the Kremlin threatened to leave the United Nations,
Washington should lift no finger to prevent it. The central conclusion was that since the Soviet Union "is vulnerable to atomic
weapons, biological warfare, and long range air power . . . The
U.S. must be prepared to wage atomic and biological warfare."
There "must be constant research in both offensive and defensive
weapons" to enhance American capabilities in that direction.

This was, it should be stressed, before revolution in the Third
World had gained its subsequent great momentum and before a
CIA had been established to systematically inject itself into the internal affairs of other states. The United States was concerned
about "stability" in Western Europe, but little thought was given
to toppling pro-Soviet governments except in the so-called "satellite" countries, since there were none. By and large the confrontation between the United States and the Soviet Union was direct
and uncomplicated—and so was the single-option strategy under
study. If war should occur, Washington was thinking of only one
form of response, "atomic and biological warfare." It was as if our
hypothetical military ladder had been sheared of five rungs, only
the sixth one remaining.

III

The United States had a corner on atom bombs from 1945 to
1949. Many people point to the fact that it didn't use them as
proof that it has consistently pursued a policy of forbearance. That
does not, however, square with the bellicosity of American leaders.
"Unless Russia is faced with an iron fist and strong language,"
Truman wrote to Byrnes late in 1945, "war is in the making. Only
one language do they understand—'how many divisions have you?'
. . . I'm tired of babying the Soviets." Nor does it square with the
retention and enlargement of the military machine.

There is a more cogent explanation as to why the Administration did not resort to war when it had a nuclear monopoly—firstly that it was already impossible to *win* an all-out war, even with The Bomb; and secondly that there was a widespread feeling that the Soviet system could not soon recover from the enormous wartime damage, and might even fall apart if left to its own devices. "Washington believed in those days," says author Richard J. Barnet, a former Arms Control and Disarmament Agency official, "that the Soviet Union was not much of a rival. It had lost so many people and so much of its productive facilities it was 'on the ropes.' " There was little anxiety therefore about the prospects of an arms race—despite what Bohr, Szilard and others were saying; as Truman put it to a Tennessee lawyer, Fyke Farmer, in October 1945, "we will stay ahead" under any circumstances.

Beyond that, however, cool reflection showed there was little hope of winning what the Pentagon calls a "strategic war." American power might appear to be absolute, as the London *Observer* underscored in these exuberant words (June 27, 1948): "It is we who hold the overwhelming trump cards. It is our side, not Russia, which holds atomic and post-atomic weapons and could, if sufficiently provoked, wipe Russia's power and threat to the world's peace from the face of the earth." Presumably the Soviets might have to "resign" from a threat of war, just as a chess player gives up when it is evident he will be checkmated. But on closer examination the idea of a nuclear victory was not so foolproof; it was not even feasible. "The United States," a former naval officer who worked on strategic projects asserts in an interview, "did not have enough weapons those days to obliterate the U.S.S.R., only enough to wound it. Meanwhile the Red Army could have seized all of Europe to the English Channel with conventional weapons. We could not have finished the job without sending in our own foot soldiers, and that was impossible." Raymond Aron, one of Europe's most authoritative writers, confirms this judgment: "United States superiority over the Soviet Union in the nuclear field was offset . . . by Russian superiority in conventional arms and by the Red Army's continued ability to overrun Western Europe in a matter of days, as during the years from 1946 to 1953, or with more difficulty in the years after 1953."

A top secret report to the National Security Council in April 1950, NSC-68, a basic document in American history that was declassified only twenty-five years later, corroborates this opinion. Evaluating Soviet forces, the document conceded that "the Soviet Union and its satellites" had the capability "(a) To overrun Western Europe, with the possible exception of the Iberian and Scandinavian Peninsulas . . . (b) To launch air attacks against the British Isles and air and sea attacks against lines of communications of the Western Powers in the Atlantic and the Pacific . . ." (By 1950 the Soviets might also, according to NSC-68, "attack selected targets with atomic weapons"—having developed their own nuclear bomb the year before.)

Simple arithmetic showed that Russia could not be wiped out with the weapons America then had. According to U.S. sources, early atom bombs of the Hiroshima type could inflict approximately the same damage as 2,000 tons of chemical explosives. Extrapolating from this figure, Nobel laureate P. M. S. Blackett estimates that to wreak the same havoc on Russia as 1.2 million tons of traditional bombs did on Germany in the peak bombing period from January 1943 to the end of World War II, would require 600 A-bombs. German morale did not break under that punishment and German production "rose steadily until August 1944." True, an atomic attack would concentrate the blow in a brief time span, but European Russia alone was eight times larger in area and three times more populous than Germany (not to mention Asiatic Russia, much larger still). To achieve comparable devastation to that suffered by Germany in 1943–45 was beyond American capability since it was producing in the first postwar years, according to Dr. Ralph Lapp, only enough nuclear material for 100 A-bombs annually. There was moreover the problem of delivery; before the intercontinental ballistic missile, U.S. bombers had two grave disadvantages, namely that they relied on Allied bases in Europe for takeoff and servicing, and they had to contend with excellent Soviet fighter planes. The ultimate decision, then, would rest on the Army, and as General George C. Kenney, Commander of the Strategic Air Force, observed: "The United States has no intention of landing mass armies in Europe and slugging it out with the Red Army—manpower against manpower. Napoleon and Hitler both made that mistake."

No one recognized the dilemma of America's position in 1945–50 more clearly than the National Security Council itself.

In NSC-68 the Council estimated that the Soviet A-bomb stockpile by mid-1950 would be only ten to twenty weapons and by mid-1954, only 200. Despite that negligible number, a U.S. victory was out of the question. "A powerful blow could be delivered upon the Soviet Union," says NSC-68, "but it is estimated that these operations alone would not force or induce the Kremlin to capitulate and that the Kremlin would still be able to use the forces under its control to dominate most or all of Eurasia. This would probably mean a long and difficult struggle during which the free institutions of Western Europe and many freedom-loving people would be destroyed and the regenerative capacity of Western Europe dealt a crippling blow."

Thus, from the very beginning, fixation on The Bomb as the cornerstone of American power was a delusion—its effectiveness could be and was countered by other means. Yet, like compulsive gamblers, the American power elites fed their delusion by putting more chips in the pot. Instead of a long look into the consequences of their miscalculation, they continued to ride the tide of every technological breakthrough—from the fission bomb to the fusion bomb, the solid fuel missile, the ABM, the MIRV—with the single hope that one of them would *guarantee* victory. And as they wrestled with the difficulty of winning an all-out war they refined their strategy to include economic blockade plus the other forms of warfare on the military ladder—CIA subversion, direct intervention, conventional warfare, limited nuclear warfare.

Even the "softer" political strategies, such as "containment" and later "détente," reflected the "win syndrome" that has been implicit and explicit since 1945. The policy of "containment," for instance, as defined by its prime architect George F. Kennan, was conceived as a means to "increase enormously the strains under which the Soviet policy must operate" and thereby cause internal problems that would lead either to "the breakup or the gradual mellowing of Soviet power." Containment would take longer than the more dramatic preventative war or pre-emptive strike, but its purpose was the same—to "win." The American Establishment, during the whole nuclear age, never abandoned the belief that military power was the ultimate power and atomic weapons the ultimate expression of that power. While relying on options less horrifying than all-out nuclear war—out of necessity—it continued to crank the nuclear motor.

The men of power, as will become evident, are in the grip of a multiple dilemma. There is as yet no true defense that will assure, in case of all-out war, that the United States survives relatively potent while the Soviet Union is reduced to ashes. The probe for such a defense, however, must be—in their opinion—continued. That means giving free rein to the scientific and engineering bureaucracy to continue its research and keeping the public in perpetual alarm over the Soviet "threat," so that Congress will vote the necessary funds. But it doesn't end there. It would be impossible to keep the public in that state of alarm if the Pentagon merely asked for additional research money but agreed to cutbacks in the production of weapons—both nuclear and conventional. Hence the government continues to ask for—and receive—greater sums for everything. The arms race rolls on, unabated.

3

The Win
Syndrome (1)

If one is seduced by the minutiae of the nuclear debate—such as
whether a "disarming first strike" (one that demolishes the enemy's "force" before he can use it) is preferable to "restrained
counter-force" (a first strike which merely destroys part of his arsenal), the essence of the nuclear arms race is lost under the chaff
of talmudic hairsplitting.

Overriding all the talk of "counter-value" versus "counter-
force"—and all the rest—have been two fundamental facts: One is
that the top U.S. leadership, contrary to its public posture, does
not now and never has sought a stalemate with the Soviet Union, a
"balance of terror." It has always sought to "win"; its quest for
victory, indeed, has been an irrepressible fixation. That is the
significance of the military ladder we have described: if there is no
hope for victory at one rung of the ladder (one particular type of
warfare), then the focus is shifted to higher or lower ones. During the Kennedy years General Maxwell Taylor advocated de-
emphasizing the nuclear option in favor of concentrating on
"brush-fire," "counterinsurgency" warfare. During the 1950's
John Foster Dulles and Eisenhower talked of "massive retaliation," but since it was a policy impossible to implement, they centered their efforts on covert CIA-type wars, and surrogate wars. At

the core of all policy making, however, has been the "win syndrome." American leaders want no stand-off with the Soviet Union, they are passionately determined to gain victory, total, complete, absolute. Circumstances may stymie their efforts, but that is another matter.

The second salient fact about America's role in the nuclear age is that it has been hobbled by a twin paradox. Its defense policy has focused around a weapon that is all-powerful, but, at least at the present, can't be used. Yet, on the other hand, to pursue this policy, it has set in motion a process which propels it toward the ultimate use of nuclear weapons by the United States as well as their use *against* the United States. Nothing like this has ever happened in recorded history. A nation that scored a technological breakthrough in the past—a superior naval vessel, a tank, an airplane, heavier artillery—ordinarily gained political and military advantages from it. But while the 8,000 megatons of bombs in the U.S. stockpile constitute more firepower than all the nations in all prior history have collectively assembled, and can kill all four billion people on earth a dozen times over, they cannot assure victory because their use invites certain annihilation in return. The general estimate by such experts as McNamara and Schlesinger is that no matter who presses the button first there will be between 95 and 120 million dead on each side. "Victory" therefore becomes the ultimate defeat, but such is the nature of the nuclear race that this must constantly be risked.

The fixation on victory has always been a characteristic of nation-states, but the present win syndrome is unique in at least five respects:

1. The search for a "win" formula has coalesced with a technology which gives two nations, and soon more, the capability to extinguish all human life.

2. The constituency which supports the win syndrome has developed an institutional structure and is immeasurably more powerful than that select group of people who were once called "the merchants of death."

3. The permanent war economy and national security state which are indispensable to the win syndrome, have restructured America's institutions and values so that in effect the U.S. has two

governments, one which retains the vestiges of political democracy, and another which is totalitarian.

4. The peaceful spin-off of fission science, nuclear energy, is simultaneously the vehicle by which many other countries—and terrorist groups—may soon own nuclear weaponry beyond any hopes of control.

5. Most ominous of all, the process is *self-propelling,* driven by a momentum that is impersonal, no longer amenable to easy containment or reversal.

What we have, in other words, is a set of gears, each speeding the one in front of it, so that as C. Wright Mills observed in 1958, "the immediate cause of World War III" may very well be "the preparation for it."

II

To speak of a "win syndrome" is not to suggest that all the people in positions of power are engaged in a conspiracy, or that there is anything approaching unanimity among them. On the contrary, many thousands of those who once served the defense machine disengaged from it as their concerns mounted. There are many people such as Clark Clifford, Robert McNamara, Daniel Ellsberg, Morton Halperin, whose views have moderated; or misplaced doves such as Richard Barnet, Leonard Rodberg, Marcus Raskin, Jerome Wiesner—to name a few—who once thought they could change things from "within" but found they were nursing an illusion.

Nor is it fair to imply that the men of power who implement the win syndrome are a brigade of Dr. Strangeloves practicing nuclear witchcraft. On the contrary, they have never planned or sought Doomsday. They would like nothing better, in fact, than to avoid war—any war. What they do want, however, is victory for the American private profit system and its imperial design. They pray for the kind of victory in which, as Sir Solly Zuckerman, Britain's Chief Science Adviser for many years, put it, "the adversary surrenders without a shot being fired." The London *Observer* (November 21, 1948) called on the West to build its forces so that "faced with overwhelming, instantly available strength, Russia might without going to war, resign herself to the position which today among all the nations of the world, she alone refuses—as a chess player resigns when it is clear that any exchange of pieces would lose him the game." But if victory could not be won so easily, American leaders and their supporters abroad wanted an outcome in which there would be as few fatalities on "our" side as possible. In the Truman era such an objective did not seem wildly out of reach, especially since the United States was expected to retain a monopoly on The Bomb long enough to establish an unchallengeable position in world affairs.

The prospects for victory, however, have been in inverse proportion to the size of the atomic arsenal. Given the imperatives of its particular win syndrome, the United States was caught in a vise: it could neither contain (let alone defeat) the Soviet Union, yet it continued to rely on the nuclear option as a hope for the future. The arsenal kept growing, and each decade the potential for human annihilation increased—sometimes by geometric progression—but the Soviet Union was not brought to brook; during much of the time, in fact, Soviet influence expanded, Western influence contracted. All that happened was that as one side escalated, the other side matched the escalation; in the end nothing had been gained and much had been lost.

III

"The decisions which we make today in the fields of science and technology," Sir Solly Zuckerman once wrote, "determine the tactics, then the strategy, and finally the politics of tomorrow." Each decision moreover seems to have set the course, or at least predisposed the course, for the next one—like a stream of water that deepens the seabed. In that sense the A-bomb begat the H-bomb, and the H-bomb paved the road for the ICBM, MIRV, cruise missile, and so on. In each case new weapons systems were the product of three factors: scientific research which showed they were feasible, a constituency which promoted them, and an international crisis—real or synthetic—which helped secure public approval.

Unfortunately the very awesomeness of technology blotted out political insight, so that in each critical moment the tendency was to reach for a new military miracle rather than weigh social or diplomatic solutions. In Truman's view, for instance, it was the atom bomb that would make the Russians obeisant, but when that proved to be a gross miscalculation he simply approved the next sensation offered by technology—the H-bomb.

The last year of the American nuclear monopoly, 1949, was the year that American policy suffered its worst setback of the postwar era—China, with more than a half billion people, seceded from the Western orbit. It was also the year that Moscow acquired The Bomb. From both ends of the strategical spectrum, then, American policy had misfired: America's A-bomb had neither terrified the Soviets into immobility, as Truman, Byrnes, et al. had expected it would, nor had it played any role whatsoever in dealing with a social revolution that Washington felt was inimical to its interests.

No one could argue that China fell from the clutches of America's surrogate, Chiang Kai-shek, for lack of military wherewithal. When the Chinese civil war was renewed in August 1945, Chiang had four million men under arms, including thirty-nine supposedly "crack" divisions trained and supplied by the United States. He also had the largest air force any Asian nation, other than Japan, had ever put together. He controlled all the major cities and three quarters of the population; and to defend that empire he received $3 billion in U.S. aid plus the weapons of a million disarmed Japanese soldiers, as well as direct American help in transporting troops.

From July 1946 to November 1947 Chiang's Kuomintang armies lost almost 1.7 million men, two thirds of them made prisoners. Mountains of American guns fell into rebel hands. Chu Teh, chief of the Maoist Eighth Route Army, told a New York *Times* correspondent, Foster Hailey: "During the last few months of fighting we have annihilated 35 Nationalist brigades. In that operation we have seized much United States equipment. It is very good. We hope to get more of it." After the Communists came to power, Western observers were amazed by the quantity of American weapons displayed. Indeed one can make a fair case that American supplies to Chiang helped the Communists more than Chiang. Former Secretary of State Dean Acheson, in a biting critique, attributed the defeat to Chiang's "gross incompetence" and a "total lack of support both in the armies and in the country."

The American response to this defeat and the Soviet atomic explosion was not to reassess obvious mistakes in dealing with foreign revolutions, but to put another chip in the military pot, the hydrogen bomb, or, as it was originally called, the Super. All the ingredients were in place for this step: research had shown there was an excellent chance the Super could be produced; the Pentagon, the Atomic Energy Commission, Edward Teller, Dean Acheson, and many others were eagerly advancing its cause; and there was the convenient crisis in East-West relationships occasioned by China, the atom test in Russia, and the overthrow of Beneš in Czechoslovakia the year before. As was to happen often in the nuclear race, such combinations overwhelmed restraint—and the go-ahead signal was given.

Scientists had known for decades that the fusion of light elements such as hydrogen—like the fission of heavy elements such as uranium—would release vast amounts of energy; fusion in fact was the method by which the sun itself produced heat and light. Edward Teller, another Hungarian-born scientist and an associate of Szilard and Fermi at Columbia University, had dabbled with plans to develop a fusion bomb in the early 1940's, but put the project aside while he joined the other physicists and engineers on the more promising fission bomb. After the war he renewed his advocacy of the Super in conferences of the Atomic Energy Commission, but the proposal lay dormant until the political crises of 1948–49.

As with the A-bomb, the debate over how to meet this crisis took place in the shadows. One group of scientists, in the minority, Teller, Ernest O. Lawrence, Luis Alvarez, and young people such as Herbert F. York, who had worked on the thermonuclear reaction test of Operation Greenhouse, began campaigning for the Super immediately after it became known that the Russians had exploded an A-bomb. "It is the hallmark of the expert professional," Herman Kahn once observed, "that he doesn't care where he is going as long as he proceeds competently." Some of those working on thermonuclear research—York, for instance—fell into this category; they were intrigued with the pure joy of scientific achievement, leaving speculation on political and social consequences to others. For some, such as Teller, by contrast, the Super fit snugly into hawkish political precepts.

Most of the leading scientists in the country feared the long-run consequences of the horrifying weapon under consideration. In the tension of the Cold War they agreed that some kind of response to the crisis was necessary, but they didn't want to open a new chapter in nuclear history. Their suggestions, York tells us, involved *"evolutionary* changes in the current" programs, increasing the production of atom bombs and "fissionable material" and researching for better delivery vehicles. But they rejected the H-bomb.

The General Advisory Committee of the AEC, made up of nine top scientists headed by J. Robert Oppenheimer, *unanimously* opposed the Super program. Eight of them (Glenn T. Seaborg, discoverer of plutonium, was out of the country) wrote a report expressing the "hope that by one means or another the development of these weapons can be avoided." The eight were divided as to whether the commitment not to produce should be unqualified or dependent on whether the Russians would also make such a commitment. There was no doubt, however, that all were uneasy. Six of the prestigious scientific figures asserted that "the extreme dangers to mankind inherent in the proposal outweigh any military advantage that could come from this development. . . . The reason for developing such super bombs would be to have the capacity to devastate a vast area with a single bomb. . . . Mankind would be far better off not to have a demonstration of the feasibility of such a weapon until the present climate of world opinion changes. . . . We see a unique opportunity of providing by example some limitations on the totality of war and thus of limiting the fear and arousing the hopes of mankind."

Two scientists, Enrico Fermi and I. I. Rabi, were more emphatic: "Necessarily such a weapon goes far beyond any military objective and enters the range of very great natural catastrophes. By its very nature it cannot be confined to a military objective but becomes a weapon which in practical effect is almost one of genocide. It is clear that the use of such a weapon cannot be justified on any ethical ground which gives a human being a certain individuality and dignity even if he happens to be a resident of an enemy country."

The most highly respected scientists in the nation, then, were pleading for a cap on the arms race, both on strategic and moral grounds, but their views were never put before the public for consideration and debate. They were, in fact, brushed aside with little ceremony. On January 31, 1950, the Truman administration, on the recommendation of a Special Committee of the National Security Council, composed of Acheson, Louis Johnson (Secretary of Defense) and David Lilienthal (Chairman of AEC), decided to go ahead anyway. "I believed," Truman wrote in his memoirs, "that anything that would assure us the lead in the field of atomic energy development for defense had to be tried out . . ." The proclivity for escalation was inherent in the situation. It would take about five years, according to scientific estimate, to produce the new weapon (actually it was done in less); what if the Russians broke through in this field before the United States? It would be years before America could catch up. In the minds of "practical" men, therefore, there was no alternative but to go ahead—just as there was to be no alternative but to go ahead with all the other technological advances. You had to match not only what the Russians were doing now, but what they might be *capable* of doing a few years from now.

The allure of technology was like a habit-forming drug, so much so that policy makers invariably opted for the most advanced and destructive of weaponry even when lesser ones were more than adequate. In November 1952, the same month that the U.S. tested "Mike," its first fusion device, at Eniwetok, it also tested "King," a *fission* bomb with an explosive yield of 500,000 tons of TNT—forty times as much as the Hiroshima weapon. Presumably "King" should be sufficient for any realistic undertaking that might ever confront the Pentagon, and in fact physicist Hans Bethe had proposed that it be developed as a substitute for the Super. But there was something still bigger and "better" available—"Mike" had the explosive equivalent of 10 million tons of TNT (10 megatons) and the Bravo explosion at Bikini, on March 1, 1954, was half again more powerful, 15 megatons; Washington refused to settle for the "old" Bomb when there was a new one available.

Moral restraint too yielded to the technological imperative. It would be wrong to say that no one in government cared about human consequences, but the moral concern about killing civilians had already eroded to the point where further erosion strained few consciences. Early in World War II, before America's entry, Roosevelt had stated to a Red Cross meeting that "the bombing of helpless and unprotected civilians is a tragedy which has aroused the horror of mankind. I recall with pride that the United States has consistently taken the lead in urging that this inhuman practice be prohibited." Unfortunately no one, including Roosevelt, paid much attention to sparing civilians thereafter, and even if they had, the atom bomb would have made the issue moot. In 1945, when targets were chosen for The Bomb by the Interim Committee, one of the specific instructions was that it be deployed against "a war plant *surrounded by workers' homes* . . . [and] without prior warning" (emphasis added). Now, with the Super, there was not the remotest chance of isolating the devastation to a limited target; blast, fire, and radiation would kill large numbers of innocent civilians many miles beyond Ground Zero. In World War I only 5 per cent of the 9.8 million dead had been civilians; in World War II, 48 per cent of the 52 million dead were civilians; in Korea the ratio of civilians killed was even higher. Now, with thermonuclear weapons, civilians would constitute almost the total casualty list.

To add insult to injury, it was all for naught. The Russians put their own hydrogen bomb chip in the military pot only nine months after the United States did, and the relationship of forces remained approximately the same. "The response the Government made in 1949 and 1950 to go ahead with the bomb," Bethe said years later, "was natural and perhaps even correct. It was said then that we were in a Cold War and we had to develop the hydrogen bomb because the Russians would develop it. Well, they sure did, but it is obvious that there would be no security. And I think it is obvious now that weapons are completely out of proportion, that they no longer have any function as a continuation of foreign policy."

The confirmation of this judgment was graphically illustrated in Korea. The Bomb, again, played no role in deciding the issue. It did not stop the North Koreans from overrunning the South, the Chinese from entering the fray when the North Koreans began to fall back under American attack, or the Russians from giving material support. It had neither actual value as a war instrument, nor blackmail value. President Eisenhower, in his famous "Atomic Power for Peace" speech before the United Nations (December 8, 1953), noted that in the eight years since 1945 the United States had "conducted 42 test explosions" making possible new generations of A-bombs "more than 25 times as powerful as the weapons with which the atomic age dawned." The warheads at United States disposal already exceeded "by many times the explosive equivalent" of "all bombs and all shells that came from every plane and every gun in every theatre of war in all the years of World War II." Yet this impressive pyramiding of nuclear armament had made absolutely no difference in Korea. In that theater, as in China, they served no function as "a continuation of foreign policy."

The Korean lesson, however, did not cause the Eisenhower administration to modify its fixation on the super-weapon, or to slow production. Though he personally had opposed dropping The Bomb on Hiroshima and was perhaps the least hawkish of postwar Presidents, Ike could not or would not dispense with the nuclear option. In his 1954 State of the Union message he warned that: "While [we are] determined to use atomic power to serve the usages of peace, we take into full account our great and growing number of nuclear weapons and the most effective means of using them . . . if they are needed to preserve our freedom." Guidelines already adopted by the National Security Council in 1953 called for placing primary reliance on nuclear rather than conventional weapons, and before he had left office almost all Army divisions were transformed into "pentomic" forces, trained for nuclear action.

Jerome H. Kahan, a Brookings researcher who later served as a senior advisor in the Kissinger State Department, estimates that during the Eisenhower years, from 1953 to 1960, "expenditures for strategic capabilities . . . probably averaged $35 billion annually" (in 1974 dollars), nearly half the total for "defense." Eisenhower never used The Bomb but he did threaten to do so on more than one occasion, and his Secretary of Defense, Neil H. McElroy, warned that in any crisis larger than Lebanon or the islands offshore China, Quemoy and Matsu, tactical nuclear weapons would be employed and would likely lead to general nuclear war.

The nuclear motor was cranked up. Eisenhower didn't shut it off—indeed he pressed more heavily on the throttle.

IV

One of the reasons the nuclear race hasn't been checked is that the weapons developed constituencies of entrenched power elites. Never in any land at any time has the production and sale of weapons been so rigidly institutionalized.

The "constituency" for pursuing atomic bomb technology in 1939 was three foreign-born scientists, Szilard, Wigner, and Einstein, who happened to catch the ear of Franklin Roosevelt. The constituency that approved the use of The Bomb at the end of World War II was far weightier. Though the actual decision to "go" with the Hiroshima undertaking was made by Truman, Byrnes (Secretary of State after July 2, 1945), and Stimson, the program had the general endorsement of a larger coterie, most of them the highest representatives of Big Business and Big Banking in government.

Stimson was an old Wall Street lawyer with strong links both to the banking community and government; his assistant, George Harrison, was on leave as president of the New York Life Insurance Company. The Secretary of State before Byrnes, Edward Stettinius, was a J. P. Morgan partner; his undersecretary, Joseph C. Grew, a member of an upper-class banking family in Boston. The chief aides at State and War included Robert Patterson, another Wall Street lawyer, John J. McCloy, chairman of the board of Rockefeller's Chase National Bank (and later president of the merged Chase Manhattan Bank), and Robert A. Lovett, partner of the Wall Street investment firm Brown Brothers Harriman (with which W. Averell Harriman, ambassador to Moscow, was also associated). Dean Acheson, who joined the government as an Assistant Secretary of State in 1941 and was to become the department's secretary and a prime architect of nuclear policy, had been a prominent member of the prestigious Washington law firm Covington and Burling, which by its own claim had represented at one time or another "twenty percent of the companies on *Fortune*'s list of the five hundred top corporations." Secretary of the Navy and later the first Secretary of Defense was James Forrestal, president of the Wall Street investment firm Dillon, Read.

These business-oriented officials were followed in the State Department by men of the same ilk representing the same interests: John Foster Dulles (of the Wall Street legal firm Sullivan and Cromwell), General George C. Marshall, Christian Herter, Dean Rusk (president of the Rockefeller Foundation), Wall Street lawyer William P. Rogers, Henry Kissinger (a project director for the Rockefeller Brothers Fund). The Secretaries of Defense included, among others, Forrestal, Lovett, Charles E. Wilson of General Motors, Neil H. McElroy of Procter & Gamble, Thomas S. Gates, Jr., who was to be president of the Morgan Trust Company in 1965, Robert S. McNamara of the Ford Motor Company. Not all these people were unreconstructed hawks; some, Stimson, for instance, had second thoughts about where The Bomb was taking America. But collectively, as spokesmen for The Establishment, they launched an era of American history in which The Bomb was the strategic linchpin.

Next came a battery of constituencies whose interests were narrower: the military seeking to recover status, the corporate goliaths in quest of profits, academia looking for research grants, the labor hierarchy poking for jobs and dues, and sundry others whose commitment was either ideological or material. The Bomb acted as the coagulant for these varied interests, and they in turn huckstered The Bomb.

It is noteworthy that the ardor for The Bomb generated from self-interests that had nothing to do with The Bomb's utility as an instrument of foreign policy. For the military leadership, for instance, the atom was no lurid passion. Many military leaders, as noted above, were less than enthusiastic about Hiroshima, and somewhat muted in their admiration for the atom generally. Their biggest preoccupation in the first years after the war was to regain ground they had lost—the Army had been slashed from 8.3 million men to below a million in 1947; the Air Force (though not yet an independent branch), from two and a quarter million to less than a third of a million; only the Navy had grown, and just slightly. The big item on the officer class agenda in those days was universal military training (UMT), which would put the nation's youth under the military thumb: each young man reaching eighteen, except the physically handicapped, would be inducted into the services for a few years, then required to take training a few nights each month and every summer for many years thereafter.

Members of Congress, however, kept asking why the services needed so many troops if they had atom bombs capable of killing 75,000 at one blow. UMT, despite the enormous sums and personnel lavished in the campaign to sell it, was destined for defeat. The military would have to take second best, *selective* service, a much less stringent control of the younger generation.

The high brass, therefore, soon was pursuing atomic weaponry with ever increasing fervor—first, because it gave them an opportunity to recoup status, and second, because that was what the civilian establishment wanted. With the help of many others, the brass created a public climate for atomic armament, and while they did not invent anti-Communism, they fanned its flames as a means of increasing support for The Bomb. Thousands of Pentagon propagandists, film-makers, lobbyists, spread the word and heated the tensions, on the theory—as Derek Shearer writes—that "if the world is threatened by international Communism, then naturally the United States must maintain an overwhelming military force to combat the threat . . ." It would be false to say that the three branches were united. They often engaged in fierce inter-service rivalry ("It was sometimes hard to tell," said one wag, "whether they were fighting Communism or fighting each other") to get as big a share as possible of the nuclear assignment. Whatever their scuffling, however, and their different approaches to strategy—based on each service's weapons mix—they were singularly united on the overall objective of "more."

Unlike the military, the corporate brass needed little coaxing. Long before World War II had ended, key figures in industry were suggesting the need for an alliance of Big Business and the military in a "permanent war economy." Charles E. Wilson, president of General Electric, speaking to the Army Ordnance Association in January 1944, urged that the machinery for such an economy be established immediately because "the revulsion against war not too long hence will be an almost insuperable obstacle for us to overcome in establishing a preparedness program . . ." Under his plan every large firm would choose a liaison man with the armed forces (to be commissioned a colonel in the reserves). The role of Congress would be "limited to voting the needed funds," while industry and the armed services would jointly decide how the funds should be used. Military preparedness, said Wilson, "must be, once and for all, a continuing program and not the creature of an emergency."

It was not difficult to divine what was the motive here, even if Wilson and others of his type are credited with the best intentions. In due course this fervor for the militarist society would be rewarded with billions for research and many more billions for procurement—something business had never before enjoyed in peacetime. According to an estimate by former Senate Foreign Affairs Committee chairman J. William Fulbright, some years ago, military spending provided "the livelihood of some 10 percent of our work force." Approximately 22,000 prime contractors and 100,000 subcontractors depend on the Pentagon for at least part of their business, and some depend on it entirely. Corporate support for the nuclear arms race was not based on strategic calculation, so much as on self-interest. If the President had decided to scrap The Bomb and increase correspondingly the production of planes, tanks, and land mines, that would have suited industrialists just as well. They gave their blessings to The Bomb because that was the channel for profits under existing circumstances, not because it did or did not make political sense.

A particularly dynamic element that was co-opted for the win syndrome, oddly enough, was the scientific community, the physicists, biologists, chemists, and engineers who work directly on the ultra-modern weapons, as well as the social scientists and theorists who give it a rationale. It is not that the scientists were united behind official policy; on the contrary, thousands—including many of those who first developed The Bomb, such as Szilard—refused to participate in anything relating to the arms race. But they were either weeded out of the decision-making process or they weeded themselves out. "The physicists," said J. Robert Oppenheimer, "have known sin," and not a few were doing penance for having associated with atomic bomb technology in the first place.

But, as Ralph Lapp observes, "a not inconsiderable part of the scientific community adapted itself to the Pentagon's $8 billion per year funding of research and development. The corrupting influence of secret activities invaded the campus, creating pockets of the military-industrial complex in the university domain." These pockets were the propellants of what a chastened McNamara eventually called "a kind of mad momentum intrinsic to the development of all new nuclear weaponry." The imperative of technology became, again in Lapp's words, that "if a weapons system *could* be made, then it *would* be made . . ." (emphasis added). The scale of this "mad momentum" can be gauged by the fact that as of 1973 the federal budget was sponsoring and paying for 19,000 separate research, development, test and evaluation projects, more than half the funds for this purpose (56 per cent) going for "missiles, aircraft and satellite systems" related to nuclear war.

The perniciousness of a permanent war economy with so many constituencies working on its behalf is that it is self-reinforcing. It is almost totally free of public control, and substantially free of control even by government leaders. Key military officers, the National Security Council, the President, and a few committee chairmen in Congress may make the decisions on strategy but, in large measure, the weapons available determine the strategy, and the weapons available come into being by a process that is little related to political analysis. Each weapons system is its own justification—if it can muster the required support from the military, industrial, and scientific constituencies.

"We just do what the government asks; we build what they want," a General Electric vice-president is reported to have told a college audience. Such humility is praiseworthy, but the way a weapon is born is not quite that simple. Each year the Pentagon awards a mountain of defense contracts ($38 billion in 1974), a portion, large or small, going to each of the fifty states. Members of Congress, not unexpectedly, apply whatever pressure they can to have orders allocated to their own industrial constituents. A Senator or House member with influence can achieve wonders; the late Mendel Rivers of South Carolina, when he was chairman of the House Armed Services Committee, boasted that he had brought to his district 90 per cent of its lush defense facilities, including a Marine Corps air station, an Army depot, a shipyard, a Navy training center, two Polaris missile facilities, a Navy supply center, two Navy hospitals—a payroll, all told, of $200 million a year, with many thousands of people dependent on it for a livelihood.

Thus, to begin with, the congressional elite and the military bureaucracy invariably develop a common bond and a common instinct to escalate the arms race. The bond is so strong that from

1949 to 1968 not a single appropriation or authorization bill was reduced on the floor of either the House or Senate, a truly remarkable record considering how many bills for social improvements were cut or excised in that same period. Khrushchev describes in his memoirs a discussion he had with Eisenhower at their 1959 Camp David meeting on how the military budget is set on both sides. In America, Eisenhower explained, "my military leaders say, 'Mr. President, we need such and such a sum for such and such a program.' I say, 'Sorry, we don't have the funds.' They say, 'We have reliable information that the Soviet Union has already allocated funds for their own such program.' So I give in." The Soviet premier said "it's just the same" in his country. If there is any resistance left in the White House Office of Management and Budget, it soon disappears if a Soviet "threat" can be conjured.

Money, therefore, is no problem. Scientists and engineers working for either the Pentagon or private industry have merely to come up with a promotable weapon and its fate is assured. That is not much of a problem either. Prior to World War II the government was spending almost nothing on military research and development (R & D); in 1947 (exclusive of AEC research) it allocated a half billion dollars for this purpose (four times what all other government agencies were receiving); by 1975 the figure was close to nine billion (again excluding the nuclear energy commission and space agency). Most of that R & D money goes to the 100 big corporations which do about two thirds of all defense work, the lion's share to the top twenty-five such as Lockheed, General Dynamics, General Electric, etc., who carry off roughly half the military orders.

Within these corporate organizations are thousands of retired officers—2,072 in 1968, according to Senator William Proxmire—plus innumerable civilians who once worked for the Pentagon, often buying the weapons systems they now sell. For example, former Assistant Secretary of Defense Thomas Morris went directly from his post as chief procurement officer for the Pentagon to a top job with Litton Industries. In his last full year with government Morris and his subordinates approved a 250 per cent jump in Litton's defense orders, from $180 million to $466 million. As a Litton executive, dealing with men in the Pentagon who once worked for him, he was expected to do even better. "Morris' vice-

presidency of Litton," commented Proxmire, "can be viewed both
as a payoff for the huge Pentagon business shifted to Litton in
1968 and an assurance of immense future influence for Litton."
Litton had quite a few other men besides Morris with a similar history, including forty-nine retired high-ranking officers on its payroll, retired General Carl A. Spaatz on its board of directors, John
H. Rubel, a former Assistant Secretary of Defense, as a senior
vice-president. This is an alarming situation, strongly hinting that
aggrandizement has been more important than patriotism in stok-
ing the fires of preparedness. Moreover, the trend is for the great
corporations to entrench themselves, since almost all of their contracts are awarded without bidding—simply by negotiations between the Defense Department and a selected corporation it feels
can do the job. A study made in 1966 showed that of the biggest
twenty-five defense corporations twenty-one had been on the top
list a decade before. There is little turnover.

Within each of these giant firms there is an interesting mechanism for getting a contract. The Pentagon itself may ask a corporation to submit a proposal for a weapon or a weapon improvement, but as a Washington sales representative told David E. Sims,
"if you wait around until the RFP [Request for Proposal] comes
out, you're dead." Usually, Sims points out, the suggestion comes
from three closely interrelated organs within the corporation.
"There is a long-range requirements analysis office, a larger engineering office dealing in advanced programs, and, more important, a sales/marketing organization." The first of these groups,
made up of engineers, social scientists, and other specialists, tries
to analyze what the military will be asking for in years to come.
Sometimes this same group at Lockheed, or Boeing, or General
Electric, has already prepared—under contract—long-term analysis
of expected military threats and consequent military requirements
for the Pentagon itself.

Based on these analyses the advanced engineering group "pre-
pares detailed technical studies that can become either Unsolicited
Proposals or responses to RFP's." In other words, it synthesizes
the research and development work under way in its company to
come up with an appealing plan for a new or modified weapon. At
this point the sales/marketing organization takes over, assigning
its staff to sell the.Unsolicited Proposal to the general or admiral

in whose jurisdiction it falls. So specialized is the selling technique that the Pratt & Whitney Division of United Aircraft, Sims reports, has one man to promote the F-15, another for the AMSA (Advanced Manned Strategic Aircraft), and so forth.

Each of the three constituencies in this arms procurement process (plus the labor union hierarchy, which wants to protect jobs) has a powerful incentive for escalating the arms race. The ultimate disaster for these forces is disarmament, and the second worst disaster is a defense posture which calls for stability—such as a true deterrence strategy whose needs can be met with a couple of hundred missiles. Their very existence depends on shaking things up, finding excuses for new weapons or better varieties of old ones.

Robert C. Aldridge, who was an aerospace engineer for Lockheed, gives us a striking insight into how "defense industries keep the business coming." "With regard to keeping the business going," he writes, "the weapons industry has learned a lot from Detroit. If we examine the progression of sea-based ballistic missiles, for example, the yearly (or bi-yearly) model changes look a lot like automobile model changes. The 1,200 nautical mile range Polaris A-1 missile of 1960 was lengthened two and a half feet to reach out another 300 miles, and came out in 1962 as the Polaris A-2 model. Next came the A-3—still the same diameter but with improved propulsion and triple-header bomb load—and it was deployed in 1964. The next model change enlarged the circumference and carried many reentry bodies which would be directed to different targets." President Johnson found a new name for this model, after he was inaugurated, the Poseidon—after a Greek god of the sea—and everyone involved sought to give it a rationale. First, it was said that the Poseidon was essential "to confuse Soviet anti-ballistic missile defenses." This was a thin rationale to lean on since anti-ballistic missiles—either American or Russian—never amounted to much and have recently been scrapped. The final pretext adopted was insidious. "Pentagon planners," writes Aldridge, "apparently foresaw that the deterrent theory based on second-strike retaliation against such vulnerable targets as cities and industrial parks would not hold up as a credible excuse for making fancier weapons. Stronger justification was needed. The Pentagon supplied it in the form of a new strategic doctrine—called 'counterforce'—which implies the first use of nuclear weapons."

Aldridge, who was heavily involved with the Poseidon program, is convinced that the various "gaps" that are periodically "discovered" by military intelligence and heralded by politicians and press in scare warnings, are stratagems for proceeding with ever newer, more expensive, and "better" weapons. The "bomber gap" of the 1950's fathered the B-52 plane; the "missile gap" of 1960 (peddled by Kennedy) was the excuse for the Polaris submarine and an increase in ICBM's. James Schlesinger's allegation that America needed a "counter-force capability" because the Russians were acquiring one—the "counter-force gap"—is of the same genre, with the single purpose of expanding research, development, and production of new models of weaponry. Significantly, three years before Schlesinger was openly talking of "counter-force," Lockheed was already developing counter-force weapons such as the Trident missile, on which Aldridge was a leading engineer.

The President of the United States, powerful as he is, cannot alter this system of creating and deploying more and more instruments of death. He cannot possibly know of the thousands of projects "in the pipeline"; and short of cutting the military-industrial complex down to size he cannot reverse the trend for "more." The public of course is in an even worse position, not knowing either what is in the pipeline, what is planned, or what mistakes are being made—because all of it is marked "secret." A thousand little conspiracies go on behind its back of which it is completely unaware and which it cannot restrain. For example, when there was some discussion during the SALT negotiations in 1970 of banning MIRV's (multiple independently targeted re-entry vehicles), Lockheed and the Navy put their heads together to find a substitute for the MIRV'ed Poseidon which was nearing the production stage. "Fearing unfavorable reactions should the study become generally known," Aldridge writes, "classification management declared that mere knowledge that such an activity was in progress was secret information. The task force was given a code name and the people of this country were never the wiser."

The public knows only what is infrequently leaked about such matters as weapons failures, poor designing, waste, bad performance; all of it is stamped "classified" or "secret." More, the public is trained, by ceaseless propaganda about the need to "guard" secrets and national security, not to question its leaders in this area.

In the vast majority of instances the only "security" guarded is the security of those who prod the nation toward higher military peaks without rhyme or reason, or who miscalculate the value of a new weapon. Very little of it can possibly be secret from the Soviets.

v

In a democratic society every interest group not only should have the right to form alliances to further its cause, but should be encouraged to do so. It is a mark of social strength when a senior citizens' organization is created to lobby for national health insurance or larger social security payments; or when an ad hoc coalition comes together to protest higher telephone rates. It is something entirely different, however, when *government* uses public funds to sell its pet projects, or when a constituency *subsidized* by government does so. For scientists to establish a federation to agitate against the arms race is one thing, but for government to underwrite a scientific group that agitates in favor of the arms race is quite another matter. The essence of democracy, as our forebears clearly understood, is that a citizen or a citizens' group must be given protection against the very government that serves them, because the government is so immeasurably more powerful that an individual or group cannot stand up against it. Hence we insist that the government must prove an accused guilty; he does not have to prove himself innocent. Government may not invade our privacy, tap our telephones or enter our premises without judicial warrant, or force the press to publish what the government wants it to publish.

But when a military machine with a $114 billion budget, a defense industry with $40 billion in procurement, and a scientific and engineering community with $9 billion R & D money at its disposal, join hands in their own self-interest to "sell" a weapon such as the B-1, the ABM, or the Minuteman III, that is a manifest subversion of the democratic principle. The government's own money is being used to brainwash the populace, and when this is compounded by secrecy, we have an array of power not only difficult to challenge, but *impossible* to impress with rational argument.

The constituencies which benefit from the arms race spend incalculable millions each year—whose source ultimately is the federal treasury—to give the arms race its intellectual rationale. The Pentagon has thousands of civilian and uniformed persons to lobby, advertise, and huckster its cause—back in 1951 Senator Harry Byrd put the figure at 3,022; today no one can possibly tell how large the public relations force is because many on the Pentagon payroll serve in dual capacities. Industry, academe, and the military, in a joint effort, underwrite hundreds of university centers, private research corporations, and a host of think-tanks such as RAND which constantly elaborate "good" reasons for the arms race to continue. Conversely, those who are unenthusiastic about the arms race have difficulty getting a postage stamp. Edward Teller and his associates receive limitless sums for the Livermore Laboratory at the University of California, which specializes in nuclear research, but when Professor Kenneth Boulding, then with the University of Michigan, tried to wangle $250,000 for his Center for Research and Conflict Resolution to study unilateral initiatives that might slow the arms race, he was turned down. His project had to subsist on a $30,000-a-year budget raised by the school from private sources.

The voices we hear most often, therefore—and by a ratio of thousands to one—are the voices of the pro-military segment of our society. Part of the Treasury dollar which goes to the defense corporation winds up in dozens of semi-private institutions as "position papers" that are circulated far and wide to prevent such "catastrophes" as rejection of the B-1 bomber or the ABM. Along with the monies that go to the think-tanks, those funds buy the brains which are in effect the fourth branch of the armed services, and provide the raison d'être for the arms race. It is this intellectual segment of the nuclear constituencies that invariably finds a justification for the Pentagon's quest for "more"—either (1) that the Russians have outpaced us, (2) that the Pentagon and President must have "multiple options," or (3) that deterrence is "unstable," not working. What they sell most of all is fear—combined with the ironic promise that if America is strong and determined there will be nothing to fear. "It is part of the general pattern of misguided policy," General MacArthur told the Michigan State Legislature on May 15, 1952, "that our country is now geared to an arms economy which was bred in an artificially induced psychosis of war hysteria and nurtured upon an incessant propaganda of fear." Early in the Cold War one of the key figures in Congress, Senator Arthur Vandenberg, expressed the opinion that if the United States was not to be diverted from preparedness, it was necessary "to scare the hell out of the country." The intelligentsia identified with the arms race do just that.

"Is there any limit to the nuclear race," Edward N. Luttwak, a Pentagon consultant and associate director of the Washington Center of Foreign Policy Research at Johns Hopkins, was asked in a 1975 interview. "There is no race," he replied. "That's a cliché. American expenditures on strategic weapons have been declining since 1959, every year but one, and its megatonnage is 40 per cent less than ten years ago. The B-52 used to carry 25-megaton bombs, now it carries bombs of one to four megatons. The most powerful Minuteman missile has three warheads of only 170 kilotons each."

The same plaint was heard from Colonel Jack Frisbee (ret.), a pleasant man who edits *Air Force* magazine and has taught at the Air Force Academy and West Point. "The arms race," he says, "is a one-sided affair. Warsaw Pact forces are much larger than NATO forces, and NATO is falling apart. While the U.S. has reduced its nuclear pile steadily since 1968, the Russians have increased theirs." He warns against accepting "the figures that the CIA compiles. Its estimate of Soviet spending is much lower than those made by any other intelligence agency. It has been consistently wrong."

The unassailable impression is that poor Uncle Sam is falling far behind—and must repair the balance. The "facts," however, are somewhat out of context. Strategic spending by the United States fell for some years because the military changed from a delivery system based on big bombers to one based on missiles—and bombers are far more costly to maintain than missiles. Similarly, the megatonnage of American warheads has been reduced, according to Herbert Scoville, who once worked for the Pentagon and CIA, because it was found that with improvements in accuracy the big weapons, such as a 25-megaton bomb, were unnecessary. "Two one-megaton bombs," says Scoville, "can do the job as well or better than one 25-megaton bomb. In total, however, the U.S. has many more strategic warheads than the Russians (the figure today is 9,000 to 3,500), and in tactical warheads there is just no comparison. We're way ahead."

Luttwak refuses to put a finite figure on the number of warheads we need. He concedes that a "minimal deterrent" of 100 missiles "is adequate to protect the territory and political integrity of the United States. But it is inadequate to protect our allies. The international predicament is not a bus you can get off at will. In the real world, unlike the unreal one, you have to respond to many situations—a threat to Israel, to Asia, or to Western Europe—and you can never have enough options, because each situation is different. You find that your options are either too strong or too weak, and you have to adjust with a different blend of weapons." On this theory there is no end to what we need, because military science, like everything else, is imperfect: there can never be an option that is just right, neither too strong nor too weak.

A more important figure in the nuclear firmament, Albert Wohlstetter, who served as associate director of projects at RAND, is a master at proving that "the thermonuclear balance, which it is generally supposed would make aggression irrational or even insane," is "in fact precarious." It is falling out of line, becoming unstable, he writes in a January 1959 issue of *Foreign Affairs,* because "we must expect a vast increase in the weight of attack which the Soviets can deliver with little warning and the growth of a significant Russian capability for an essentially warningless attack. . . . At a critical juncture in the 1960's we may not have the power to deter attack." Again, poor Uncle Sam is falling behind. If the Russians can incinerate us "with little warning" we had better do something and do it fast—because there is a "lead time" of six to eight years between conceiving a weapons system and deploying it.

Change a few commas and catch phrases and this has been the sermon of the nuclear theorists since they first came on the scene. They always plan, as ex-Senator Fulbright says, "not on the probable, but on the *worst* possible contingencies." Russia might not yet have a certain weapons system, but if there is some chance, however remote, that it will develop it, the strategists argue for the United States to begin work on a counter-weapon at once. In testimony before Congress, John S. Foster, Jr., director of Research and Engineering at the Pentagon, put it this way: "We are moving ahead to make sure that, whatever they do, or *the possible things we imagine they might do,* we will be prepared . . . we see possible threats on the horizon, usually not something the enemy has done, but something *we may have thought of ourselves that he might do,* and that we must therefore be prepared for" (emphasis added). Thus, even though the Soviets put a low priority on improving their bomber fleet, the SAGE continental air defense system was installed at a cost of $18 billion on the chance that they might. The Pentagon argued—incredibly—that the expenditure was necessary to deter Moscow from *planning* a better bomber plane. Similarly the F-14 plane was developed to withstand a supersonic bomber attack on American aircraft carriers, though the threat, in the opinion of the Senate Defense Preparedness Subcommittee, was "either limited or does not exist." The Poseidon missile for submarines was designed to penetrate the Soviet TALLINN system, then believed to be an anti-*missile* defense. When it was found that the TALLINN was far less ambitious, simply an anti-*aircraft* defense, the Poseidon should have been scrapped, since its purpose was gone. Instead, it was redesigned for more accuracy, as a hedge against the new Soviet SS-9s.

On this basis it is absolutely excluded that the nuclear race can ever end; the fertile minds at the think-tanks and in R & D can always envision another threat a few years hence or in the distant future—such as a war between missiles on the dark side of the moon—which requires an upgrade on our weapons systems. And they can—and do—come up with scenarios for waging nuclear war that sometimes boggle a rational mind. (Herman Kahn, in his book *On Escalation,* spells out forty-four "rungs" of escalation, ending up with such interesting ones as "slow-motion counter-'property' war," "slow-motion counterforce war," "slow-motion countercity war," "countervalue salvo," "augmented disarming attack," and finally the "spasm or insensate war" in which someone pushes the button in an "automatic, unthinking, and uncontrolled" fashion.)

It is an endless process, seemingly—like a circular assembly line. The United States tries to envision what the Russians may be able to invent; and its scientists and engineers try to find an antidote for something the adversary does not yet have but will be producing six to eight years from now. The Russians, invariably behind, try to keep up, and meanwhile the men and women at the think-tanks devise new scenarios and new strategies to deal with future possibilities that require still more innovative inventions.

Alain C. Enthoven and K. Wayne Smith wrote a book some years ago (1971) asking *How Much Is Enough?* Former Deputy Defense Secretary David Packard apparently has given the answer. When asked what the word "sufficiency" means, he shot back: "It is a good word to use in a speech. Beyond that it doesn't mean a goddamned thing."

4

The Win
Syndrome (2)

If the object of American policy has been to prevent the Soviet
Union from expanding its power it has obviously not succeeded.
Russia may still be second to the United States, but in military
and economic terms, as well as world influence, it has built a formidable edifice, and it is certainly not falling apart. Why then has
the United States shied away from making war against the
U.S.S.R.? The United States twice in this century took to the
battlefield to stop German expansion, and simultaneously, in
1941–45, to stop Japanese expansion. Why hasn't it done so
against the Soviets? If Washington has had an irrepressible fixation
on winning, and in addition has had such a sizable advantage in
nuclear weaponry, it would seem logical that it should try to do to
the Russians what it did to the Germans and Japanese.

In a 1960 article on the "nature and feasibility of war and deterrence," Herman Kahn, a weapons and strategy expert who
spent eleven years at the RAND Corporation, posited a hypothetical scenario which sheds some light on this subject. We always
have to consider, he argued, "damage versus commitments."
"Imagine," he wrote, "that the Soviets have dropped bombs on
London, Berlin, Rome, Paris, and Bonn but have made no detect-
able preparations for attacking the United States . . ." The ques-

tion then is how shall the United States respond? Should it "fulfill its obligation and strike the Soviets" with atomic warheads? That depends, says Kahn, on the extent of the "damage" Washington must expect in return. "No American that I have spoken to who was at all serious about the matter," he writes, "believed that U.S. retaliation would be justified—no matter what our commitments were—if more than half our population would be killed." What then would be a tolerable price to pay for the privilege of eviscerating the Soviets? "I have discussed this question with many Americans," says Kahn, "and after about 15 minutes of discussion their estimates of an acceptable price generally fall between 10 and 60 million dead."

Many people considered Kahn a colorful crank when he wrote these, and similar, words in two books on nuclear strategy, but he was in fact part of the mainstream of U.S. strategic thinking and highly respected at the Pentagon and elsewhere. The dilemma he poses, of "damage versus commitments," bedevils policy makers. They recognize that "a thermonuclear balance of terror is equivalent to signing a nonaggression treaty that neither the Soviets nor the Americans will initiate an all-out attack." Yet while shackled by this unhappy stalemate they seek avidly to break it. They grope for that one, big technological breakthrough that will give them so commanding an advantage that the Russians will either have to give up beforehand or be defeated in such a way that America's own losses will be tolerable—say, "10 to 60 million dead." Since that is not yet possible they can only grit their teeth, escalate their investment in technology (and hardware) . . . and wait. They cannot as of today win a strategic war (and they know it), but they must not stop the arms race if they are ever going to find such a way. Therein lies the anomaly of the win syndrome.

Virtually every general, Defense Secretary, or other administration spokesperson who testifies before Congress describes American strategic goals in the following terms, almost word for word: "to deter aggression at any level and should deterrence fail, to terminate hostilities in concert with our allies, under conditions of relative advantage while limiting damage to the United States . . ." (General Earle G. Wheeler, Chairman Joint Chiefs of Staff, before Senate Defense Preparedness Subcommittee, 1969). Or, "Our forces are designed primarily for deterrence.

However, it is conceivable that deterrence might fail for a number of reasons. . . . It is necessary, therefore, that our future nuclear forces be sufficient in size and capability not only to deter a deliberate enemy decision to attack, but, should deterrence fail, to insure that the United States and its allies emerge with relative advantage, irrespective of the circumstances of initiation, response, and termination" (Defense Department document inserted into the record of the Senate Subcommittee on Arms Control, September 11, 1974).

There are three phrases common to all such statements— "should deterrence fail," "relative advantage," "limiting damage." "Should deterrence fail," translated into less circumspect English, means that we must reckon on total nuclear war as a realistic possibility. "Relative advantage" means that if it happens we, the United States, must come out of it better than the Russians. "Limiting damage" means, further, that our casualties must be small enough so that we can continue functioning as the world's leading nation. This is the win syndrome, a posture that will not accept standoff even if finally the "firebreak" must be crossed from conventional to nuclear war. In psychological terms it reveals a suicidal impulse as well as a loss of touch with reality, reminiscent of that famous remark by the U.S. officer at Ben Tre who said, "We had to destroy the village in order to save it."

Back in 1968, General Earle G. Wheeler, Chairman of the Joint Chiefs of Staff, engaged in the following exchange with Senate Defense Preparedness Subcommittee counsel James T. Kendall:

KENDALL: "Are you concerned that in some way we may now be in or approaching a stage of *unconditional* mutual deterrence whereby neither side would dare to use strategical nuclear weapons under any circumstances?" (emphasis added).

WHEELER: "I do not think we have reached that stage, nor do I think we will necessarily reach it if we exert our brains and if we have the will not to permit it to happen. I think that we have the resources to maintain superiority. I do not see this unconditional mutual deterrence."

One would think the general (and the subcommittee) would be pleased that a plateau has been reached—"unconditional" deterrence—where neither side dares attack the other. Instead Wheeler was distressed. He wanted "superiority," not stalemate—a capacity to win, not just keep matters at the status quo.

Well, said Kendall, "suppose the number of casualties that Secretary McNamara discussed should suddenly be doubled [to 160 million of the 200 million U.S. population]. . . . Obviously you would have no country left, neither of us." Wheeler's reply is typical of a large segment of the brass and its civilian friends: "Mr. Kendall, I reject the 'better red than dead' theory, lock, stock, and barrel."

The late Senator Richard B. Russell, chairman of the Senate Armed Services Committee, stated it even more forcefully some years ago. "If we have to start all over again with Adam and Eve, then I want them to be Americans and not Russians, and I want them on this continent and not in Europe."

II

What began as a delusion, that The Bomb assured American preponderance into the twenty-first century, has metamorphosed into a game from which the players cannot escape. The evidence is all against them, but they cannot weigh the evidence because a powerful force is driving them from behind—the military-industrial-academic-labor-congressional-government complex. As the race proceeds, the search for peaceful alternatives is bypassed, the inherent assumption that military power, especially nuclear power, makes us strong, crowds out speculation as to whether, somewhere along the way, we may have taken the wrong turn. Instead, each crisis acts as a pretext for escalating the race, precisely because the previous crisis lies unsolved, and previous strategy has proven unavailing. The Warfare State simply refuses to look at itself with anything approaching political logic.

By way of example: In March 1949 John Foster Dulles, in a *U.S. News & World Report* interview, stated that he did "not know any responsible official, military or civilian, in this government or any government, who believes that the Soviet government plans conquest by open military aggression." George F. Kennan recalls that in this early postwar period "it was perfectly clear to anyone with even a rudimentary knowledge of the Russia of that day that the Soviet leaders had no intention of attempting to advance their cause by launching military attacks with their own armed forces across frontiers." The secret NSC-68 report of 1950 conceded that "the preferred technique" of the Soviet Union "is to subvert by infiltration and intimidation." If all this was true, logic demanded that American policy makers concentrate on techniques for dealing with the problems of social revolution. But their primary response in 1949 was to "go" for the Super. The result was merely to raise the stakes of the nuclear race without adding anything to national security. In fact the United States was less "secure" because the technological gap was narrowing: it had taken the Russians, as already noted, four years to catch up with A-bomb technology; only nine months to catch up with the H-bomb.

The Korean War, starting in June 1950, provided another pretext for military escalation—from expenditures of $13 billion annually to $47 billion. So did the Soviet launch of Sputnik in October 1957, which shifted the focus of the nuclear race from the warhead to the delivery vehicle. Eisenhower described Sputnik's impact on America as a "wave of near-hysteria," and Isidor Rabi of Columbia warned that "the Russians have picked up a tremendous momentum" which might help them "pass us swiftly, just as in a period of 20 to 30 years we caught up with Western Europe and left it far behind." Thus began still another great contest, the futile results of which could have been forecast with mathematical certainty.

By that time the technological community had solved some of the problems which had hobbled the military in the last half of the 1940's, most notably the problem of producing enough nuclear material—enriched uranium and plutonium—for bombs. The "warehouses" soon were full. Though actual figures were secret, scientists could make computations from congressional reports of the amount of uranium feed material going into the enrichment plants, the electric power used, and capital investment. Lapp in 1960 estimated that the United States had 350 *tons* of fissionable material, give or take 20 per cent, enough to fabricate 70,000 Hiroshima bombs. Linus Pauling, using a similar method, placed the figure higher. The costs too, by now, were manageable, insignificant in fact: a million dollars for a one-megaton bomb (seventy-five times the firepower of the Hiroshima warhead), $1.1 million for ten megatons, and $1.2 million for 100 megatons.

Scientists had also unlocked the door to miniaturization, fitting small atomic devices to cannon, mines, and other battlefield weapons; and had discovered how to control atom splitting so that fission could be harnessed to the production of electricity. Each of these had important strategical implications. Eisenhower, Defense Secretary Charles E. Wilson, and others were convinced that, with miniaturization, nuclear devices were virtually indistinguishable from conventional weapons and might therefore be deployed for a "limited" war.

The "mad momentum" of technology hatched ever new military strategies, but something seemed to be missing in each one. Six months after the Korean War reached an unhappy stalemate in July 1953, Secretary of State John Foster Dulles delivered his famous "massive retaliation" speech before the Council on Foreign Relations to punctuate American "toughness" and "determination." Should there be a "new aggression" like Korea, he said, or if the Russians took liberties in Europe, the Eisenhower administration would retaliate "instantly" and with all its "strategic" power. The Kremlin was told, in effect, that if it were to cross any line considered vital to U.S. interests it would be wiped out. "The Line" became part of the American lexicon—a Line beyond which Moscow moved at the peril of extinction. John Fischer, editor of *Harper's,* had recorded in 1951 that "the Line of Containment has held, under great pressure in Greece, Indochina, Turkey, Berlin and Yugoslavia. We have suffered one major defeat—China—but that may yet be recovered . . ." The very fact that anyone was talking about a "Line" in the 1950's reflected a setback from the exaggerated hopes of the 1940's. Now Dulles was saying it would be breached no further, even if it took a nuclear war to hold it.

"Massive retaliation" sounded magnificently awesome, and it could be shown with facts and figures to be quite feasible: the general estimate as of 1953–54 was that the Pentagon was hoarding 5,000 warheads as against 300 or less in the Soviet pile. But it was a delusion of active minds, led astray by wish-fulfillment. "The essential element of the situation," wrote British Nobel prize physicist P. M. S. Blackett in 1954, "is the far greater development of the offensive power of atomic warfare than of the countermeasures against it." The Soviets might have only a few bombers that could pierce American defense, but it would be enough to make life in the States very unpleasant. Charles J. V. Murphy in a 1953 series for *Fortune,* calculated that should Moscow dispatch its planes over American soil "U.S. interceptors and anti-aircraft artillery could bring down between 15 and 20 percent of the bombers—if the bombers came over in daylight. If they came at night, the kill ratio would be a fraction of one percent." Enough would perform their mission to make such a war devastating. A frequently heard estimate of that period was that if the Soviets could drop 250 H-bombs on the United States it would cause 70 million deaths, plus injuries for millions more. Cut the figures in half or a quarter and the prospect was still terrifying. Of course Russia would also be annihilated, but that was small comfort. Moreover, the Red Army in the meantime could not be prevented from occupying all of Western Europe. Would the United States then bomb the land, and kill the citizens, of its closest allies? The idea was simply preposterous, and though Eisenhower and Dulles talked of "massive retaliation" it was never more than a bluff—as the 1956 events in Hungary proved. "Say what you want about Ike," a former Pentagon staffer said in an interview, "he couldn't be kidded by the think-tankers. He knew war better than they did." Western Europe was still hostage to Soviet defense, a circumstance which not only nullified the American nuclear advantage but sent tremors throughout Europe.

The futility of the "massive retaliation" doctrine was so obvious that the Council on Foreign Relations assembled thirty-three experts, headed by Gordon Dean, former chairman of the Atomic Energy Commission, and under the direction of Henry Kissinger, to study the problem of "foreign policy in a nuclear age." Its conclusions were put before the public in a sensational 1957 book by Kissinger, *Nuclear Weapons and Foreign Policy,* which, among other things, picked apart the one-option policy of massive retaliation. "We should leave no doubt," wrote the future Secretary of State, "that any aggression by the Communist bloc may be resisted with nuclear weapons, but we should make every effort to limit their effect and to spare the civilian population." The obverse of "massive retaliation" was to be "limited war." "We could announce," Kissinger continued, "that we would not use more than 500 kilotons explosive power unless the enemy used them first . . ." We would also refrain from striking "the enemy retaliatory force or enemy cities located more than a certain distance" from the battle, say 500 miles, and that in this zone we would not use nuclear weapons against "cities declared open and so verified by inspection." It was all calm and cool-headed, like a philosophy dissertation: both sides would fight a restrained nuclear war with tactical weapons such as the Davy Crockett (a bazooka missile), the Long John (with a ten-mile range), the Corporal and Sergeant (with seventy-five-mile range) and the Pershing (500-mile range), each used in turn, as the fighting became more fierce. But both American and Russian cities would be untouched.

The trouble with this cerebral scenario, it soon became clear, was that our own allies (and theirs as well) would be left in a shambles. War games by the Pentagon to simulate conditions on the battlefield confirmed this judgment. In Operation Sage Brush, played in Louisiana, 275 nuclear weapons were "employed," ranging from a tenth to twice the power of the Hiroshima bomb; the results showed that there was no such thing as a "limited" war for the particular area involved. A similar game for Western Europe, Operation Carte Blanche, in which 335 bombs were used, indicated that 5.2 million of Germany's 49 million people would be dead or wounded within two days. Presumably, if the war lasted as much as three weeks there would be no live or healthy people left in Germany, just 33 million wounded—with few doctors or hospitals to care for them. How the Pentagon would cope with this state of anarchy is unknown, but it is clear beyond dispute that a "limited" war for the United States would be a "total" war for Germany, ending its existence as a nation. Even Kissinger, in a 1961 article titled "A Reappraisal," conceded that a limited war could not be kept limited. (Jimmy Carter expressed a similar view in the 1976 election campaign.)

The desire for victory was so intense, however, that despite the existing stalemate, periodic voices continued to be heard for preemptive attacks or first strikes.

"The United States," said Fleet Admiral Chester W. Nimitz in January 1958, "would not survive on the basis of purely defensive policy of massive or graduated deterrents. These will at best hold the strong terrain. The United States must combine its defensive deterrent strategy with a military attack strategy that reduces the Soviets' strength well below that of the Free World . . ." On

March 2, 1959, Defense Secretary Neil H. McElroy stated, according to the New York *Herald Tribune,* that "American policy remains not to strike the first blow that would lead to war, but that policy could change . . ." The men who made decisions were ill at ease not because the policy of deterrence had effectuated what it was supposed to effectuate—a military stalemate, a balance of terror—but, on the contrary, because the stalemate was not of their choice, and they couldn't seem to find a way around it.

As late as 1963 Colonel Albert P. Sights, Jr., of the Air University, was writing that "we can win a nuclear war." "Defeat," he argued, "will surely come to those who think they cannot win. . . . A nation rightly demands no less of its leaders than plans for winning all armed conflicts, including nuclear ones. True, a government may elect to stop short of victory, but its armed forces must be prepared nonetheless to go the full distance if required." His formula for victory was simplistic, "an aerial blitzkrieg of unprecedented power and efficiency, one that will overwhelm the enemy's air defenses and destroy his offensive air forces wherever they may be found"; but his zeal and conviction that our "air power can do the job" were not atypical. The only trouble was that none of these win proposals could be made even remotely feasible by any realistic calculation of what would happen in a nuclear war.

III

Since the strategy of massive retaliation, despite its bellicose rhetoric, was clearly feeble, the sharp-minded Kennedy team that took office in January 1961 decided on a grab bag of options, under the rubric "graduated response." It was not that they spurned the atom—on the contrary, Kennedy increased military expenditures in his first year by $6 billion. Nor did they have compunctions about threatening nuclear war, as evidenced by the October 1962 Cuban missile crisis. But it dawned on key officials, Kennedy in particular, that the source of Soviet strength was its ability to chip away at the world status quo piece by piece, studiously bypassing the atom. In an April 1961 speech to the American Society of Newspaper Editors, Kennedy showed a keen appreciation of the problem, if not the means of dealing with it. "We face a relentless struggle in every corner of the globe," he said, "that goes far beyond the clash of armies or even nuclear armaments. The armies are there, and in large number. The nuclear armaments are there. But they serve primarily as the shield behind which subversion, infiltration, and a host of other tactics steadily advance, picking off vulnerable areas one by one. . . . The message of Cuba, of Laos, of the rising din of Communist voices in Asia and Latin America—these messages are all the same. The complacent, the self-indulgent, the soft societies are about to be swept away with the debris of history. . . . We intend to reexamine and reorient our forces of all kinds—our tactics and our institutions here in this community."

Whatever that re-examination might produce, Kennedy evidently recognized there were places where the nuclear stick was grossly irrelevant. He also seemed to recognize the hazards in wielding that stick: in a book published the year before he became President, he argued that "inevitably the use of small nuclear armaments will lead to larger and larger nuclear armaments on both sides, until the world-wide holocaust has begun."

But if JFK understood all this, the "graduated response" doctrine concocted by himself, McNamara, General Maxwell Taylor, and a small brigade from the RAND Corporation, simply constituted a decision to *build up everything*. In General Taylor's pithy language, the purpose was to "deter general war, to deter or win local war, and finally to cope with a general war if deterrence fails." The nuclear threat was to be retained as an American "shield" and used after a "pause" if all else failed; but there would be a much heavier concentration on conventional and counterinsurgency forces, as well. "If we are to assure that the disastrous big war never occurs," Taylor had written, "we must have the means to deter or to win the small wars."

Presumably, the "graduated response" doctrine (which included McNamara's counter-force), gave the United States a maximum "win" potential, all the more so since the Kennedyites were the beneficiaries—like Truman and Eisenhower before them—of still another technological revolution, this time not in the warheads per se but in the means of delivering them. The cumbersome bomber, which required a pilot and forward bases in Europe, and was "slow" (400 to 500 miles an hour), was to be replaced in priority by a pilot-less missile, which sped to its destination at 9,400 miles an hour and could not be shot down by an enemy plane. Emplaced in an underground silo or in a nuclear-powered submarine, it was also far more difficult to "kill" than the old bomber.

As early as 1957 the scientists and engineers had begun providing the Pentagon with one new generation of ballistic missiles after another, giving the offense a still wider edge over defense. The first one, a two-stage vehicle, with three-rocket engines, and fueled by liquid oxygen and kerosene—the Atlas—weighed 120 tons, was 85 feet long, and accurate, with a relatively small warhead, within 2 miles of its target. Next came the Titan, also liquid-fueled, slightly larger with somewhat greater thrust; and still later, the Minuteman, a solid-fueled vehicle, much smaller and lighter than either of its predecessors (54 feet long, 33 tons in weight) fitting a silo only 10 feet in diameter and 80 feet deep, and having a range of 6,000 miles. The world was now introduced to the space age, and the technological miracle of something called an intercontinental ballistics missile (ICBM).

Concurrently, the Navy came forth with a rocket, called the Polaris, only 26 feet long, fitted with a 600-pound warhead that packed two thirds of a megaton of explosive power, fifty times more powerful than the Hiroshima bomb. In a sense this was an even more sensational development than the Air Force's missiles, because the Polaris was to be fired from a moving submarine undersea, which was next to impossible to apprehend and destroy. It was—and remains—what the strategists call "invulnerable." Even if the Russians could wreck every one of America's 1,000 Minutemen before they were set off and could "kill" every bomber stationed in Europe or Asia, the forty-one Polaris submarines with a range up to 2,500 miles could still annihilate Soviet cities from one end to the other. In subsequent years the Navy replaced the Polaris with the Poseidon missile, each capable of carrying fourteen individual warheads, individually targeted to a different area (MIRV'ed), and is currently working on the Trident submarine, each of which will be armed with twenty-four missiles that can hit targets 4,000 miles away and will, in the words of Senator Thomas J. McIntyre (D-N.H.), "compound the Soviet's anti-submarine warfare problems tenfold and will therefore insure the survivability of our massive sea-based retaliatory force through the rest of this century." The Trident, because it can roam so large an area of ocean, is virtually immune to Russian sensors. In due course too the Air Force "hardened" its missile silos—put more concrete around the vehicle, making it more resistant to incoming Soviet missiles—and MIRV'ed them, equipped them so they can carry three, four, five, six warheads each, individually targeted to different sections of the enemy's terrain.

Yet, with all the new weapons and the improvement in conventional war capability, the McNamara-Taylor-Kennedy "graduated response" doctrine was no more viable than Dulles' "massive retaliation" or Kissinger's "limited nuclear war." Giving the Pentagon all the options from A to Z offered as little hope for victory as threatening the enemy with wholesale and immediate liquidation. The doctrine, as is now well known, failed abysmally in Indochina, where the United States and its allies were driven from the scene in April 1975. It did seem to accomplish its purposes in the Cuban missile crisis of 1962, when the Russians were forced to withdraw intermediate-range missiles they had secretly emplaced on the Caribbean island. But even that was not as sweeping a victory as it appeared to be at the time. It failed of its political goal—to disembowel the Castro regime. A secret quid pro quo, moreover, pledged there would be no further American-sponsored campaigns to invade Cuba.

Beyond that, however, it is now clear that there wouldn't have been a Cuban missile crisis to begin with if McNamara hadn't unsheathed his "counter-force" saber earlier that year. Morton Kondracke, a Chicago *Sun-Times* correspondent, documents this thesis in a *Washington Monthly* article published seven years later. "There are more than a few people in Washington, around at the time," he writes, "who believe that the U.S. never would have got into the crisis in the first place had it not been for McNamara's rattling our rocket superiority and implying that the United States intended to use it in a realistic war game." Air Force Chief Curtis E. LeMay applauded the counter-force speech and the retargeting of U.S. missiles against Soviet rocket sites, but "others at the Pentagon—particularly in the Navy were aghast" that the Kennedy administration was seriously thinking (as the President himself wrote two weeks earlier in a magazine article) of striking first "in some circumstances." Nikita Khrushchev's response was to condemn the

McNamara speech as "a camouflage for nuclear war," place ads in American newspapers warning that the United States was "preparing for a nuclear war," "harden" Soviet missiles so that they would be less vulnerable to a surprise attack—and station the missiles in Cuba.

Whether the 1962 confrontation was a victory or a standoff, Kennedy himself recognized that it wasn't the kind of experience a reasonable person would want repeated—"even the fruits of victory," he said, as already noted, "would have been ashes in our mouths." Toting the score for the "graduated response" strategy, it was a failure at every level. The "brush-fire" war option was running into one pitfall after another, McNamara's and General Taylor's rhetoric to the contrary notwithstanding. "Victory" in a strategic all-out war with Russia, it was clear, would be pyrrhic—"ashes in our mouths." A "limited strategic war" in Europe would reduce the terrain of our allies to the same "ashes," as repeated "war games" played by the Pentagon itself showed. And moreover there was the question as to whether the Soviets would accept the kind of restraints "limited" nuclear war specialists were talking about. Khrushchev warned on more than one occasion that he would never abide by such rules, and in fact they were patently impractical. The American scenario envisioned a Soviet conventional attack on NATO in Europe, to which NATO and the United States would respond with atomic arms—to "repair the balance." But what if the balance turned against the Kremlin, wouldn't it too try to recoup its lost position by dispatching its own super-weapons wherever it would hurt the American side most—including ultimately New York and Detroit? "That it would prove possible, in the event of an atomic war," wrote George F. Kennan, "to arrive at some tacit and workable understanding with the adversary as to the degree of destructiveness of the weapons that would be used and the sort of target to which they could be directed, seems to me a very slender and wishful hope indeed."

One of the prime problems in the limited strategic war scenario is communication. There is no way for an enemy to tell, with anything approaching certainty, whether the bomb heading his way is the beginning of an all-out attack or just a limited one. It takes approximately thirty minutes for an ICBM to devastate a missile silo across the ocean, but only five to fifteen minutes to reach a nuclear submarine in the Mediterranean or a site near Moscow—if launched from Europe. If the United States, let us say, contemplated a "first strike," its missile from Omaha would have to be set off at 9:00 A.M. whereas its missile from Britain would be hurtled into the stratosphere at 9:15 A.M. The generals watching radar signals in Moscow couldn't possibly know, therefore, whether the missile they pick up some minutes after 9:00 A.M. is the forerunner of hundreds to come ten or twenty minutes later, or the only one. But since the cost of making a mistake would be ruinous, they would have to operate on the assumption that it is the beginning of a total attack—and respond in kind. Presumably the American President could get on the "hot line" and tell his Soviet counterpart that this was a "limited" attack, but would he be believed in the state of certain hysteria that would ensue? It is hardly likely. Nikita Khrushchev was not mistaken when he observed that in a war between the Warsaw Pact and NATO nations "neither side could be expected to concede defeat before resorting to the use of all weapons, even the most devastating ones." General Louis H. Wilson, Commandant of the U. S. Marine Corps, made a similar point in an interview with George C. Wilson of the Washington *Post.* "In the early stages" of such a conflict, he said, the United States might be able "to send messages" to an adversary by firing small nuclear weapons. But on the battlefield "it would be very difficult to contain" a war of this kind.

Nor was it reasonable to expect Moscow and Washington to observe Henry Kissinger's 500-kiloton ceiling, if for no other reason than the fact that there was no way to judge, while the fighting was going on, how powerful the warheads were. "The United States does not have, and the Soviet Union presumably does not either," says a report of the Federation of American Scientists (April 1975), "a system for instantaneous damage assessment in nuclear war. If a missile destroyed a city, or missed a city, or landed near a missile silo, there are not a series of sensors that—before being destroyed—report immediately the extent of the damage. Nor do we now have a method of determining—when missiles in flight are reported—where those missiles are headed and may land. Thus during the period of warning of enemy attack, the President would not be sure what was happening." Neither would the Kremlin, if the situation were reversed. "And since only minutes would be available, one can expect only confusion in higher circles"—the kind of confusion that might very well trigger total war, even when one or both sides want to "limit" it.

IV

In the hands of the Russians, The Bomb has been a response, not a challenge. To say that is neither to defend nor condemn Soviet behavior. It is simply a fact: virtually every technological innovation in the nuclear arms race has originated in the United States, and in the one or two instances when the Soviet Union scored a breakthrough first—with Sputnik, for example—the United States quickly overcame the disadvantage and forged ahead with seven-league boots. The Russian leadership, too, wanted to "win" but the "win syndrome" in the U.S.S.R. pivoted on an entirely different axis: to link its fate with the growing national and social revolution that nibbles away at the Western world's periphery. The nuclear initiative has come from America, which deployed advanced instruments of war in unending profusion.

The trouble has been that in each asymmetrical situation, America's superiority could be nullified—not by Soviet defense, because there was no physical defense against The Bomb by either side, but by other means. In the first decade or more of the nuclear age, Moscow overcame its shortcomings by holding Western Europe hostage to its conventional might. It was also able to add just enough warheads, short-range and long-range missiles, as well as tanks and planes for traditional warfare, to stymie hopes for a low-cost victory. It has been throughout a game of seesaw, which so far at least has been unwinnable.

Not long before Kennedy came to office the United States acquired a weapons system which by all odds should have tilted the scale decisively in its favor. In 1960 the first nuclear-missile submarine, the Polaris, was put to sea. The mating of the nuclear reactor with the traditional submarine represented a revolution in naval warfare of greater significance than the changeover from oars to sails, or from sails to steam. A glob of uranium the size of a golf ball, two pounds in weight, provided as much energy for the submarine as 3,000 tons of coal or 460,000 gallons of fuel oil had previously. Where the diesel-powered sub could travel underwater for only a few hours at a time before coming to the surface to run its engines, nuclear propulsion made it possible to remain submerged—and at far greater depths—indefinitely. The nuclear power plant produced oxygen from seawater, so that the only limitation on the amount of time the submarine was forced to stay below the surface—traveling from one ocean to another (including the Arctic)—was dependent on the supply of food the ship could carry, and the ennui of the sailors. A typical nuclear sub may remain under sea nowadays for two months at a time. More, whereas the most powerful weapon of the pre-nuclear sub, other than the torpedo, was a sixteen-inch shell with 50 to 500 pounds of TNT, the present Polaris sub can discharge missiles with warheads having the explosive power of 500,000 to 1,000,000 *tons* of TNT.

"The submarine," writes former New York *Times* military expert Hanson W. Baldwin, "has become the modern 'capital ship,' or principal ship, of nuclear war . . . Its new-found importance can be emphasized dramatically by one statistic: from 1960 to 1963, the personnel assigned to submarines in the United States Atlantic Fleet increased from 8,000 to 15,000 officers and men . . ." The first nuclear sub, the *Nautilus,* was built in 1954; by the end of John F. Kennedy's abbreviated term in office thirty-five such vessels had been commissioned, and more were being planned or constructed. Today, as noted, the United States has forty-one nuclear submarines, ten of the Polaris class and thirty-one newer Poseidons. Each of the American vessels of this type usually carries sixteen missiles, each missile with ten to fourteen warheads, or a total of 160 to 224 warheads. "Just one nuclear submarine," writes Phil Stanford of the Center for Defense Information, "can destroy any country on earth."

But advantageous though this may have been for the United States, it was an advantage quickly lost—exactly as might have been expected. C. P. Snow once observed that "societies at about the same level of technology will produce similar inventions. In military technology in particular, where the level of the United States and the U.S.S.R. is very much the same [and] where the investment of scientists and money is also similar, it would be astonishing if either society kept for long anything like a serious, much less a decisive, lead. . . . It is quite unrealistic, and very dangerous, to imagine that the West can expect a permanent and decisive lead in military technology over the East as a whole. That expectation is a typical piece of gadgeteer's thinking. It has done the West more harm than any other kind of thinking. History and science do not work that way." The first Polaris in the United States went to sea in 1960; by 1965 the United States already had thirty-three undersea nuclear vessels, as against nine for the Soviet Union, but as of 1974 the numerical advantage had turned the other way around, forty-eight for the Russians, forty-one for the Americans. While this disparity is more fictional than real— because the United States submarine missiles are MIRV'ed, while the Russian missiles carry only one warhead each—the gap certainly will soon be closed in that respect too. The latest Russian sub, the Delta, had a missile with a 4,000-mile range, not far out of line with the projected U.S. Trident, which initially will carry delivery vehicles with a 4,500-mile range.

Despite Washington's technological successes, the nation remained vulnerable to attack. A couple of years after the ICBM and nuclear sub were deployed McNamara alerted Congress that "fully hard Soviet ICBM's and nuclear-powered ballistic missile-launching submarines would considerably detract from our ability to destroy completely the Soviet strategic nuclear forces. . . . Even if we were to double and triple our forces we would not be able to destroy quickly all or almost all of the hardened ICBM sites. And even if we could do that, we know of no way to destroy the enemy's missile-launching submarines at the same time."

There just was no means by which America could win a general war; its efforts had to be confined to smaller ventures aimed at weakening the Soviet alliance—such as the Vietnam intervention. "From the end of World War II until quite recent times," General Maxwell D. Taylor, chief architect of the Kennedy-Johnson strategy, wrote in 1966, the main military concern "was to keep ahead of our opponent in numbers and quality of nuclear weapons and delivery devices. . . . Since that time, we have moved rapidly in the direction of better preparation for nonnuclear war . . ." That too of course was to be a failure—though Taylor does not yet admit it—but it indicates how difficult the problem of global strategy had become. Far from guaranteeing the kind of victories originally envisioned at the dawn of the fission-fusion era, nuclear power mired the military and civilian leaders in desperate confusion.

V

McNamara left his post before the end of the Johnson administration a chastened and disillusioned figure. His civilian defense program—about which more later—had proven to be an undiluted fiasco (the twenty RAND people who devised the program evidently understood its uselessness as much as did the general public, because not one of them built a shelter for his own home). The Vietnam "brush-fire" war fared even worse, leaving behind only a spate of statements by generals and Defense Secretaries that in retrospect are ludicrous ("French victory is both possible and probable," Defense Secretary Charles E. Wilson, 1953; "the guerrilla threat in Vietnam has receded to a point where one single territorial regiment could handle it," Lieutenant General S. T. Williams, 1959; "the corner has definitely turned towards victory," McNamara, May 1963; "we have stopped losing the war," McNamara, November 1965). The Secretary's nuclear strategy, including the "counter-force" doctrine, had shown itself to be an exercise in futility.

Toward the close of his incumbency, McNamara presented to Congress new figures on what might happen in a nuclear exchange. He computed the results that might accrue under three different circumstances: (a) where the United States did nothing to improve defense, (b) where it spent $9.9 billion for anti-missile devices to protect twenty-five cities, and (c) where it spent $19.9 billion to protect fifty cities. The computer print-out was extremely disheartening: if the Soviets struck first and the United States retaliated, the result would be the same in *all three postures*—120 million American dead, 120 million-plus Soviet dead. The expenditure on defense would be for naught. If the United States struck first and the Soviets retaliated, the situation would be somewhat worse in relative terms—100 million American dead under Posture A, 90 million under the other two postures, BUT "only" 70 million Russian fatalities. The reason the Russians would lose less if the United States struck first was that many of its weapons would be expended on their missiles, leaving less to destroy their cities.

In any event, both societies would lose three quarters of their industrial facilities, leaving them hopelessly unviable.

With all that, however, and with evidence from some of the best minds in the nation that the military ship was off course, the mad momentum of the arms race could not be stopped. The constituencies promoting it were too compelling. "I have calculated," wrote atomic pioneer Ralph Lapp in 1968, "that as few as 45 ballistic missiles can strike at 60 million Russians living in 200 Soviet cities. No, my arithmetic is not nutty—each missile can be armed with from three to ten nuclear warheads targeted on individual cities. The total megatonnage in this hypothetical attack amounts to only 21 megatons—roughly one thousandth of that once carried by our SAC bombers." But though America already had many times that number of missiles and hundreds of times that megatonnage, it was not enough. It was not enough because, in spite of the fact that the game was self-defeating, the players refused to stop playing it in hopes of still finding the weapon or combination of weapons that would finally augur victory.

VI

The next doctrine to emanate from Washington was called by Nixon's Defense Secretary, Melvin R. Laird, a "spectrum of conflict." It was a refinement of the McNamara doctrine of graduated response. America must be prepared, said Laird, to fight a "strategic nuclear war" (all-out), a "theater nuclear war" in Europe (with the help of French and British nuclear weaponry), a "theater conventional war" in Europe, and a "sub-theater or localized war." Except for the rhetoric there was little innovation here. Perhaps the Administration was so preoccupied trying to "win" in Vietnam it had neither the resources nor the will to elaborate anything better.

The only new element added to the military calculus in the first few Nixon years was the campaign for an anti-ballistic missile (ABM). It was a charade by decision-makers thrashing about without sense of direction. What the ABM was supposed to do was give the United States a true defense against incoming missiles, something that had been deemed impossible for more than a decade. The scientists and think-tankers had been discussing an *anti*-missile missile since 1954 on the theory that if you could "kill" the enemy's missiles in flight you had a near perfect "win" formula. The United States in this hoped-for nirvana, would save all or almost all its people and property ("damage limitation"), while the Soviet Union would be laid waste by the Pentagon's *offensive* missiles. On paper the idea was most attractive. But the plan had already been vetoed by Eisenhower and rejected by Kennedy because, among other reasons, there was no radar system adequate for the task. Lyndon Johnson, perhaps because he was losing the war in Vietnam and wanted to recoup public esteem, revived the hope of an ABM defense in 1967–68 when he bludgeoned $1.9 billion out of a suspicious Congress to develop the Sentinel program. Nixon, however, was prepared to go further, at an initial cost of $7.2 billion, exclusive of the price of warheads.

As even its proponents knew, however, the Safeguard system (a modified version of the Sentinel) was little more than an exciting fantasy. The Safeguard required two kinds of radar to track the enemy's ICBM's in their last ten minutes of flight; and the most complex computer system ever devised, with twenty data-processing units and a capacity equal to 100 large commercial computers. Once the radar "found" the incoming missile it would be intercepted by a Spartan (with a range of a few hundred miles) that would "kill" it in the stratosphere, or the Sprint that would "kill" it in the atmosphere, both from the radiation of their explosions, x-rays in the case of the Spartan, neutrons in the case of the Sprint. Fully deployed, Safeguard would consist of twelve sites in the continental United States and one each in Hawaii and Alaska.

The program was so flawed, however, that not even the Pentagon, in a most vigorous propaganda effort, could sell it. Assuming everything was in good order—the radars, computers, Spartans, and Sprints—the Russians could make the system unworkable either by sending up decoys and other objects that would make the computers inoperative; or by neutralizing the radars with jamming devices on the incoming missiles; or by lowering orbit trajectories to evade U.S. radar.

Military systems, however, do not work *perfectly*. That defect alone would make the ABM useless, for if even a small number of enemy missiles came through it would be enough to cause untold fatalities in the United States. According to Dr. Daniel Fink, a former Deputy Director of Defense Research and Engineering, the normal missile used in offense was reliable 41 to 65 per cent of the time. Defensive missiles (ABM's) would be considerably less trustworthy. The radar and computer elements were even more "high-risk," according to Dr. Abram Chayes of Harvard. There was a three to one chance that at least one radar would be out of commission at any given time, thus allowing a considerable number of enemy weapons to hit their targets unhindered. Additionally, the Soviets had only to increase the *number* of their offensive missiles to overwhelm the Safeguard system. A few billion in expenditures for more delivery vehicles and warheads would render the ABM valueless. Even the Nixon people recognized these flaws, for they fell back on the argument that if not of great value against the Russians, the ABM might be useful against *the Chinese.* Nixon continued to ask for funds for the anti-missile missile, but he was forced to concede finally that "although every instinct motivates me to provide the American people with complete protection against a major nuclear attack, it is not now within our power to do so."

Under President Ford the ABM sites were entirely abandoned—after an expenditure of billions.

5

Towards Armageddon

When James Schlesinger was appointed as Defense Secretary in May 1973 he inherited an impressive technological harvest—MIRV's, MARV's, the automated battlefield, cruise, Trident, B-1, mini-nukes—some already deployed, others in advanced research. Yet there still seemed to be no way to weave all this military wealth into a "win" strategy; the problem remained that while offensive capability was total, defensive capability was nil; while the United States could destroy the Soviet Union, it could not simultaneously save itself from destruction. This was the same problem that had confounded strategy for the better part of two decades, and had caused think-tankers and government officials to range far and wide seeking a way out of the dilemma—massive retaliation, limited nuclear war, graduated response, counter-force, and McNamara's last hurrah "mutual assured destruction" or MAD.

The strategists found themselves with a mix of three elements that were not compatible, yet interrelated and indispensable to each other. First was "The Threat"—you had to threaten the Soviet Union with all-out war, lest it take liberties in other types of action where the odds were in its favor, such as conventional war or guerrilla wars by its allies. "Our atomic deterrent forces," General

Maxwell Taylor wrote in a 1958 memorandum for the National Security Council, "would be the shield under which we must live. This shield would provide us protection, but not a means of maneuver." The "atomic deterrent," in other words, stays the enemy's hand, so that—hopefully—he doesn't send aid to surrogates and allies, and more important, doesn't take advantage of American preoccupation to initiate little wars of his own elsewhere or attack the United States itself.

That of course has always been a feature of the military planning, that each side assesses what are the enemy's reserves and what he can or cannot do with them. The "reserves," even though not in use, invariably affect the outcome, and never more so than under present circumstances. In the scenario described by Edward Luttwak for a war in Korea the North Koreans invade South Korea with conventional weapons, the United States calls in planes from all over the world to demolish the North with conventional bombs, and if that is not enough takes the next step, a nuclear shelling. Suppose, however, that Russia decides to compensate for the loss of an ally with an adventure of its own, say against neighboring Turkey or oil-rich Iran. To discourage the Soviets, Washington would have to make clear in advance that it is prepared to devastate the U.S.S.R. itself—and might just be "crazy" enough to do it. The Russians must be made to accept a victory by the United States in Korea, but must not be allowed to square the record with a victory of their own. Otherwise there is no "win," only a trade-off.

This state of affairs did not obtain in the early days of the Cold War, when America held a monopoly. The Bomb, it was thought by many, would bring direct results—such as confining the Soviet Union within its own borders or at worst no farther out than Eastern Europe. It was to be an instrument of international blackmail (as all weapons are to one extent or another), which, if it didn't succeed, would lead—in James Byrnes's phrase—to "measures of last resort," i.e., actual war. But after the United States lost its monopoly, The Threat forfeited its sting until it finally assumed a *psychological* more than a physical character. All threats obviously have a psychological element, but in most instances those who threaten are willing to follow through with action if their threat is not taken seriously. In this instance the threat is a bluff because each side knows that action means double suicide. The only question really is how the bluff can be made believable. This has been the dilemma of the nuclear age, at least since the late 1950's, that The Threat was credible only if Moscow could be convinced that Washington, *in some circumstances,* was ready to pay the price of America's own demise.

The burden that Defense Secretaries carried twenty years ago was that it was *difficult* to devise a strategy for *total* victory against the Soviets. Schlesinger's problem was that it was impossible. The situation itself was "no-win." Victories or stalemates could be recorded on the lower rungs of the military ladder—in CIA wars or wars through surrogates—but ultimate victory against the other superpower was out of reach. "Victory" itself meant defeat, if defeat is defined as loss of national coherence and national will.

As far back as 1946, some theorists concluded that the military function was no longer to plan how to win wars, but how to avoid them. "Thus far," wrote Bernard Brodie and his colleagues at the Yale Institute of International Studies, "the chief purpose of our military establishment has been to win wars. From now on, its chief purpose must be to avert them. It can have almost no other useful purpose." The simple deterrence advocates in the nuclear age felt that the capability to deliver 100, 200, or 400 nuclear weapons on the enemy would deter him from attacking the "free world," and was all that the military could aspire to.

"The modern—or post-1945—strategists," by contrast with the "classical" strategists, notes Colonel Richard L. Curl in the Winter 1975 *Strategic Review,* "although usually accepting that force *exists* as an element in international affairs, have believed that force could be eliminated or at the very least intelligently controlled. Thus they took the threat of the use of force as a major element in the definition of strategy, and devoted their time to determining how wars could be avoided."

The people, however, who held the *simple* deterrence theory—the one the public wrongly believes to be American policy—were eased out or eased themselves out of government. They became either critics with little influence, or, more often, quiet bystanders. The men who predominated in policy making used the *word* "deterrence"—because of its non-aggressive connotation—but they meant something entirely different than simple, or stable, deterrence. In their lexicon, as defined by Colonel Curl, deterrence is "a *derivative* function and not the goal itself" (emphasis added). It is the "shield" General Taylor talks about. It is part of a holding operation until a true defense ("damage-limitation") can be found and all-out wars can again become winnable, as in the pre-nuclear age. The purpose of "derivative" (or "unstable") deterrence is not to avoid war, but to prevent the enemy's reserves from coming into play during wars of lesser destructiveness.

The Threat, then, is designed to stay the enemy's hand by convincing him that there *are* circumstances which would cause the United States to launch a nuclear war. The Threat is constantly repeated so that the Soviets will not miss the message. "Strategic bombing [i.e., an atomic attack on Russia itself] has a high priority in our military planning," General Omar Bradley, first Chairman of the Joint Chiefs of Staff, said in October 1949. "I don't think we ought to use this thing [The Bomb]," said Harry Truman, *"unless we absolutely have to."* Eisenhower, according to one of his advisors (quoted by C. J. V. Murphy in *Fortune,* March 1956), "made it clear from the beginning that defense strategy plans were to recognize the existence of atomic weapons and the fact that *they would be used if needed."* "We would propose," said McNamara (February 22, 1963), "to use nuclear weapons or any other weapons wherever we felt our vital interests require their use." "We and our allies together," said Richard Nixon, "must be capable of posing unacceptable risks to potential enemies . . . Potential enemies must know that we will respond to *whatever degree is required* to protect our interests. They must also know that they will only worsen their situation by escalating the level of violence." (All emphasis added.)

The Threat, however, loses its muscle with repetition. As a quarter of a century of experience has proved, it did not prevent the Soviets from coming to the aid of guerrilla or revolutionary allies, with the possible exception of Cuba in 1962, and even there the outcome was questionable. Nor did it prevent Communist (and neutralist) expansion. When The Bomb was first being developed, Communism was confined to a single country with 190 million people, and virtually all of Asia, Africa, and Latin America was a colonial or neo-colonial appendage of the Western powers. Three decades later Communism embraces fifteen countries with more than a third of the earth's population, and if you include Third World nations that are lukewarm or unfriendly to the West, such as Algeria, India, Tanzania, Libya, more than half the world has escaped the status quo that The Bomb was supposed to guarantee. The Threat was ineffective, yet it was felt necessary to continue making it. It was the only thing approaching a "defense" that the think-tankers could hatch. Every few years, however, they had to modify or strengthen The Threat because unless it was credible it was meaningless.

It was a risky business in itself since it required that the contenders build up gigantic mechanisms for monitoring and threatening each other, thereby increasing the danger of war by accident or miscalculation. As Professor Lloyd J. Dumas of Columbia University points out in a May 1976 article for the *Bulletin of the Atomic Scientists,* from 1950 to 1973 "there have been at least 63 serious accidents publicly reported involving major mass destruction weapons carrier systems, or an average of more than 2.5 severe accidents per year." Most alarming of these was the crash of a B-52 bomber near Goldsboro, North Carolina, carrying two 24-megaton weapons. One bomb was intact when removed from the wreck, but the other had come very close to exploding: five of its six interlocking safety systems had been triggered. Had the last one been tripped as well—say at a height of 11,000 feet—"all standard housing within 12.5 miles" would have been destroyed and "all flammable materials within a 34.5 mile radius" ignited.

At Palomares, Spain, on January 17, 1966, another B-52 had crashed with four big hydrogen bombs aboard, and at Thule Bay, Greenland, on January 21, 1968, still another B-52 with the same number of weapons fell into the bay, melting seven-foot thick ice. There had been, in addition, at least four instances of "false warnings"—where radar or other systems were misread. On October 5, 1960, NORAD (North American Air Defense Command) received a warning that "a missile attack had been launched against the United States"; it took fifteen to twenty minutes to discover that "the radars, apparently, had echoed off the moon." During 1971 there were three similar incidents, one of which took forty minutes to correct. Had these mistakes not been caught in time there is no telling what might have happened, but it certainly would not have been pleasant.

The second element in the strategy mix was "damage limitation," how to save enough lives and property, should war break out between the superpowers, for America to remain a viable nation. This too was related to The Threat, because unless the Soviets perceived that America was taking steps to husband its main resource, people, it would conclude that the Pentagon was bluffing. The paradox here was that there was a disparity between the price and the profit. A conventional war such as Vietnam might cost 55,000 lives and $160 billion in wealth—an enormous cost—but it was well within the "damage" range that American leaders could absorb. To chance total war for the same objective, or for the defense of a General Park in Korea, was something else again. There was a *physical* defense against a guerrilla, a tank, or a bomber (the M-16 rifle, the machine gun, the anti-tank gun, the anti-aircraft missile), but no physical defense whatsoever, as the ABM debate showed, against an intercontinental ballistics missile, or a submarine-launched missile. The enemy would know that we knew there was no conceivable way to limit "damage," just as we would know that he knew.

American scientists, of course, were working on the problem of defense, and not a few strategists were confident it would be solved before long. Colonel Richard L. Curl, Staff Engineer of the Army's XVIII Airborne Corps, believes "it is a virtual certainty that a technological answer to the ICBM will be forthcoming in the near future which will assure a virtually 100 per cent impregnable defense. This is an easy prediction to make because the forerunners of such a system are already realities and the march of technology appears unstoppable. For example, laser technology, while not in itself the answer, is on the verge of merging with nuclear physics to produce the 'graser'—the amplified gamma ray. . . . A 'graser' tied to current state-of-the-art phased array radars offers promise of destroying an incoming barrage of warheads in microseconds, simply and cheaply." A perfect defense of this type would change the whole calculus of war, since "damage" to America would be negligible, whereas "damage" to the Soviets would be total. The incentive for a first strike—or the blackmail that could be exacted with that capability—would be irresistible.

However, the "graser" was not yet with us, and no one could tell whether the Russians had on the drawing boards a "de-graser" or other means to make it ineffective. Meanwhile the men at the helm had to steer towards a realistic strategy with the full knowledge that in today's world their nuclear arrow was bent. The only "damage-limitation" plan that offered even the slightest chance of saving lives was the civil defense program—as weak a reed to lean on as a cornstalk during a tornado.

The third element in the strategy mix was the operational one—which type of war or wars constituted what General Taylor called "the active elements of our military strategy." In the McNamara-Taylor scenario the United States was prepared to fight two and a half wars simultaneously—one in Europe, another in Asia, and a "half" war in Latin America. But the weight came down on "brush-fire" "counterinsurgency" wars with conventional weapons; it was here that Kennedy's (and Johnson's) "best and brightest" hoped to earn super-profits. They built up their capability in that area—and plunged into the morass of Southeast Asia, hoping that The Threat of counter-force, repeated by McNamara until 1965 or thereabouts, or MAD in the latter years, would frighten Moscow into inaction. As events proved, it didn't. If the United States, then, in addition to being stymied on the nuclear front had no way of winning lesser wars, it was in a sorry state indeed. Back in 1960, when he was an associate professor at the University of Virginia, Schlesinger urged, in a book titled *The Political Economy of National Security*, that we reconcile "ourselves emotionally to the need for the continual exercise of power to protect our interests . . . We must become adjusted to the heavy costs of limited warfare as a condition of life . . ." Should even that channel be foreclosed, American power—in his view—would decline precipitously.

Unfortunately, the Pentagon's depressing record in Vietnam greatly magnified the new Secretary's task. Three months before he took the post, Henry Kissinger had signed a peace treaty with Le Duc Tho that the Nixon administration hailed as "peace with honor," but which was in fact a setback without parallel in American history. As with China a generation before there was a cascade of excuses for not winning, ranging from the "soft" position that the Army was poorly trained for fighting guerrillas to the abrasive charge that Washington's refusal to bomb Hanoi "into the stone age" or invade the North represented a deliberate policy of "no-win." Whatever the cause of the miscarriage in Vietnam, the image of American invincibility was badly battered and the McNamara-Taylor strategy of "graduated response" severely tarnished.

Schlesinger's task was to fabricate strategy to the measure of these handicaps. He took to that task with typical determination and self-confidence. "Much of what passes as current theory," he said, "wears a somewhat dated air—with its origins in the strategic bombing campaigns of World War II and the nuclear technology of an earlier era when warheads were bigger and dirtier, delivery systems considerably less accurate, and forces much more vulnerable to surprise attack." A man of eloquent circumspection in public but excruciating bluntness sometimes in private (the first time Nixon met him years back, he told underlings, "I don't want to see that guy in my office again"), he concocted a comprehensive strategy which has the merit of being coherent, if not necessarily realistic.

What he proposed essentially was to make total war credible by making limited tactical war and limited strategic war (what in our hypothetical ladder corresponds to the fourth and fifth rungs) *operable,* "the active element." The Schlesinger Doctrine, observed Herbert Scoville, former Deputy Director of CIA and former Assistant Director of ACDA, was "part of a very planned campaign to acclimate the American public and to get better support for a new policy in which our country would consider using nuclear weapons much more freely than we have in the past." What the new Secretary was actually calling for was a breach in the "firebreak" between conventional and nuclear weapons—a barrier that had held for three decades. In a sense that was inevitable—as the quality of nuclear weapons improved, as the technological wonders piled up, and the pressure by the arms race constituencies mounted for a "win" formula. But it also narrowed the gap between the *threat* of nuclear war and the *actuality* of one, for it is an anomaly of The Threat that it is more believable as it comes closer to being actualized.

II

The Schlesinger Doctrine—still official policy though he himself is gone—was foisted on the American people in much the same way as Lyndon Johnson enlarged the war in Vietnam, in bits and snatches and always by minimizing each step upwards. Speaking to the Overseas Writers Association on January 10, 1974, Schlesinger, as already noted, matter-of-factly announced "a change in targeting strategy as it were." Because "both sides now have, and will continue to have," he said, "invulnerable second-strike forces [such as the nuclear submarine] . . . it is inevitable, or virtually inevitable that the employment by one side of its forces against the cities of the other side in an all-out strike will immediately bring a counterstrike against its own cities." Since each superpower has the wherewithal to deter the other, "the range of circumstances in which an all-out strike against an opponent's cities can be contemplated has narrowed considerably. . . ."

Having thus made the point that "strategic forces" to strike at the other side's cities serve little purpose, the Secretary concluded that *"one wishes to have alternatives for the employment of strategic forces . . ."* (emphasis added). But why does the United States need an "alternative" for its "strategic forces," if they are "virtually" valueless? The answer of course is that the militarist mind seeks a use for everything: if the missiles and submarines for an all-out war against the Soviet Union have no realistic function at the moment, why not utilize them, if necessary, in a "restrained," "limited" war against the Soviet Union?

In his annual Defense Department Report a few months later the Secretary hinted at what was really in his mind. "The concept that has dominated our rhetoric for most of the era since World War II," he said, "has been massive retaliation against cities, or what is called assured destruction." Left with that single terrifying option, might not an American President hesitate to take it? Might he not be paralyzed as his finger rested on "the button," lest the man on the opposite side of the world, who had his own button, push it in return? "If we could all be guaranteed that this threat [of MAD] would prove fully credible (to friend and foe alike) . . . we might also agree that nothing more in the way of options would ever be needed," said Schlesinger. "The difficulty is that no such guarantee can be given."

From here on the reasoning becomes even trickier. Deterrence, MAD, cannot be guaranteed because "we ourselves find it difficult to believe that we would actually implement the threat of assured destruction"; and since "we" might hesitate to take such shocking action, "there can be no certainty that, in a crisis, prospective opponents would be deterred from testing our resolve." In other words total war is so horrifying that the enemy may conclude that we won't launch it; that being the case he may decide the risk of retaliation is so small it's a good gamble to attack us first. No one asked Schlesinger why it didn't work the other way around: The United States concludes that Russia lacks the resolve for so monstrous an attack, the United States initiates a surprise all-out offensive on Russia.

That, however, is only one of the minor illogicalities of the Schlesinger Doctrine. The true purpose of his dissertation was to affirm a need for "selective response options—smaller and more precisely focused than in the past." That would require, on the one hand, beefing up conventional forces to fight *automated* wars with remotely piloted drones, unmanned aircraft, and laser-guided weapons, but, more importantly, beefing up the tactical and strategic forces for fighting less than all-out, "controlled," wars—something like the Herman Kahn scenario for step-by-step escalation. As George C. Wilson of the Washington *Post* described it, the President would reserve to himself the option to "wound rather than kill." That "could mean that in a war the President would give an Army colonel permission to set off nuclear mines to stop Soviet troops marching towards West Germany; order a B-52 bomber pilot to fire one of his SRAM nuclear-tipped missiles at a single Russian refinery or factory; radio a submarine skipper to shoot a missile at a Soviet airfield; approve the launch of a few Minutemen ICBM's to knock out the communications center for Soviet rocket forces without hitting cities in the process."

Under this "make nuclear wars small" strategy, writes Wilson, "Army theoreticians—to the disgust of some battle-hardened officers who know that actual combat is often mass confusion—are holding secret meetings in the Pentagon these days, for example, to sing the praises of the new warheads that destroy only the target —nothing else." This is called "zero collateral damage," and falls under the heading of what Schlesinger and the others, in their exotic jargon, call "restrained counter-force." Instead of a maximum attack on an adversary's forces Schlesinger would order a minimum attack, then wait for the other side to respond—either with his own minimum attack or with a plea for negotiations. If he decides to continue, the United States continues, escalating a little but not to all-out dimensions. To repeat Senator Stuart Symington's rejoinder: "You talk as if the Joint Chiefs of Staff of the Soviet Union and the Joint Chiefs of Staff of the United States were together in this thing and started to play a game of chess."

In the lexicon of the trade there are essentially three kinds of counter-force—the term for attacking the opponent's military forces rather than his cities. One is the "disarming first strike," defined by Robert Sherman, in the *Strategic Review* (Spring 1975), as an "attack sufficient to reduce the adversary's *total* retaliatory capability to a level one considers tolerable." Neither the United States nor the Soviet Union *today* has anything approaching that capability. A second variety is the "damage-limiting counter-force," in which our side retaliates against the other's military targets so as to "reduce our total damage to a point which, even though above the 'acceptable' level, would be lower than we would otherwise sustain." (Sherman is contemptuous of this notion, on the grounds that "if we place our adversary's weapons in a 'use them or lose them' situation" the chances are more than likely that he will use them.) The third species, restrained counter-force, is a means of "sending them a message," in Schlesinger's words, "a series of measured responses to aggression which bear some relation to the provocation, have prospects of terminating hostilities before general war breaks out, and leave some possibility for restoring deterrence."

If the Russians were willing to play Schlesinger's game of a controlled nuclear war, presumably they would be sufficiently intimidated to keep out of situations such as Vietnam, Angola, Korea, or what have you. The threat of "wounding" rather than "killing" is more formidable than the all-out threat because the Russians know that Washington wouldn't flinch from action where its "damage" cost would be tolerable.

It is very heavy thinking, except that the Russians are not likely to play, and there are few people anywhere who believe a limited nuclear war can be kept limited. Oddly enough one of the best rebuttals to "restrained counter-force" came from the pen of Henry Kissinger in a book, *The Necessity for Choice*. He may or may not still hold to that view, but his 1960 words are lucid and incontrovertible: "While it is feasible to design a theoretical model for limited nuclear war, the fact remains that 15 years after the beginning of the nuclear age, no such model has ever won general agreement. . . . The Air Force thinks of it as control over a defined air space. The Army considers it vital to destroy tactical targets which can affect ground operations, including centers of communication. The Navy is primarily concerned with eliminating port installations. . . . Since disputes about targets are usually settled by addition—by permitting each service to destroy what it considers essential to its mission—a limited nuclear war fought in this manner may well become indistinguishable from all-out war."

Another disquieting feature of "restrained counter-force" was that the "damage" could be far more substantial than the Ford administration perceived. In briefing a Senate Foreign Relations subcommittee on September 11, 1974, the then Secretary estimated that if Moscow struck at U.S. "ICBM fields alone" with a single one-megaton bomb per silo—leaving aside the forty-five SAC bomber bases, the command and control facilities, various support bases, and of course the cities—"the number of fatalities [would be] up to about 800,000." Another million and a half would "fall ill as a result of radiation sickness coming from fallout," but they would recover in due time. It wouldn't be nearly as bad as generally believed. "Very limited and quickly terminated nuclear exchanges," Schlesinger said in his annual report, "could result in fatalities much lower than from some of the traditional conflicts we have experienced."

The Senate subcommittee which first heard the report was indelicate enough to ask the Office of Technology Assessment to recheck the figures. An ad hoc panel, chaired by MIT president Dr. Jerome Wiesner and including many experts who once worked for the Pentagon, concluded that the Pentagon-Schlesinger estimate of 800,000 dead was "unrealistic." It had assumed, for instance, that the Soviets would level only one missile against each silo, whereas they were perfectly capable of striking each one with three or more. It had assumed that the bombs would be detonated in the air, minimizing the fallout hazard, whereas detonation on the surface of the earth would endanger life and health, according to Richard L. Garwin, who has been associated with nuclear development since 1950, "as far as 1,000 miles in the downwind direction from the military targets." It had assumed favorable winds, instead of a weather pattern for the month of March, "when the winds tend to spread fallout to great distances." Taking these factors into consideration, the number of fatalities would be not 800,000 but "in the range of 3.5 to 22 million"—and that left out of account death from "fires, long-term radiation exposure, the interactive effects of the loss of communications, hospital facilities, etc." It also failed to mention—as one of the experts, Sidney D. Drell, pointed out—that such an attack "would result in some 800,000 Canadian fatalities alone, and a total Canadian casualty figure of 1.2 million, or about 5 per cent of their total population."

Nor did Schlesinger's reassuring figures take into account the toll from a condition of anarchy in many places, with millions of corpses to be buried, many millions seeking shelter, and about five million injured clamoring for medical aid. "The seemingly rigorous models of nuclear deterrence," observed Fred C. Ikle, ACDA Director, "are built on the rule: what you can't calculate you leave out." Dr. J. V. Neel of the medical center at the University of Michigan (testifying September 16, 1975) showed how impractical it was to expect treatment for the large number maimed by blast, radiation, and fire. His own facility, one of the best in the country, "can handle exactly 10 acute [burn] patients at a time." Clearly medical treatment would be unavailable for hundreds of thousands, a condition made to order for wholesale riots. A Reuters dispatch of September 20, 1975, from Ankara, Turkey, tells of a small civil war in the village of Saydamli, center of an earthquake that took 2,350 lives two weeks before. Villagers, it seems, fought with guns to get their hands on the sparse number of tents being distributed to the homeless. How much more turbulent would the situation be in an America ravaged not by a couple of thousand casualties but with 3.5 to 22 million dead and 5 million injured.

Schlesinger offered no protest when his figures were challenged. Neither, however, did he, Congress, President Ford, or anyone else in high office change a comma in their new strategy.

III

In the Schlesinger schema, the back-door dividend from "restrained counter-force" and "selective response" was that it embellished The Threat with an aura of realism—and greater menace. This was quintessential because The Threat was the closest thing to "defense" in the Pentagon arsenal. "In the past," Henry Kissinger wrote in 1957, "the strategy for avoiding defeat was roughly identical with that which aimed for victory." In the thermonuclear age, however, defense rests on the *psychology* of affrightment, how well the United States can convince its adversary not that it *has* the weapons to kill him—that is quite obvious—but that it will *use* them. What made previous threats, back to "massive retaliation," vague and implausible, was that it was difficult to imagine an American leader (or a Soviet leader) making the leap directly from conventional war to all-out nuclear war. Experience had shown that the American colossus had backed away from implementing The Threat during a number of severe crises in the Communist world—the East Berlin uprising, the Hungarian events, Czechoslovakia. In evaluating the price and the profit, cool (or paralyzed) heads had opted for rhetoric instead of action. But if the United States were to move across the threshold actually to use nuclear arms in a limited way, or if it displayed unshakable determination to do so, the all-out threat would also become more credible. From conventional war to nuclear war is a quantum jump; from one type of nuclear war to another is far less painful on the psyche—and the Russians doubtless would recognize that.

The "credible threat" is perhaps the weirdest aspect of military strategy in the nuclear age, for it depends not on reality but the *perception* of reality. "No threat is stronger," Kissinger once observed, "than the belief of the opponent that it will in fact be used." If the enemy doesn't cower, The Threat is worthless. We must maintain military "equivalence," constantly upgrading the quantity and quality of weaponry, Schlesinger told Congress in the summer of 1974, "in order that we not only have the equivalent physical capability to the other superior power, but also in order that we be *perceived* as equal by all parties around the world . . ." (emphasis added). That perception is doubly important because of what it "does to our own will." If we feel and act strong, others will think of us as strong. If we don't, allies will conclude that we may not defend them, and enemies that they are free to roam at will. Whether or not the weaponry serves any purpose in the substantive sense, it must be deployed to convince the world that we will "match" our enemies, will raise the ante as necessary. Leslie H. Gelb of the New York *Times* summarizes the Schlesinger approach this way: "Like the true Thucydidean historian that he is, he goes beyond the Strangelove scenarios of nuclear war to *perceptions* of the strategic balance. His question is always, 'How will others see the balance?' and, 'Will others not regard imbalances favoring Moscow as a sign of disintegrating American will?'"

In the end it resembles a game of "Chicken." As Bertrand Russell described it, Chicken "is played by choosing a long straight road with a white line down the middle and starting two very fast cars towards each other from opposite ends. Each car is expected to keep the wheels of one side on the white line. As they approach each other mutual destruction becomes more and more imminent. If one of them swerves from the white line before the other, the other, as he passes, shouts 'Chicken!' and the one who has swerved becomes an object of contempt."

Schlesinger's "selective response" strategy certainly makes the game of Chicken more interesting, because the enemy is always held in a situation of uncertainty. He doesn't know whether he will be attacked with conventional arms or with nuclear arms, and if nuclear arms, just how far it will go. "One of the major aspects of U.S. deterrence around the world," Schlesinger said, "is the volatility, to some sense the unpredictability of American reactions." In the words of Stefan Leader of the Philadelphia *Inquirer* (July 20, 1975) this statement was meant to "plant a seed in the mind of other countries that we just might be crazy enough to use" nuclear weapons. As any psychologist will affirm, there is no great line of demarcation between "acting" and "being." Schlesinger made The Threat more credible simply by bringing the world closer to the brink.

This unfortunately is not a game that can be played forever. The Threat is part of the calculus of actual nuclear war, if only because Chicken must be played to its outer limits, a little closer to the moment of impact all the time. It is high-risk adventure which in a time of attenuated crisis can—and must eventually—transform threat into reality. The Threat can be credible only so long; after that it loses its force and must be refurbished to appear more menacing.

In the process of refurbishing, however, the arms race gains additional momentum. That is so because to give The Threat credibility, the U. S. Government must "scare the hell" out of the American people, to establish a public climate favorable to more armaments and more armament research. Washington dare not appear conciliatory, even when it has—for one reason or another—entered into certain accommodations. "Détente," said Defense Secretary Donald Rumsfeld in March 1976, does not mean "the Soviets are our friends—that we can trust them, and that they will conduct themselves the way we do in our country, that they believe in freedom and individual God-given rights of man, that they will not continue to support 'just wars of national liberation' or that they will not continue to develop substantial military strength to serve their interests." The Soviets must be pictured as untrustworthy, evil, cunning, and even worse—as catching up to us and surpassing us. Thus every year at budget time a general or a Defense Secretary suddenly discovers that there is a "bomber gap" (1956–57), or a "missile gap" (1960), or, as in 1975–76, that the Soviets have overtaken the United States in military power. Since no one outside government has access to the facts the hysteria can be maintained long enough to secure funds from Congress for new projects. Actually there never was a "bomber gap" or a "missile gap"—Senator Symington has shown that the missile force available to the Kremlin in mid-1961 was only 3.5 per cent what the intelligence sources had estimated, and the number of bombers only 19 per cent.

The Ford administration 1975–76 claim that Moscow was "outspending us" for defense by 30 or 50 per cent was achieved by the dubious technique of computing Russian military expenditures in *dollars*. The CIA and Pentagon asked themselves, "What would it cost to buy the Soviet defense establishment in the United States at U.S. prices?" The pay of an American private is $383 a month, and with upkeep the cost to the U. S. Government is about $10,000 a year. The wage of a Russian soldier is negligible, and with upkeep runs to only $1,700 a year—one sixth the American cost. By computing the annual wage costs of the Soviet Union's 4.4 million troops at $10,000 instead of $1,700 its military expenditures can be made to loom far larger than they really are. By this and similar sleight of hand it was determined that in 1975 Russia was spending $107 billion a year (in 1974 dollars) and America only $79 billion. "When the calculations are done with rubles," however, Congressman Les Aspin points out, "the United States is the bigger spender." If you reduce the American private's wages from $383 a month to what Soviet privates receive, and do the same for the cost of tanks, planes, etc., the gap turns out to be the other way around. More, if you compute what damage the Pentagon can inflict on the Soviet Union the whole thing is absurd. "Even if the Soviets successfully carried out a devastating attack on our forces," writes Aspin, destroying 50 per cent of our submarine-launched missiles, 90 per cent of our land-based ICBM's, and 80 per cent of our B-52 nuclear bombers, "the United States would still have about 3,100 surviving warheads—and that is 10 percent more than the Soviet arsenal has now, before an attack. . . . The United States would still have enough surviving warheads to drop 13 on every Soviet city of more than 100,000 people."

Lies and deception clearly are a necessary factor in making The Threat credible. It is foolhardy to assume that it is an empty gesture, simply because nuclear arms are too horrible ever to be employed; as ACDA chief Fred Ikle notes, "The usability of nuclear weapons is built into them." In time The Threat becomes a "self-fulfilling prophecy."

6

Breaching the Firebreak

Having spent more than a trillion and a half dollars on its military machine in the first three postwar decades, and having researched and developed every conceivable weapon that human ingenuity could devise, by 1974 the United States inevitably had the capacity to fight any kind of war, any place. Schlesinger's "selective response" strategy reflected that wealth in weaponry, but it was something more, for while it prepared for every contingency from relatively minor conventional war to total nuclear war, the "active element" was a giant leap to tactical war with nuclear weapons and the automatic battlefield.

Other Defense Secretaries and Presidents had discussed tactical nuclear wars in this or that situation; what was new in the Schlesinger Doctrine was that it stated it as the centerpiece of policy and made clear that there would be little hesitancy about implementing it in the future. Secretary McNamara, in making his appropriations request for 1964, stated that tactical nuclear weapons, no matter how small, were "extremely destructive devices and hardly the preferred weapons to defend such heavily populated areas as Europe." They were, moreover, no substitute for conventional forces. Presidents Kennedy and Johnson, as the Congressional Research Service notes in a November 1974 study, "also subscribed heartily to the so-called firebreak theory that held that wartime detonation of any nuclear device would lead to a strategic exchange, and therefore, that the real threshold in escalation lay not between the use of tactical nuclear weapons and strategic weapons but rather between conventional warfare and nuclear warfare."

In his book *The Strategy of Peace,* Kennedy had written that "inevitably the use of small nuclear armaments will lead to larger nuclear armaments on both sides, until the world-wide holocaust has begun." This did not prevent Kennedy from taking the risk two years later in the Cuban missile crisis, or considering it for a number of other situations; but he would not affirm "limited nuclear war" as a policy. Johnson, in answer to Goldwater during the 1964 election campaign, stated plainly: "Make no mistake. There is no such thing as a conventional nuclear weapon. For nineteen peril-filled years, no nation has loosed the atom against another. To do so now is a political decision of the highest order, and it would lead us down an uncertain path of blows and counterblows whose outcome none may know." In the one kind of situation where tactical nuclear weapons might be necessary—"Any attack by conventional forces [which] puts Europe in danger of being overrun"—the Kennedy administration posited a "strategic pause" doctrine in which a period of time would elapse, giving the enemy time to reconsider before the United States would respond with "small" atomic devices.

But the pull of technology and the frustration of Vietnam began to change the outlook of militarists during Melvin R. Laird's tenure as Defense Secretary under Nixon. "Our theater and tactical nuclear weapons," Laird stated on March 15, 1971, "add to the realism of deterrence of theater conventional wars in Europe and Asia; the Soviets and Chinese Communists cannot be sure that major conventional aggression would not be met with the tactical use of nuclear weapons." Thereafter, the pressures against the barrier between conventional and nuclear arms mounted, in concert with the deterioration of the American image for invincibility as a result of Vietnam. The pressures reached a peak under Schlesinger.

If the name of the game was "perception"—that America must not only be strong, but must be perceived as strong—the "little war" in Vietnam was a traumatic experience. "At this stage of history," Walt Rostow, chairman of the State Department Policy Planning Council, wrote in 1964, "we are the greatest power in the world—if we behave like it." By 1974, however, it was evident that the United States wasn't behaving like it. The irregular forces of a small country with only 20 million people and a gross national product of $4.7 billion, aided by the regular forces of the North, with 23 million population and an even smaller GNP, $1.6 billion, were effectively resisting the United States with a population of 200 million and a GNP 250 times as large—and getting away with it. "The stature of the U.S.," noted Schlesinger, "has been diminished, at least temporarily, by what's happened in Vietnam."

It was against this background that the Secretary, abetted by Kissinger, Ford, and later Rumsfeld, elaborated the policy of "selective options." *Parade* magazine (June 15, 1975) correctly defined it as being "prepared to fight various kinds of limited nuclear wars with Russia instead of just one big war." From now on, said the Defense Department chief, it will be "necessary to go for the heart of the opponent's power; destroy his military forces rather than being involved endlessly in ancillary military operations . . . Action must be more vigorous from the outset . . ." A hint as to what "vigorous" meant was contained in Schlesinger's comment to the Washington *Post* (June 21, 1975) that "we have deployed in Korea tactical nuclear weapons as is, I believe, well known." (The general estimate, by such experts as Barry Schneider, then with the Center for Defense Information, was that the Pentagon had 700 such weapons in South Korea.) President Ford, by studied ambiguity, confirmed that the option of "first use" of atomic bombs was again in the forefront of policy-maker minds: "This is a matter that has to be determined," he said, "if and when there would be any requirements for our national interest." Tactical atomic war was definitely not being "foreclosed."

In well-orchestrated remarks of that time the direction of policy was made impressively clear. Kissinger, also stung by the Indochina debacle, called for a "stern and abrasive" foreign policy. Retired General William Westmoreland, who had directed the ill-fated venture in Southeast Asia, expressed the opinion that "the use of several small yield nuclear weapons conceivably could have put an end" to the Vietnam War. A military officer in Seoul,

Korea, told a press conference that in case of hostilities, nuclear "options" would be considered "seriously." President Park Chung Hee of South Korea told columnists Rowland Evans and Robert Novak that "South Korea could and would develop its own nuclear weapons." In June 1975 a report was leaked to the press that Strategic Air Command (SAC) crews were being given special "limited nuclear war" training. And another retired general, Mark Clark, who commanded American and UN forces during the Korean War, told an audience at a commemoration ceremony in Seoul, that the United States hereafter must avoid "a war of Communist aggression without the determination to win it and win it fast, with whatever means are necessary."

More eloquent than what public officials were saying was what the Ford administration was doing. There was an obvious acceleration of limited nuclear war training. According to the Washington *Post*'s military expert, George C. Wilson, Air Force bomber crews were provided a new "mission folder" and given a crash course in carrying out approximately twenty-five different types of limited nuclear war missions—as against "less than a half dozen types of missions for firing nuclear weapons" in the past. The "Limited Nuclear Option training covered in the mission folders now under study," Wilson reported (June 15, 1975), "goes all the way from hitting only a few Soviet facilities such as refineries and factories to destroying 80 percent of the facilities in various categories." The "selective response" strategists evidently left themselves a wide range for escalation.

Nor were their sights confined to limited wars in Europe. In the midst of the Arab oil embargo on December 2, 1974, *U.S. News & World Report* advised its readers that "top-level administration policymakers" were reviewing a war game called Operation Alkali Canyon 73 that had been conducted by 9,000 Marines from Camp Lejeune, North Carolina, sixteen months before, simulating desert warfare. Alkali Canyon 73, in which "Soviet-armed Yarmonian troops" were pushed back by the Leathernecks after five days of fighting in intense heat, was a useful study for the "policymakers," the magazine reported, because "of the possibility of armed action by the U.S. if the oil crisis becomes unmanageable." Kissinger made the threat of a Middle East attack specific the following month when he told *Business Week* that military action was not excluded if the OPEC nations threatened "some actual strangulation of the industrialized world." The diversification of training in limited nuclear wars clearly had a purpose.

The arsenal of tactical atomic arms and delivery systems, moreover, was so extravagant it was difficult to assume they were not for ready use. Leaving aside the 8,500 strategic weapons, the Pentagon had at its disposal 22,000 tactical weapons, widely dispersed over the globe. In Europe 2,250 aircraft, missile launchers, and nuclear cannon were equipped to deliver 7,000 warheads (as against 3,000 to 3,500 in the Russian stockpile). Their firepower might constitute only 6 per cent or thereabouts of the total 8,000 megatons available to the American military machine, yet their TNT-equivalent of 460 million tons was, as Barry Schneider points out, "roughly 35,000 greater than the nuclear weapon that destroyed Hiroshima in 1945." They were emplaced in every NATO country but Luxembourg, Norway, Denmark, and France (which had its own supply), and they included, in addition to air-to-surface bombs, such short-range weapons as 3,030 155mm and 203mm artillery shells, 380 depth bombs, and 300 atomic demolition munitions. For delivery the Pentagon had a choice of approximately 500 fighter-bombers and at least four different kinds of surface-to-surface missiles (Lance, Sergeant, Honest John, and Pershing).

The tactical weapons and delivery systems elsewhere were scaled down to the assumed need, but there were a total of 1,700 on Asian territory (Turkey, the Philippines, South Korea, etc.), not to mention the 1,500 aboard ships of the Pacific Fleet, and about 10,000 kept at home, presumably for replacement and supplement, as necessary. "One risk of developing tactical nuclear weapons," writes Schneider, "especially those now euphemistically called mini-nukes, is that they may create the illusion that a limited war can be fought. Small weapons such as the 155mm nuclear artillery projectiles have already been introduced. The trend is for more of the same. As smaller, 'cleaner,' and more accurate tactical nuclear weapons are added to the U.S. arsenal, they will add to the dangerous illusion that tactical nuclear weapons can be used with no risk of escalation."

II

Schlesinger's contribution to the chorus for tactical nuclear war was to give it form, rationale, and the requisite rhetorical vagueness so as not to alarm the American people beyond the breaking point. It was a significant step, one of the most portentous of the nuclear age.

"What we need," said the Secretary in his 1975 report, "is a series of *measured responses* to aggression which bear some relation to the provocation" (emphasis added). The major flaw in the American posture, as he perceived it, was that there have been no "sufficient options between massive response [which is 'less and less credible'] and doing nothing." Consequently he called for building up virtually all military capabilities. Concretely that meant "as a minimum" we needed "to maintain a conservatively designed reserve for the ultimate threat of large-scale options"— and that was exactly what the Pentagon was doing. "We" have "a reserve capability for threatening urban-industrial targets" (all-out war); "we are acquiring selective and discriminating options . . . to deter another power from exercising any form of nuclear pressure" (limited nuclear wars); and "simultaneously . . . we and our allies are improving our general purpose forces" (for conventional war).

But having made provision for the whole range of options, Schlesinger explains where the primary emphasis must be placed. He may be a leading exponent of the win syndrome, but he is not on that account a pepper-shot strategist with no sense of relative values. He is realistic enough to know where the best and the worst dividends are to be found. The worst, of course, is all-out war, because "neither the United States nor the Soviet Union now has a disarming first strike capability," nor are they likely to have one, he says, "in the foreseeable future." Since we cannot destroy the enemy's missiles and nuclear submarines before they unleash their megadeath, the strategic all-out war is obviously not the place to look for profit. He acknowledges that it may take place anyway, through "accidents and unauthorized acts . . . especially if nuclear proliferation should increase." He foresees the possibility, as well, that "conventional conflicts could escalate into nuclear exchanges; indeed, some observers believe that this is precisely what would happen should a major war break out in Europe. Ill-informed or cornered and desperate leaders might challenge us to a nuclear test of wills." And though he believes that the chances of a "massive surprise attack on our forces" are "close to zero under existing conditions," he does not rule it out. But he contends with something approaching religious zeal that nuclear wars are *containable,* and this is the distinguishing characteristic of his doctrine. He appears convinced that "we may be able to bring all but the largest nuclear conflicts to a rapid conclusion before cities are struck. Damage [i.e., deaths] may thus be limited and further escalation avoided."

This is the essence of the Schlesinger Doctrine and though it sounds moderate, it paves the way for a leap into the void that humankind has evaded for three decades. By reducing the *size* of a nuclear exchange it aspires to contain nuclear war and thereby make it practical. Back in 1964, Republican candidate Barry Goldwater introduced the term "conventional nuclear weapon," and suggested that America's six divisions in Europe could be reduced by "at least one third" if NATO commanders were authorized to fire tactical nuclear weapons on their own. In more prolix prose, spiced with great erudition, Schlesinger proposes the same thing—"conventional nuclear weapons," using them as if they were merely ordinary weapons with a bigger bang. He wants no more Vietnams, with 55,000 dead Americans and 300,000 wounded, and hundreds of thousands protesting in the streets of Washington every few months, thereby "paralyzing" the national will—as Henry Kissinger has often said. He proposes to use the military arm instead as an operable weapon to exact concessions from the other side (what is called "international blackmail"), and if that blackmail doesn't work, to fight "small" wars to quick victory with "limited damage."

This concept of the practicability of limited nuclear wars is a natural outcome of three decades of historical development; ever since technology made it feasible strategists have been thinking of it. Schlesinger was certainly not wrong when he pointed out to Martin Agronsky in an interview on WETA-TV (July 11, 1975) that the United States has deployed tactical nuclear weapons in Europe and in Korea "since the 1950's" and that America's top leaders, going back to Eisenhower in 1958, had refused to rule out "first use of nuclear weapons under some circumstances." What was new was that Schlesinger supplied an intellectual raison d'être and expressed it as a policy. We will respond with nuclear bombs, he said on ABC's "Issues and Answers," wherever aggression is "likely to result in defeat in any area of very great importance to the United States." Does that include Korea? he was asked. "We cannot exclude Korea," he replied. And while the scholarly Pentagon chief maintained that his program made total war less likely, Senator Edmund Muskie was closer to the mark when he charged that "you encourage the development of limited war as an acceptable kind of conventional military involvement. And when you escalate the possibilities to that level, it seems to me you escalate the possibility for ultimate nuclear war." If Schlesinger's Doctrine was designed to avoid total war, it in fact assured it.

III

The paradox of American strategy in the nuclear age, Henry Kissinger wrote some years ago, lies in the fact that "the enormity of modern weapons makes the thought of war repugnant, but the refusal to run any risks would amount to giving the Soviet rulers a blank check." The "more powerful the weapons, the greater the reluctance to use them." Recognizing this paradox, the policy makers and scientists decided early in the game to develop weapons less powerful and therefore more usable.

In the summer of 1948 a group of scientists conducted a series of conferences at the California Institute of Technology, called Project Vista, to review, as Morton Halperin describes it, "what uses nuclear weapons could be put [to]. The situation considered was implicitly (if not explicitly) that of local warfare. As a result of Project Vista the United States began to take seriously the potential of the uses of tactical nuclear weapons, and a process began which was ultimately to see tactical nuclear weapons become standard equipment for American military forces."

Concurrent with work on the "big" nuclear technology—the H-bomb, the intercontinental ballistic missile—scientists strove also to develop weapons ranging from as little as a tenth of a kiloton (100 tons of TNT-equivalent) to 400 kilotons (about thirty times as powerful as the Hiroshima bomb) for tactical employment in localized wars. A series of tests in 1951 showed that sub-kiloton bombs were indeed producible, contrary to claims by strategic warfare exponents that it was a mistake to divert scarce nuclear material for that purpose. Anyway, scientists soon discovered the means to overcome that deficiency too; whereas the United States had been strapped for nuclear material in the late 1940's, it now had a sufficiency both of uranium and enrichment facilities to fabricate both big bombs and little ones without straining national resources.

It is most revealing, incidentally, how the competition between scientists leads to escalation of research facilities and new instruments of war—another indication of the self-propelling character of the present arms race. Until the early 1950's the United States had one nuclear weapons laboratory, at Los Alamos, New Mexico. But a dispute between physicist Edward Teller and the Los Alamos administration under Norris Bradbury caused the former to seek support in high places for a second facility. Despite initial opposition by the AEC, Teller was able in due course to win the endorsement of Secretary of the Air Force Thomas K. Finletter, among others, and the Livermore Laboratory was launched at the University of California under the directorship of Herbert York in September 1952. In its first year of operations the second laboratory was allotted a budget of $3.5 million and a staff of 698; five years later the respective figures were $55 million and 3,000; ten years later, $127 million and 5,000. Livermore was to produce—in addition to strategic weapons—a great variety of tactical nuclear weapons in the 1950's.

Given the prospect for a specialized weaponry, the generals and think-tankers could not resist improvising scripts for its potential use. In an article for the *Saturday Evening Post* (October 15, 1949), General Omar Bradley, Chairman of the Joint Chiefs of Staff, urged that tactical atomic warheads be placed in Europe to redress the balance between relatively weak Western armies and the considerably stronger Soviet forces. By 1953 NATO was training officers in the use of these weapons, and the first nuclear cannon (the 85-ton 280-millimeter model) was being deployed in Europe to fire atomic shells. On the intellectual front, nuclear thinkers, including William Kintner, George Reinhardt, Ralph

Lapp, Bernard Brodie, Frank Sackton, Richard Leghorn, and many others, were debating the pros and cons of this form of warfare, and some were designing fanciful scenarios such as the one by Arthur Hadley (*Reporter*, April 19, 1956), which called for a mobile brigade, equipped with tactical nuclear devices, that would fly around the world to snuff out civil and other disturbances initiated by Moscow and Peking.

In October 1953 Eisenhower gave sanction to a National Security Council recommendation that tactical bombs be employed if the occasion warranted, to counter conventional attacks. He explained that "where these things are used on strictly military targets and for strictly military purposes, I see no reason why they shouldn't be used just exactly as you would use a bullet or anything else." This theme held fascination for many people of that period, including Admiral Arthur W. Radford, Chairman of the Joint Chiefs of Staff, who informed the country that "today, atomic weapons have virtually achieved conventional status within our Armed Forces."

The most coherent attempt to give limited nuclear war a status of priority, interestingly, came from the pen of a thirty-four-year-old German émigré who had only recently received his Ph.D. from Harvard, Henry Kissinger. After being turned down for tenure in Harvard's Department of Government, the future Secretary of State signed on in March 1955 with the Council on Foreign Relations—the most prestigious foreign policy institution of The Establishment—to act as study director for a thirty-four-man group looking into the failings of American policy. Among those with whom he served were top figures in the rarified world where decisions were made, Gordon Dean (a former Atomic Energy Commission chairman), David Rockefeller, Thomas K. Finletter, General James M. Gavin, McGeorge Bundy, Paul H. Nitze, General Walter Bedell Smith, and a host of others. After a year and a half of joint probing, Kissinger distilled the study into a book, *Nuclear Weapons and Foreign Policy*, which became an instant best seller and his springboard to fame.

"Limited war," wrote Kissinger, "has become the form of conflict which enables us to derive the greatest strategic advantage from our industrial potential. It is the best means for achieving a continuous drain of our opponent's resources without exhausting both sides. . . . The argument that limited war may turn into a contest of attrition is in fact an argument in favor of a strategy of limited war. A war of attrition is the one war the Soviet bloc could not win." He was convinced—at that time—that Moscow could accept the game as being in its own interests; "an energetic diplomacy addressed to the problem of war limitation," he wrote, "can serve as a substitute for lack of imagination on the part of the Soviet General Staff." The Russians might not feel at ease with this type of operation, but Kissinger (like others subsequently) felt Moscow could be inveigled to adopt the parameters of limited war. Indeed, he envisioned a situation where each side would maintain inspectors on the territory held by the other *during* the atomic exchange, so that neither exceeded arbitrary levels of kilotonnage. "A war which began as a limited nuclear war," he asserted, "would have the advantage that its limitations could have been established—and what is more important—understood—well in advance of hostilities."

This is a remarkable hypothesis, indicating how far from reality realistic theorists can range. The scenario, as Kissinger foresaw it, would proceed thus: "We could announce that Soviet aggression would be resisted with nuclear weapons if necessary; that in resisting we would not use more than 500 kilotons explosive power [the equivalent of about thirty-five Hiroshima-type bombs] unless the enemy used them first; that we would use 'clean' bombs with minimal fallout effects for any large explosive equivalent unless the enemy violated the understanding; that we would not attack the enemy retaliatory force or enemy cities located more than a certain distance behind the battle zone. . . ."

In other words, if our side were losing—if it were being overrun by Soviet tanks—we would resort to nuclear weapons of limited explosive yield on targets not yet fatal to the enemy, but enough to turn the tide. What, however, if the Soviets took the same tack? If they now realized they were losing, wouldn't they raise the level, say by launching one-megaton bombs at cities and bases behind our lines? David Landau, one of Kissinger's less adulatory biographers, asks a number of pertinent questions that none of the limited strategic war advocates have ever adequately answered: "Why would the Soviets agree to limit their own possible response to a form of warfare in which they would face certain defeat? More fundamentally, how could it ever be possible, in a situation of total hostility, for either side to believe that the first use of nuclear weapons by the enemy was not the beginning of total war? And how did Kissinger ever think that diplomacy could settle questions of such strategic importance when he himself proclaimed . . . that 'The emphasis of traditional diplomacy on "good faith" and "willingness to come to an agreement" is a positive handicap when it comes to dealing with a power dedicated to overthrowing the international system'? . . . His confidence in the possibility of limited-war diplomacy was at best naive and at worst quite dangerous."

George F. Kennan, no neophyte in foreign affairs, makes the same point in his book—appearing at about the same time—*Russia, the Atom, and the West.* "That it would prove possible, in the event of an atomic war," Kennan writes, "to arrive at some tacit and workable understanding with the adversary as to the degree of destructiveness of the weapons that would be used and the sort of target to which they could be directed, seems to me a very slender and wishful hope indeed." P. M. S. Blackett, a British Nobel prize winner, after a scathing review of the Kissinger model, concludes that it is "plain poppycock—and very dangerous." Kissinger himself, in a book published eight years after his first one, *Problems of National Strategy,* nullified his main thesis—that the Russians could be educated to the self-control needed for a limited nuclear war. "No one knows," he wrote, "how governments or people will react to a nuclear explosion under conditions where both sides possess vast arsenals." And former Secretary McNamara, long after he vacated his office, was even more direct: "Once you use them you use everything else; you can't keep them limited; you'll destroy everything."

In the 1957 Kissinger book as in so much else connected with the nuclear race, there is a dreamlike quality of wish-fulfillment. What is inimical to the dream is brushed aside. Even as Kissinger was writing his opus the American military had convincing evidence that a limited strategic war against Russia was not feasible if for no other reason than that it would render defunct the very nations we were trying to save. The two 1955 Pentagon war games mentioned previously, Operation Sage Brush and Operation Carte Blanche, showed, as P. M. S. Blackett put it, "that no such thing as limited or purely tactical nuclear war was possible in such an area." Germany would have been paralyzed within a week of "limited" war and would certainly cease to function within a couple of weeks. What might appear as "limited" war for American theoreticians was very much total war for Western Europe. Not surprisingly the people of the Continent were never as enthusiastic about this sort of "defense" as the American think-tankers.

IV

The campaign to "conventionalize" nuclear weapons, however, continues. "I think we have to make the underlying calculation about nuclear war," Schlesinger told a Senate subcommittee on Arms Control in March 1974, "intellectually acceptable." And since there was such a fearsome outcry against the draft and human "damage" in Vietnam, an array of guided weapons has been prepared for *automated* warfare which will require few troops, keep the death toll close to zero (hopefully), and undercut public opposition. It will also disregard the barrier between conventional and nuclear weapons, blending them into a single military pattern.

The principle that the Pentagon now follows is to substitute firepower for manpower, technology for troops. The relatively small U. S. Army, said General Creighton Abrams, Army Chief of Staff, in 1973, cannot "match potential enemies man-for-man and weapon-for-weapon in many areas of deployment." The way around this obstacle, Abrams claimed, was to achieve a "qualitative edge that will provide our smaller forces with the combat advantage necessary to insure success." Kissinger, when he was still a professor at Harvard, had expressed a similar view in a Rockefeller Brothers report, noting that U.S. limited war capability was hobbled by "our lack of mobile forces capable of intervening rapidly and of restoring a local situation before matters get out of hand." When McNamara became Secretary of Defense, he ordered an armada of big jets into production, including C-5A Galaxy planes (capable of carrying 130 tons) and 284 Lockheed C-141's. The function of these giant airships was Rapid Deployment, to transport a fully equipped army to problem areas speedily for quick and decisive battles, not unlike the "mobile nuclear brigade" that Arthur Hadley outlined in 1956, but of course much more sophisticated. This was to be, at last, a practical way of "winning"—though in small bites rather than a single gulp.

Once on the scene, as the Pentagon envisions it, automated machines will take over from human beings the job of reconnaissance and killing. "On the battlefield of the future," General William C. Westmoreland said in 1969, "enemy forces will be located, tracked, and targeted almost instantaneously through the use of data links, computer-assisted intelligence evaluation and automated fire control. With first round kill probabilities approaching certainty, and with surveillance devices that can continuously track the enemy, the need for large forces to fix the opposition physically will be less important." The troops will be in the rear, handling computers, not rifles. Sensor-equipped unmanned aircraft, drones, will feed data into computers; other drones or the same one will fire rockets and bombs. "The drone," General Abrams asserted, "would carry television cameras and infrared sensors which can be monitored at a ground station. Once a target was identified, personnel at the ground station would be able to activate on-board lasers to illuminate targets for attack by laser-guided weapons." No GI would face fire.

Meshing with the automated battlefield concept is the "mini-nuke" program, which Air Force General Edward B. Giller told the Joint Atomic Energy Committee in 1973, would provide the Pentagon with thousands of small atomic shells at about $100,000 each—a few billion in toto. These would be of low yield (a fifteenth or twentieth of the Hiroshima bomb each), but equipped with precision guidance for what is expected to be pinpoint accuracy—and in some cases could be carried by one man in a knapsack. According to former NATO commander General Andrew J. Goodpaster, the lower-yield and more accurate mini-nukes "could increase military effectiveness while reducing possible collateral damage [human deaths]," as well as give such weapons "*acceptability* in NATO planning" (emphasis added). Michael T. Klare, a critical writer, observes that "by categorizing mini-nukes as front-line weapons that could be used to avert an all-out thermonuclear exchange, these strategists hope to promote the 'thinkability' of atomic warfare."

The campaign to "conventionalize" nuclear weapons—even if

they have to be made smaller and much lower-yielding—has become a major preoccupation in major militarist circles. But like similar obsessions in the past, this one too rests on the assumption that Moscow will play by *American* rules, and that it will not be able to catch up for a long time. Both expectations, however, are vain. America will not keep the big lead in automated weapons for very long, as indicated by the fact that Soviet precision-guided missiles—such as the SAM-7, the Snapper, the Swatter, and the Sagger—were remarkably effective for the Egyptians in the October 1973 Arab–Israeli war, as Klare states, "against even the most advanced and powerful offensive weapons."

Of greater consequence is that the Russians refuse to promise they will be restrained by American-imposed ceilings. Schlesinger himself has conceded, the "Soviet military doctrine does not subscribe to a strategy of graduated nuclear response." Moreover, since their bombs are bigger and "dirtier" than our "small" nuclear warheads and mini-nukes, they would inevitably inflict a higher than expected level of casualties in any exchange and thereby impel hostilities to the next escalation. The only way the Kremlin could bestow feasibility on limited wars would be to sit them out, and that is hardly a practical likelihood.

Civilian and military strategists, nonetheless, refuse to be discouraged. There is a future, they think, for *small* nuclear wars, and the Soviets will ultimately be guided to accept that fact. "The notion that a nuclear firebreak if ever breached, must inevitably lead to escalation to the top," says Schlesinger, "has been supported neither in American military planning nor doctrine nor policy statements." Presumably if American leaders hope that controlled warfare won't explode into uncontrolled warfare, it won't happen. There are hundreds of experts in the Pentagon itself, the National War College, and the think-tanks, however—as astute as the advocates of limited nuclear war—who would deny that such wishes are fulfillable. And for a nation of 215 million people to gamble its existence on it is folly indeed. "Once you get into that sort of thing," Phillip J. Farley, a former Arms Control and Disarmament Agency official points out, "you'd be one step from holocaust."

V

One step from holocaust or not, however, limited nuclear war has been weighed and contemplated—secretly—more often than is generally realized. We now know of at least a half-dozen crises in which Washington seriously considered such action. One such incident, made known like most of these long after the event, was revealed by Roscoe Drummond of the New York *Herald Tribune,* and Gaston Coblentz of the New York *Times* in their 1960 book *Duel at the Brink.* Georges Bidault, French Foreign Minister, told the two writers that in 1954, when his nation was reeling in Indochina, Secretary of State Dulles made two offers of atomic weapons to France. The first called for "one or more atomic bombs to be dropped on Communist Chinese territory near the Indochina border . . . The second is recalled as an offer of two atomic bombs against the Viet Minh forces at Dienbienphu."

Four years later, when there was some question whether Chiang Kai-shek's Nationalists could hold onto two islands, Quemoy and Matsu, near the Chinese mainland, the American Joint Chiefs advised Eisenhower that the islands could not be held unless we were prepared to use nuclear bombs. "This turned out to be a gross over-estimation of the threat and an underestimation of our own conventional power," writes Bernard Brodie, a former senior staff member at RAND. But it was seriously considered and tentatively approved by the National Security Council.

In September 1966, thirteen years after the Korean War had come to an inconclusive end, Eisenhower revealed another near miss. He had threatened, he disclosed, to use nuclear bombs back in 1953: "I let it be known that if there was not going to be an armistice . . . we were not going to be bound by the kind of weapons that we would use. . . . I don't mean to say that we'd have used those great big things and destroyed cities, but we would use them enough to win and we, of course, would have tried to keep them on military targets, not civil targets." While the former President would not say that the United States should ever initiate a massive nuclear attack on the Soviets—except in retaliation—"this does not mean that in sticky situations that you couldn't use a proper kind of nuclear weapon sometime."

Theodore Sorensen, chief aide to Kennedy during his abbreviated administration, reports in his biography of the slain President —four years after the fact—that during the Laotian crisis of 1961 the Joint Chiefs of Staff had recommended, as a first step to bring the Pathet Lao to brook, "landing of American troops in Thailand, South Vietnam and the government-held portions of the Laotian panhandle. If that did not produce a cease-fire they recommended an air attack on Pathet Lao positions and tactical nuclear weapons on the ground. If North Vietnamese or Chinese then moved in, their homelands would be bombed. If massive Red troops were then mobilized, nuclear bombs would be threatened and, if necessary, carried out. If the Soviets intervened, we should 'be prepared to accept the possibility of general war.' "

Another aide, Arthur Schlesinger, Jr., tells us—again four years after the event—that during a 1961 crisis over Berlin, "everyone agreed that a Soviet blockade of West Berlin would have to be countered first by a western thrust along the *Autobahn*." But "there was disagreement between those, like General [Lauris] Norstad [supreme commander of NATO], who wanted the probe in order to create a situation where the West could use nuclear weapons and those, like Kennedy and McNamara, who wanted the probe in order to postpone that situation. And, while everyone agreed that we might eventually have to go on to nuclear war, there was disagreement between those who favored a single definitive salvo against the Soviet Union and those who favored careful and discriminate attack." No one, in other words, was "foreclosing the option" of using atomic weapons; the differences were simply over timing and intensity.

There always seems to be someone in high councils whose instinctive reaction is to "reach for The Bomb." During the October 1962 missile crisis, when in the words of Robert Kennedy the world was brought "to the abyss of nuclear destruction and the end of mankind," the debate before a special "Executive Committee of the National Security Council" (Ex Comm) was over whether to impose a blockade on Cuba or hit it with an air strike. But "one member of the Joint Chiefs of Staff . . ." Robert Kennedy recorded in his book on the crisis, "argued that we could use nuclear weapons, on the basis that our adversaries would use theirs against us in an attack."

The proclivity for escalation seems to be an inseparable feature of international crises; a military (or civilian) leader who feels he is not winning as quickly as he should, or is taking too many casualties, or faces defeat, thinks it only natural to expand the war and reach for the most destructive weapon in his arsenal. In November 1950, during the Korean War General MacArthur, fearful that the Chinese, who had just entered the fray, would overwhelm his troops, proposed that the United States retaliate by expanding the war into China—place a blockade around its ports, strike its cities from the air, unleash Chiang Kai-shek's Formosan troops to invade the mainland, AND consider using nuclear weapons on North Korea. There were substantial reasons for rejecting this advice: America had only a small number of atomic weapons; it was husbanding them for a possible *strategic* war against Russia itself, should the Soviets take advantage of American preoccupation in Asia to strike, say, in Europe; and the UN allies, in particular Britain, were fuming at the prospect. But a flock of geese almost fulfilled MacArthur's hopes.

On November 30, 1950, while American troops were being pushed back by the Chinese in Korea with impunity, Harry Truman stated at a press conference that the United States and the United Nations would "take whatever steps are necessary to meet the military situation." Did that "include the atomic bomb?" he was asked. Unwilling to deny that he had already rejected an atomic plan, lest it give heart to the enemy, he replied that it included "every weapon that we have." Has "active consideration" been given to its use? "There has always been active consideration of its use." Coming on the heels of a call by Secretary of the Navy Francis P. Matthews in August for a preventative war, and a boast —and proposal—by General Orvile Anderson, Commandant of the Air War College, that the Air Force was ready and waiting to drop The Bomb on Moscow, America's allies were understandably disturbed that Washington was writing the scenario for Doomsday.

One of them, Prime Minister Clement Attlee of Great Britain, hastened to Washington to express his shock and get the facts directly from the White House. As luck would have it, on the third day of Attlee's visit the Pentagon's early-warning radar system in Canada, according to the then Secretary of State Dean Acheson, "picked up formations of unidentified objects, presumably aircraft, headed southeast on a course that could bring them over Washington in two or three hours. All interception and defense forces were alerted." In the midst of all kinds of furious preparations one of Acheson's "senior officers burst into" Acheson's office. "He wanted to telephone his wife to get out of town, and to have important files moved to the basement. I refused to permit him to do either and gave him the choice of a word-of-honor commitment not to mention the matter to anyone or being put under security detention. He wisely cooled off and chose the former. When we reached the White House, the soon to become Secretary of Defense Robert A. Lovett told us that the unidentified objects had disappeared. His guess was that they had been geese."

In these, as in so many other situations, chance plays an important role. When there are opposite proposals before a President, to use or not to use nuclear armament, any one of innumerable circumstances can tip the scale either way—faulty intelligence (as in the above "geese" crisis), the President's mood, friendship with the author of a proposal, a gathering anxiety that America may be defeated (as in MacArthur's case), or an incident that forces the issue. At the peak of the 1962 missile crisis, for instance, just as it appeared that a settlement was at hand, the Cubans shot down a U-2 plane, killing its pilot, Major Rudolf Anderson, Jr. This could have been the justification for President Kennedy to end negotiations and proceed with the invasion of Cuba; in this instance restraint overcame recklessness, and the news was suppressed lest it add fuel to the fires. On the critical day, when the "Ex Comm" was arguing over two opposing drafts of a letter to Khrushchev, one of which would have enlarged the war and the other of which would—and did—end it, "everyone," according to Robert Kennedy's version, "was tense; some were already near exhaustion; all were weighted down with concern and worry." Those present—the leaders of a nation on the brink of nuclear war—"almost seemed unable to communicate with one another . . ." It is horrifying to speculate what might have happened in this electric atmosphere if the participants had yielded to their malaise and exhaustion.

Finally, there is the case of Vietnam, the most unpopular war in American history. Until 1976 it was always believed that employment of The Bomb in that misadventure had never been seriously considered. But early in 1976 General William C. Westmoreland,

commander of the American forces in Vietnam, published an au-
tobiography, *War in Vain,* shattering still another illusion. During
the siege of the surrounded Marine base at Khe Sanh in 1968, it
seems, President Johnson had queried the chairman of the Joint
Chiefs of Staff, General Earle Wheeler, whether he would have to
use nuclear weapons to hold that base. If so, said the President,
"he had no wish to be faced with it." Nonetheless Westmoreland
formed "a small secret group" in Saigon, to study the contingency
of "nuclear defense of Khe Sanh." "Although I recognized the
controversial nature of the subject," writes Westmoreland, "and
that employing nuclear tactical weapons would be a political decision, I nevertheless considered that I would be imprudent if I
failed to acquaint myself with the possibilities in detail." He rea-
soned, said the general, that "if Washington officials were so intent on 'sending a message to Hanoi,' surely small tactical weapons would be a way to tell Hanoi something, just as two atomic
bombs had spoken convincingly to Japanese officials during World
War II."

Johnson's concern of course was political, that recourse to tactical nuclear weapons would raise the temperature of the anti-war
movement, already much too heated for his comfort, to the boiling
point. We can guess, but we may never know whether, in the absence of this wide-scale protest, Johnson would have acceded to
the pressure. In any case, the general who headed the armies on
the scene remains convinced "that the use of a few small tactical
nuclear weapons in Vietnam—or even the threat of them—might
have brought the war to an end." Many others, no doubt, shared
that view, including a large segment of the public.

VI

Responding to an ABC-TV interviewer (July 6, 1975), Secretary Schlesinger argued that if limited nuclear war broke out
"there would be very powerful incentive to suppress the conflict
before it became destructive [*sic*]." As proof he alluded to "the
Vietnam experience," in which "there were powerful forces that
prevented major escalation," either nuclear or non-nuclear. But
the evidence seems to be the other way around: in every conflict
that Washington engaged in the trend was to increase the stakes.

More TNT tonnage, for instance, was dropped on Vietnam than on Germany in World War II, and there was no flinching from the use of gas, defoliants, and napalm, though they were morally reprehensible and legally dubious. The "powerful forces" that inhibited "major escalation" were not the human beings at the helm in Washington, but a combination of two *impersonal* "forces":

1. That employment of nuclear weapons, though they might bring a temporary advantage, could not in the instances where they were considered offer adequate odds for victory—not in Vietnam, Korea, Quemoy-Matsu, Laos, Berlin, or Cuba.

2. That the psychological barrier between conventional and nuclear weapons has not yet been broken.

Administration leaders, however, seek to correct both "defects." The first is being dealt with by developing a technology that telescopes nuclear war into a smaller and less destructive package—in the hopes that the Russians will see the wisdom of controlled warfare. The second difficulty is expected to erode with time, just as the unacceptability of other horror weapons eroded with time. "If weapons work," writes a British scientist, J. P. Perry Robinson, "they will be used. Despite initial repugnance, the crossbow, gunpowder, flame-throwers and napalm all eventually became part of conventional warfare." There was considerable hesitancy about employing the crossbow in the twelfth century, and those who did faced excommunication from the Church. Gunpowder, invented two centuries later, also "went through a long period of moral opprobrium before becoming assimilated." Moral revulsion greeted flame-throwers, napalm, and other incendiary weapons, but ultimately they crossed the line into the "thinkable." People, Robinson notes, "became accustomed to these developments, and the weapons became conventional."

The same fate probably awaits The Bomb once the government can give it a proper rationale; the mini-nukes, especially in the light of the Vietnam experience, may be the avenue making nuclear war "thinkable." There will be no scarcity of crises, in the future as in the past, moreover, in which tactical warheads will seem like a quick solution to distressing "little" problems; and the win syndrome militates in favor of "first use" not too many years from now.

It is naïve to believe that the horror of this prospect will stay the hand of the button-pushers. The argument is often made that poison gas was deemed so frightening that the nations of the world outlawed it, in effect, by common consent. Unfortunately, that isn't exactly accurate. As Robinson records: "there were in all between one and two million CW (chemical warfare) casualties" in World War I, from chlorine, mustard, and other gases. Failure to use them subsequently on a similar scale was not due to moral constraint but to three problems that couldn't be adequately resolved. One was the matter of wind ("quite a small change in weather conditions can necessitate a ten- or even a hundredfold increase in the number of CB [chemical-biological] munitions needed for a particular mission"). Another was that protective measures, such as gas masks, were not foolproof. Finally there was the danger that such agents "can remain active and dangerous in the environment for a period of anything between minutes and years." In a cold assessment of the potential profits and losses, the latter outweighed the former—especially since better results could be achieved by other means. "These problems," Robinson notes, "exist even today, despite intensive endeavors in the weapons laboratories to mitigate them."

Even so, where one nation has had the CB agents and the enemy didn't, the tendency was strong to use them—by the Italians in Ethiopia, 1935–36; by the Nationalists in China, 1937–45; by the Egyptians in Yemen, 1963–67; by the United States in Indochina after 1964, where herbicides, defoliants, tear gases, and agent CS were employed; and by the British in Northern Ireland more recently. "If weapons work they will be used." The argument that Doomsday will be bypassed because it is too horrible to contemplate is not persuasive. Theologian Reinhold Niebuhr was closer to the truth when he observed many years ago that "it is the business of military strategists to prepare for all eventualities and it is the fatal error of such strategists to create the eventualities for which they must prepare."

7

Flight
from Reality

In his book *The Fifty Minute Hour,* psychoanalyst Robert Lindner describes one of his patients, a government research physicist, who was normal in all respects except that he fantasized living part of the time on a mythical planet, Srom, in another galaxy. Day after day he set down his adventures on Srom and other planets he visited from Srom, a compendium in all of 12,000 typed pages, 82 full-color maps "drawn to scale" of "23 planetary bodies in four projections, 31 of land masses on these planets . . . the remainder of cities on the various planets," plus "161 architectural sketches and elevations . . . all carefully scaled and annotated, 12 genealogical tables, an 18 page description of the galactic system in which Kirk Allen's home planet was contained, with four astronomical charts"—and so on. Certainly this was so fanciful that no one, let alone a trained psychoanalyst, would put any stock in it. Nonetheless the fantasy was sufficiently compelling that Lindner himself got caught up in it and could hardly wait for each arrival of his patient to learn the latest chapter in his adventures. "In the beginning," writes Lindner, "it was a game . . . but eventually it ceased to be a game . . . My participation in Kirk's psychosis disturbed somewhat that mental equilibrium on which I have always prided myself and brought me within sight of psychological distress." It was only with a great effort of will that Lindner finally disengaged himself from the hallucination of his patient.

American leaders, seeking a way around their recognized weakness, the absence of an effective "damage-limitation" program, have also fallen into a fantasy, not unlike Dr. Lindner's. "Damage-limitation"—reducing casualties to tolerable levels—was necessary, they felt, to make The Threat of retaliation, "if deterrence fails," credible. But there are only three possible ways to "limit damage" under present technological conditions, none of them promising.

One is to destroy the enemy's land-based and sea-based missiles before launch—and that is impossible. Another is to destroy the missiles while in flight, through an ABM system—and that, as shown above, is also impossible. The third is "civil defense," to find shelter for the American people where they can be protected from blast, fire, and radiation if war breaks out. That is not impossible, but the notion that it can save enough lives for the United States to remain a viable society is a fantasy. Yet, since there was nothing else on the horizon, the authorities resorted to the fantasy. Their calculations of what would happen if we build up civil defense, and their assurances that Americans can survive a total war are no less surrealistic—as we shall soon see—than the hallucinations of Dr. Lindner when he was impelled into the wild dreams of his patient.

What is ominous in this state of affairs is that a leadership which allows itself to lose touch with reality not only manipulates the public, but is in turn manipulated by its own elaborate deceptions. It downgrades the dangers and it exaggerates the safety factor, as if nothing more were afoot than a game.

Relatively small sums of money have been allocated to civil defense, mostly because the American citizenry has refused to be inveigled into the charade. But the civil defense saga is worth reviewing in detail nonetheless because more than any other feature of the nuclear arms race it reveals that flight from reality which everyone concedes can be the trigger for nuclear war.

II

Until the Russians acquired the H-bomb and missiles, civil defense was a game of postulating for the future rather than an active preparation for the present. After World War II a civil defense board was established under Major General Harold R. Bull to study what would happen to the United States if a nuclear attack were unleashed. It was not an imminent danger, since the United States still had a monopoly, but just for the sake of scholarly study General Bull formulated a plan for dealing with an attack by weapons as large as 50 kilotons (four times the firepower of the Hiroshima bomb). How would we defend ourselves? The answer in the Bull Report was to build "blast shelters"—improved versions of the bunkers and air-raid shelters that dotted Germany and Britain during the second war. The experience of Hiroshima had shown that only 15 per cent of the immediate deaths in that tragic city had been caused by radiation; defense, therefore, was needed primarily against blast, the great explosion itself. By 1950, when the monopoly disappeared, the focus moved somewhat beyond theory and a Civil Defense Act was passed to plan for blast shelters. It was still felt that "defense" of civilians was possible.

By 1954, however, U.S. tests in the Pacific—with hydrogen bombs—had proved that local radioactive fallout extended over an area far larger than that affected by blast. The deadly dust from the explosion of the *Bravo* in the Bikini Atoll, says Herbert Scoville, who was one of the experts measuring radioactivity, "was a big surprise to us." It spread over an area of 7,000 square miles (as against only 300 for the effects of blast). At the last minute the wind shifted from an expected northerly direction to the east, where ten Task Force ships were within thirty miles. The crews were forced to go below decks and speed away from the scene, while spray equipment washed the decks with tons of water. A Japanese tuna boat, ninety miles from Ground Zero, was not so lucky; its twenty-three fishermen fell ill as a result of radiation effects (one is reported to have died). Had the ship been ten miles further south all would have perished. A hundred miles from the explosion point, a deserted island was saturated with eight times the lethal dose of radiation within four days. The scientists learned much they had not known before about strontium 90 and other radioactive materials. It was apparent that civilian defense would have to be geared to fallout, rather than blast. A new theory and a new cult developed as a consequence. The blast shelters became a relic for military museums and the panacea became "evacuation," removing millions of people from the cities. Evacuation arrows dotted the highways from coast to coast, offering the illusion that in the ten or twelve hours it took the Soviet bombers to get here there would be plenty of time to head for safety a few dozen miles from Los Angeles, Chicago, and New York. As late as January 1959 New York State's Civil Defense Director, who had evidently never seen a morning expressway jam, was still claiming that "every person in New York City could be moved to the country within 50 hours."

Herman Kahn, in his widely read book *On Thermonuclear War*, tried to illustrate graphically how civil defense could effectuate victory. With an adequate program, he argued, "we could evacuate our cities and place our forces on a super-alert status, and thus put ourselves in a much better position to strike first and accept the retaliatory blow. We might then present the Soviets with an ultimatum."

Then in 1957 there was another rude awakening: the Russians had put their first satellite, Sputnik I, into the stratosphere and soon, it became evident, the nuclear warheads would be delivered by missiles that would arrive on target in thirty minutes, rather than many hours. There was no time for evacuation. The Naval Radiological Defense Laboratory came forth with a plan to build fallout shelters for everyone at a cost of $38 billion—and save 99 per cent of American lives, it said, in an all-out nuclear war. Even Eisenhower's Civil Defense Administrator, Val Peterson, thought this a little too much. "We don't think so," he said. "We think you can save approximately 60 percent. In a thermonuclear war there are no means of saving all of the people. It simply can't be done." Dr. W. E. Strope, then head of the Military Evaluation Group of the Naval Radiological Defense Laboratory, was equally pessimistic. It made little difference, he said, whether you were five miles or 100 miles from the impact point of a half-megaton bomb; you would have little protection. "If you had a completely safe shelter and came out eight days after an attack and stayed out 24 hours you would still get sick. . . . In this same region it would be two years before the intensity would drop to a point where it would meet the peacetime AEC tolerance for gamma radiation." Air Force General Curtis LeMay contended he would not "put that much money into holes in the ground to crawl into. . . . I would rather spend more of it in offensive weapons in the first place." And to the credit of John Foster Dulles he convinced President Eisenhower that shelters were not only a mirage but would vitiate America's image as a peace-loving nation.

III

Throughout the nuclear age Americans have comforted themselves with the notion that "our leaders must know what they're doing." The saga of civil defense confirms instead that it has been frustratingly difficult to reconcile the win syndrome with reality. The assumption that a couple of hundred million people could be manipulated like robots for a game of "defense by threat" inevitably proved to be foolhardy.

Sometime in 1960 the Pentagon called a top secret meeting of a dozen or so highly influential leaders, including Governor Nelson Rockefeller of New York, one of the most aggressive exponents of fallout shelters. The consensus at the meeting was that the State Department needed "muscle" in its negotiations with the Soviet Union. Unless we could *prove* to the Russian leadership that we were ready to fight, they might disregard our deterrent, and our diplomats would have no bargaining leverage. We had to make deterrence "credible" (how that word keeps coming up!) and the only way to do it was to commit our people to a large-scale shelter program.

Whether shelters could or could not save lives was considered secondary to making our military position "believable." Frank B. Ellis, director of the Office of Emergency Planning, observed that the program would be a method of "strengthening our leadership at the conference tables of the world." General Lyman L. Lemnitzer, Chairman of the Joint Chiefs of Staff, said that it "bears an essential relationship to military strength. . . . The extent to which we have the ability to defend against an attack, is an essential element of our overall deterrent. . . . It provides further unmistakable evidence of serious determination on our part." The purpose of a civil defense program, these men believed, was primarily to enhance military and diplomatic power. Saving lives, while desirable, was a subsidiary objective.

When Kennedy took office in January 1961 there was again mounting pressure for civil defense, from Rockefeller—who was expected to run for President in 1964—from Representative Chet Holifield, a powerful figure in Congress, from the Pentagon and others. The pressure grew after the Bay of Pigs debacle in April, and the subsequent crisis over Berlin. Amongst the Kennedyites were many who thought civil defense was ridiculous—Arthur Schlesinger, for instance. But how could the Administration explain to the nation that it had no defense in case of all-out war, and how could it strike a position of impotence in the face of demands by potential presidential rivals and assorted hawks to show American muscle?

Kennedy, ever the politician, decided to go with the tide—but with slightly more realism than was encompassed in the proposals of Rockefeller, Edward Teller, Herman Kahn, et al. Under the direction of Carl Kaysen a moderate formula was devised—not to build fallout shelters to make deterrence "credible" or give diplomacy needed "muscle"—but simply as "insurance." Just as one buys insurance against loss in a fire, so citizens and the government would build or identify shelter spaces, at a small cost per person, that might save people from the perils of radiation. The responsibility for "defense" was shifted from an independent agency, the Office of Civil and Defense Mobilization (OCDM) to the Department of Defense itself, and the budget was lifted from approximately $60 million a year to $700 million.

Government agencies began marking out corridors and basements in skyscrapers, subways, and other edifices as community shelters, and citizens were asked to build private shelters in their yards or basements, and stock them with food, water, and a dosimeter. U. S. Steel began marketing a $1,800 prefabricated shelter capable of accommodating six persons. General Mills marketed a new food called MPF, Multi Purpose Food, with which shelter residents could allay their hunger for $2.50 a gallon. The United States Chamber of Commerce—never one to turn its back on Pentagon philosophy—issued a circular, "Fiction and Fact About Family

Fallout Shelters," which was no small boost to the new shelter manufacturers. "Civil defense," it said, "supplements military defense." It urged Americans to disregard anti-civil defense propaganda and "build family fallout shelters in their homes."

Before long the industry was blossoming like a rosebud, hopes high and firm. In November 1961 forty shelter manufacturers formed the National Shelter Association with Frank Norton of the Chicago area as president. Norton predicted there would soon be 200 firms catering to the demand, and judged that the industry had a $200 billion potential that would attract a thousand new companies. He expressed the hope that with proper government support business would sell $30 billion worth of shelters and accessories in 1962 alone. The Wonder Building Corporation in Chicago, whose executive vice-president was the former national director of the civil defense program under Eisenhower, Leo A. Hoegh, sold 7,500 shelter units in that area alone by October 1961 and made an arrangement with a feeder plant for rapid expansion.

Even the labor movement was swept into the act, particularly the building trades unions. The south Florida *Labor Tribune* of September 28, 1961, reported on "action taken by building trade unions on the Pacific Coast to explore the idea of financing and constructing nuclear fallout shelters for sale at nominal prices to individual home owners and renters." This, said the *Tribune*, would not only provide "needed work to union craftsmen," but would "attest to the readiness of American Trade Unions to spring to the defense of their country." "No group of citizens," wrote New York *Times* columnist James Reston, "is showing more solicitude for the future well-being of the nation [than the builders of fallout shelters]. The Iron and Steel Institute, the cement manufacturers, and the makers of brick and other clay products are all vying with one another to make a better shelter, and the National Lumber Manufacturers Association has produced a dandy little number [made] out of wood, which, as everybody knows, doesn't burn." Patriotism it seems has a thousand faces.

The industry-labor campaign attested again to the self-generating character of the arms race. Patriotism and the dollar were supplemented by still another spasm of fraudulent anti-Communism, to harden the nation's will and sell shelters. Hoegh's company distributed a mimeographed brochure which among other things quoted a Soviet leader, Dmitri Manuilsky, to the effect that "war to the hilt between Communism and the free world is inevitable." Another brochure asked: "Do you predict a nuclear war?" and answered: "No, but I'm not predicting that there will not be one. As long as you have a Khrushchev, and as long as you have the Communists openly saying they must dominate the world, there's a good chance you will have one. Every two or three months the Communist leaders threaten to bury us. Some day they might try it. Hitler did." One shelter company carried an advertisement prominently contrasting two quotations. President Kennedy: "It is the responsibility of every man to protect his family"; and Soviet Premier Khrushchev: "We will bury you." The government itself was hardly less crude. An OCDM student manual contained a section on the "conflict of ideologies" which gave this picture of Soviet thinking:

"'Peace' means the final rule of Communism. Unpleasantness, disagreements, and wars are those things which must be endured to gain this 'peace.' The goal of Russian Communism is world domination. This is to be achieved by political and economic means if possible. Otherwise, war is an instrument to be used at the opportune time and when success by this means appears probable."

It became evident before long that the American people were not quite as manipulable as their leaders thought. They might be "anti-Communist" enough to tolerate the expenditure of more money for weapons, but they were not ready to live a couple of weeks in gruesome shelters—the poorer models of which were to be only four feet high—in order to send the Communists a message. To begin with there was the discomfort: one experiment after another revealed that middle-class America was not prepared to place itself in solitary confinement. Mrs. Jeanine Perkins, who with her husband and two children spent a week in an experimental shelter in Washington, D.C., recorded in her diary on the last day: "I'm so sick of it here. I just hate it"; and then an hour before coming out, "One more hour . . . just wait 'til they open the door. I'll rush out like a wild woman." Despite the fact that she had daily contact by telephone with a civil defense official and on Sunday received a telephoned sermon from her minister, it was unbearable.

There were other problems which the planners, in their penchant for "idiotic arithmetic"—as James R. Newman, chief intelligence officer for the U. S. Embassy in London during World War II, called it—had overlooked. You might have a good, even an adequate shelter in your yard, but of what value was it if you were at your office when the word came that bombs were hurtling your way? There would be only thirty minutes—in the case of a submarine nuclear attack, even fewer minutes—to drive home through dismaying traffic jams, assemble your children and wife, and go underground. Even then you might find that someone had seized your shelter and barricaded the doors; it was a situation made to order for hysteria and meanness.

"Recently," noted Governor Edmund G. Brown, Sr., of California, the "public has been alarmed by groups and individuals who say they will resort to violence in the event of nuclear war. These guerrilla bands have announced that they will not hesitate to shoot down citizens entering areas designated by the selfish as their own. . . . This reversion to cave-man barbarism is a cause of concern to every thinking American . . ."

In a Chicago suburb a shelter builder told *Time* he intended to mount a machine gun at the entrance and shoot down anyone who attempted to force his way in. Another entrepreneur announced plans to build community shelters on a "key club" basis, hiring a policeman for each entrance. In Las Vegas the civil defense chief, J. Carlton Adair, urged formation of a local militia of 5,000 men to repel an "invasion" by citizens from Southern California. In case of nuclear war, he said, they "would come into Nevada like a swarm of locusts." The police chief of Bakersfield, California, told the Chamber of Commerce that if war came "the greatest danger to Bakersfield would not be from an atomic bomb or its fallout but from the hundreds of thousands" of survivors fleeing Los Angeles. The chief reassured his audience that he had plenty of policemen to divert the "invaders" to the desert. In upper New York State, a doctor of philosophy who once served in the German Army had his picture taken in front of a lavish shelter with an Enfield rifle in his hands. A resident of Santa Barbara, California, had his shelter built in the dead of night by workmen disguised as sewer repairmen; and when he climbed into it after the laborers had packed their tools and gone home, found his secret hole filled with water—an excellent reservoir when it rained but worthless to hide from fallout. In Milwaukee, a shelter builder promised prospective customers his trucks would carry no markings—"for secrecy"—and his workmen would pose as TV repairmen. "Are we preparing to fight the Russians," asked journalist I. F. Stone, "or each other?"

Instead of heralding a nation united and ready to die in order to "defeat Communism," the debate over fallout shelters emphasized confusion and immobility. "By far the strongest single objection [to shelters]," reported pollster Samuel Lubell, "is the thought that 'if those big ones fall, a shelter won't be worth anything,' or, 'if you're going to die, you might as well die quickly.'" The Gallup Poll (October 28, 1961) confirmed these observations: nine out of ten people so far had done nothing, not even stored food. Even the top government officials seemed to have little faith in the idea, for not a single one of the fourteen high officials of the National Security Council had built a shelter for his own family. Neither had Vice-President Lyndon Johnson, Attorney General Robert Kennedy, or the man in charge of civil defense, Steuart Pittman.

What the debate revealed more poignantly than at any time before or since was how unclear the nation's strategy was and how little its leaders really knew about nuclear war. There were at least two positions as to the purpose of shelters, neither of which was particularly logical. The official theory, that we needed shelters for "insurance," offered small hope for saving lives and even less for saving the economy. When Secretary of Defense McNamara outlined his plans to the Joint Committee on Atomic Energy (the Holifield Committee), on August 1, 1961, there was little enthusiasm to his words. The heart of the project—to which $93 million was allotted—was the identification of community shelter "spaces." Engineers were to survey cities and towns to find usable spaces for fifty million people in existing buildings, subways and quarries, and to stock them with water, food, and other necessities. But McNamara was quick to point out: "This does not mean the program will save fifty million lives. Again, as the 1959 [Holifield] study had pointed out, nearly 75 percent of the deaths from the hypothetical attack would have resulted from blast and thermal effects combined with immediate radiation effects." Shelter spaces would offer little or no protection against these, McNamara said, but they might "save at least ten to fifteen million lives" from the ensuing fallout. Since the Holifield report assumed that one quarter of the nation would die in an attack with 1,446 megatons (less than a third of the targets being cities), that was small comfort: 30 million, or one out of six Americans would die within a day or two even with shelters—twenty or twenty-five times as many as had died in battle in all of the nation's previous wars put together.

President Kennedy, moreover, had little faith in civil defense as a deterrent. "We will deter an enemy from making a nuclear attack," he said, "only if our retaliatory power is so strong and so invulnerable that he knows he would be destroyed by our response. If we have that strength, civil defense is not needed to deter the attack. If we should ever lack it, civil defense would not be an adequate substitute." If the enemy is "rational," the President argued, he would not attack us. Unfortunately, however, he added, "the history of this planet, and particularly the history of the Twentieth Century, is sufficient to remind us of the possibilities of an irrational attack, a miscalculation, an accidental war, or a war of escalation in which the stakes by each side gradually increase to the point of maximum danger which cannot be either foreseen or deterred." This was a formidable argument in favor of disarmament and against civil defense, but such was the nature of America's mood—inflamed by ceaseless anti-Communist propaganda—that Kennedy proposed *both* an increase in arms of $6 billion, and civil defense.

A top aide to McNamara, who refused to let his name be used, said in an interview, "One of the possible consequences of our new civil defense program is to make the Soviet Union increase its offensive preparations. But this is all to the good, for one of the ways we can win the Cold War is to get the Soviet Union to enlarge its costs of operations." If our civil defense causes the Russians to respond by spending more on arms, their economy will founder, their people will lose faith, their potential allies in the Third World will receive less aid, hence be less loyal. The measure of victory, presumably, is that we cut off two of our own fingers in order to force them to cut off a whole hand.

The Pentagon, less subtle and more outspoken, stuck to its guns that civil defense—in the words of General Lemnitzer—"is an essential element of our overall deterrent" proving to the Soviets that "we mean business; we're ready to die for our objectives." Abetted by a host of scientists and theorists, Kahn, Edward Teller, Willard Libby, the focus shifted therefore to "indirect deterrence," "hardening the national will." Assistant Secretary of Defense Pittman expressed it this way: "Our willingness to stand firm and ready to create the risk of war carries a message. It makes deterrent credible." By keeping the Soviets guessing as to whether we might or might not act "crazy"—irrationally—we stay their hand.

Adam Yarmolinsky, McNamara's closest associate, convinced himself—and others—that the Kremlin didn't have enough weapons to strike both cities and military bases and would therefore "concentrate on military targets. Few weapons could be spared for cities as such"—unless of course "the Russians got mad." Dr. Kahn echoed this thesis: "If the Russians consider attacking the United States, by and large they will not worry about their ability to kill all of the Americans. Their problem is to kill SAC [the Strategic Air Command, which controls American atomic weapons]."

Such reasoning is obviously weak, but it poured out of the Pentagon and think-tanks in torrents. We are building a stockpile of weapons, it argued, to deter the Soviets from attacking us. If they are rational they will respect this display of power and refrain from nuclear war. If by chance, however, they are not rational, they might launch such a war anyway. But, if they do, then the Pentagon is confident they won't "get mad." They will be rational enough to aim for the outskirts of Omaha, Tucson, and other bases which house hardened missile sites, rather than New York, Boston, and Washington.

To reinforce this remarkable logic the extreme hawks mounted a campaign to convince Americans that they *could* survive a war, they could defend themselves. Dr. J. C. Nunnally, a psychologist from Vanderbilt University, had already warned the government that it was creating a "paralysis of anxiety" by emphasizing the horrors of nuclear war. His advice, which *Newsweek* said was adopted by the Administration and the Pentagon, was to "supply fewer of the gory details. . . . Communicate simple, easily understood information. If the public is thus built up gradually for calamities, it can be controlled." What ensued was an avalanche of "idiotic arithmetic"—to use James Newman's term again—which shows the Military-Industrial Complex at its deceptive worst.

IV

Life magazine, then the second most widely read publication in the nation, told the American people on September 15, 1961, that with fallout shelters "97 out of 100 people can be saved." With President Kennedy personally endorsing the article in a letter on the opening page, *Life* postulated that instead of 45 million dead in a "military-objective attack," about "five million people, less than 3% of the population, would die." The article caused a sensation and became the centerpiece of a new mythology that it would be almost no problem to avoid death in a nuclear war. Dr. Willard Libby, one of America's leading scientists, proposed an inexpensive fallout shelter costing thirty dollars that he claimed would increase chances of survival by 100 times. The general figure bandied about was 90 per cent, that nine out of ten people would live through the holocaust. Two Chicago writers published a book showing how 99.5 per cent would be alive after the bombardment.

The trick in all these estimates was to make false assumptions. *Life,* for instance, assumed that the Russians, who according to *Army* magazine held 10,000 megatons of bombs in their arsenal, would use only 300 megatons, and that all the weapons would be directed against military objectives in uninhabited areas—none against cities. But the same graphs from which *Life* compiled its arithmetic (Holifield hearings, 1961, pages 213 and 216) also showed that even as small an attack as 300 megatons, if directed against cities, would leave 45 to 54 million Americans dead; and an attack of 3,000 megatons—well within Soviet capability—against population centers, would result in 120 million fatalities, two thirds of the American citizenry. Ironically, *Time* magazine, also published by Henry Luce, claimed that "an adequate national system of fallout shelters might well cut the death rate from 160 million to 85 million," but not five million as *Life* had claimed.

In the year of the shelter craze, 1961–62, it became evident how narrow were the limits to nuclear knowledge. Not only were there great gaps between what one scientist believed and what another did, but very few looked at the problem in its conglomerate form—each hazard multiplying the effects of others. It was estimated by the Atomic Energy Commission, for instance, that people would have to stay in shelters a maximum of two weeks. Just four years previously the same AEC had stated, "It is impossible to indicate in advance at what value of external dose rate it may be permissible to leave the shelter"; and Dr. Maurice B. Visscher, head of the University of Minnesota's Department of Physiology for twenty-five years, stated that "to survive fallout one must also be able to live at least a year in the shelter if there has been a real nuclear war."

In the Holifield hypothetical attack "experts" calculated that in the first two weeks a person above ground would be subject to a total of 10,000 roentgens (a measure of radiation); but that if he stayed in a better-than-average shelter, which reduced the dose by 250 times, only 40 roentgens.

According to the AEC handbook "The Effects of Nuclear War," published in 1957, a dose of 130 to 170 roentgens inflicted on a general population would result in no deaths, but a quarter of those exposed would suffer such ailments as nausea, vomiting, loss of hair, bloody diarrhea, bleeding gums, and gangrene. A dose of 270 to 330 roentgens would result in sickness for everyone and death for 20 per cent. Those who absorbed 400 to 500 roentgens would have one chance in two of surviving, and over 550 roentgens, no chance.

The 40 roentgens in the Holifield hypothetical case therefore would not be likely to kill the shelter-dweller or make him sick. (It would, however, adversely affect his life-span, his ability to reproduce, and his susceptibility to cancer and other diseases.) But if he left the shelter after two weeks to work outdoors eight hours a day on such activities as rescue work and decontamination of food, he would receive another 24 to 30 roentgens of radiation a day. At the end of five days he might be a very sick person, and at the end of ten days his chances of dying would be one in five. Thus the "two weeks" figure *might* apply to areas where the first-hour radiation (it decays rapidly) was relatively light, but hardly to all areas.

If you combine the radiation problem with the problem of damage to dwellings, the "two weeks" figure becomes totally untenable. The Holifield estimate was that 11.8 million homes—or more than a fourth the total—would be destroyed, another 8.1 million greatly damaged, and 12.5 million would be so contaminated by fallout they would be dangerous for as much as several months. Three quarters of the population would be virtually homeless. Would the person who emerged from the shelter sleep outdoors? If he did, the radiation dose would no longer be 24 to 30 roentgens a day, but 50 to 72—far too much for safety. His only recourse would be to return to his shelter for extended periods. Add the fact that children would have to stay much longer because of future genetic dangers; add the fact that anyone as far as forty miles away who looked at the fireball for an instant would be struck blind; add the fact that there would be tens of millions of sick people and only 1.6 million beds in hospitals (many of them destroyed) and that tens of thousands of doctors would either be dead or would be unable to make the rounds because of fallout danger (in Hiroshima 260 of the 300 doctors were immediate casualties and only 500 of the 1,800 nurses were available for duty after the explosion); add all this and more together and the optimistic figures of *Life,* Teller, and others disappear into the void.

Fred C. Ikle, director of the Arms Control and Disarmament Agency in the Ford administration, points out that nuclear theorists operate on the maxim that "what you can't calculate you leave out." By contrast with conventional war, where the analysts are more modest in their predictions, in the nuclear calculus "we pretend that we can analyze all that is relevant. We work with simplistic abstractions and are not too troubled by the discrepancies between these abstractions and the possible reality, a reality that is so hard to imagine." The "simplistic abstractions" from which hawkish scientists concluded in the 1960's that life would be "bearable" after a nuclear war, left out of account—among other things—what would happen to the environment. With seemingly erudite graphs and charts Herman Kahn could present a neat formula: If two million people were killed in nuclear war, the nation would be back on its feet in a year. If 20 million were killed, it would take ten years and if 80 million perished, a half century. RAND Corporation, the Air Force think-tank, presented more elaborate charts to show that after a "50-city, 1,500 megaton attack," in which 27 million people died it would take twelve years to recover—if the nation was "investment-oriented," if it gave up consumer goods in favor of building factories; and much longer if it insisted on satisfying consumer wants. Neither Kahn nor RAND asked themselves, however, whether the environment could still accommodate human life after a war.

Dr. John N. Wolfe, chief of the Environmental Sciences Branch of AEC, who did take this factor into account, was much more pessimistic. "The effects of nuclear war on man and his environment are awesome to contemplate. Thermal and blast effects, and concomitant radiation would create vast areas that would be useless to the survival of man. . . . Fallout shelters in many areas seem only a means of delaying death . . . With an environment so completely modified, the question is, where does man go after his sojourn in shelters? What does he do upon emergence?"

Listening to Wolfe, a quiet man who was not happy with his conclusions, was a staggering experience. "Fires," he said, "would vary with the type of vegetation. Los Angeles would be the biggest tinderbox because of the chaparral around it. On the other hand fire in Arkansas wouldn't modify the environment much beyond the blast area. But then you must look at the multiplicity of problems. For instance, pine, spruce, and fir trees are more susceptible to radiation than broadleaf trees. They would be killed by total doses of 5,000 to 10,000 roentgens." Destruction of trees and vegetation in hilly country would result in a cycle of floods and erosion. Water running off the barren soil carries silt and pebbles before it, and in a single season carves out great gullies and ravines. Instead of being taken up by plants, said Dr. Wolfe, water would run off into the sea, drastically reducing the supply of food.

Wolfe foresaw many other problems, especially in the relationship of human beings and animals. Rats, for instance, are less susceptible to radiation than people. The rat population at Eniwetok has survived several nuclear blasts. Thus, after an attack, rats would feed on the filth of the city and transfer disease to human beings whose resistance already had been seriously lowered by radiation and deprivation. Similarly "disease-producing bacteria in sewerage disposal units and sewers would very likely be a considerable problem because they are practically immune to radiation. They can withstand a million roentgens." Disease levels in humans, therefore, would rise appreciably. Insects, flies, bees—all more resistant to radiation than people—would wreak havoc on the balance of nature. They would not have to attack humans directly. But by killing trees or destroying wheat they would further complicate the problem of recovery.

Water supplies would be drastically cut after a nuclear war, as filtration plants were destroyed, and agricultural land would be made useless by the strontium 90 covering its soil. Crops could be grown in that soil, but it would take 40 generations of crops—forty years—before the dangerous strontium 90 were filtered out. "The point is," said Dr. Wolfe, "that nuclear war triggers a whole series of effects. If you killed bumblebees you'd have a hard time growing clover. You wouldn't get the pollination. If you destroyed the bird population you'd get an explosion of insects that birds now keep under control. I can multiply these examples a thousand times. . . . Maybe not one of these things will be difficult to handle by itself, but when they all come at once and when there are problems of food, clothing, and shelter as well—" Dr. Wolfe didn't complete the sentence.

Scientists differed on every aspect of the problems that would face America after a nuclear war, but the Administration, the Pentagon, and most of the mass media proceeded as if only those views which minimized the horror had any legitimacy. Dr. Rogers S. Cannell of Stanford University, a Department of Defense advisor, said that a two-year supply of surplus food would still be available after attack and that at least 30 per cent of cropland would be usable soon after hostilities ended. But Dr. Visscher foresaw "famine within a year." The federal government scientists failed to include oxygen tanks as part of equipment for shelters. But Dr. Ralph Lapp insisted they were indispensable, and Dr. Visscher contended that, in addition to one oxygen cylinder per person for every ten days of confinement, the shelter would have to be stocked with twenty-five pounds of soda-lime to absorb the carbon dioxide. Experts disagreed on the effects of the fallout products strontium 90 and cesium 137 on food, soil, and water. They disagreed on the amount of radiation left by a 3,000-megaton attack, ranging from an AEC estimate of 2,500 roentgens one hour after explosion, to 4,000 by Dr. Lapp, to 7,500 by the Naval Radiological Defense Laboratory.

On the matter of fire, Dr. Tom T. Stonier of the Rockefeller Institute estimated that hundreds of thousands of people in New York alone would die of the fire storm effect from a 20-megaton bomb, even if they survived blast and fallout radiation. The fallout shelters as planned, he said, would be almost totally vulnerable to heat, flame, and carbon monoxide. To be effective they would have to be airtight and stocked with tanks of oxygen. Dr. Alexander Langsdorf, Jr., a physicist at the Argonne Laboratories, stated that if the Russians knew we had adequate fallout protection they would explode their bombs in the air rather than on the surface. "From an airburst," he explained, "you get a massive fire storm which might set all Chicago on fire. Concrete fallout shelters would turn into ovens, cooking the people inside. If they didn't burn, they would probably be suffocated, because all the oxygen would be consumed."

Dr. Harrison Brown, professor of geochemistry at the California Institute of Technology, judged that a single ten-megaton bomb would set all of Los Angeles on fire. Most of the city's three and a half million cars and trucks would be "lifted and thrown like grotesque Molotov cocktails," spewing gasoline and "automobile shrapnel"; oil cans and pumps would rupture and explode, pipes would be sheared. "It seems safe to speculate," he said, "that in Los Angeles at least a twenty-five-mile radius and an unknown distance beyond it would be, within minutes, engulfed in a suffocating fire storm that would persist for a long time." The civil defense authorities, however, denied all this. A leading Defense Department scientist said that a fire storm could occur only in an area of approximately one square mile, and that in cities such as Washington, D.C., with wide boulevards, this hazard might be escaped altogether. "We think it's safe to assume," he said, "that anyone caught in the basement of a small house that was burning intensely would be in trouble. But persons in the basement of a large building that won't burn intensely or in a shelter in a relatively open area will probably be able to get all the oxygen they need."

Much of what was presented to the public as "science" was in fact a guess, and often a less than educated one. Even Herman Kahn complained to the Holifield Committee that "there is almost no work aimed directly at thermonuclear war. That is, there is no attempt to apply the data at all." A scientist who gave an extensive report on the fire danger conceded he had been studying the problem only four or five weeks. Reflecting the paucity of information about fallout, Walmer E. Strope, a Defense Department research chief, told a California audience: "We know far less than we would like to about fallout from a major weapon. The statement that we need shelters, and we need good shelters, is about the best information we have." It might have been "best," but it was obviously more of a guess than a scientific determination based on empirical facts. Had it not been for the win syndrome no government would have proposed the shelter program of the 1960's. Again, it showed the self-propelling character of the arms race, the need to manipulate minds to the continuation of that race —even if it meant presenting as scientific fact that which was gross and highly slanted speculation.

Mission-oriented scientists, working on specific tasks for the government rather than objectively seeking truth, forgot the maxim of French biologist Claude Bernard more than a century ago: "To doubt, and, in ignorance, to refrain." Instead they sold a product—to make nuclear war "thinkable." The mission determined their proclaimed "knowledge," rather than knowledge their mission. In a subtle way this too was a manifestation of that self-generating process called the arms race.

In this instance, it was a failure. American families, called on to invest hundreds or thousands of dollars each, refused to respond. The private shelter program, which seemed to have a lucrative potential for shelter builders, collapsed of its own illogic. Significantly, during the 1962 October missile crisis, when the whole world feared a general thermonuclear war and Dean Rusk commented that the two superpowers were "eyeball to eyeball," Kennedy did not ask Americans to build shelters or get into those they already had. Considering that he asserted at the end of the crisis that "the fruits of victory would be ashes in our mouth," this was strange indeed.

America's civil defense program didn't terrify the Russians into submission or into yielding political ground; it simply fortified their determination to match each escalation of the arms race with one of their own. On May 25, 1961, President Kennedy asked for the shelter program and a substantial increase in armaments. The

Soviets immediately announced their decision to keep men in their armed forces who had been scheduled for release; and hardened their attitude towards a pact to suspend nuclear tests. Premier Khrushchev, speaking to British Laborite Konni Zilliacus, said: "When we proposed negotiations and a peace treaty, we were met with saber-rattling, increases in defense budgets and armed forces, and threats of war." Acting on this thesis Moscow increased its own defense bill by $4 billion over the 1961 figure. As in physics, each action had its reaction—but the bluff of civil defense exacted no political gain of any kind, either domestically or internationally. The "will" of the American people was not "hardened"; the enemy was not cowed.

v

Civil defense lay in limbo for a dozen years after the 1961–62 debacle. It would have caused a national outcry if either Johnson or Nixon had brought it up during the Vietnam War. Asking people to build shelters while that unpopular confrontation was underway would have reinforced the notion that the Administration was ready to risk anything, including a general nuclear war, to win its objectives in Southeast Asia. Neither President was ready to go so far.

But after the Vietnam peace agreement of January 1973 civil defense was again elevated to a position of importance in the military "posture." The Nixon-Ford administration, however, avoided many of the errors of the Kennedyites. It did not ask private citizens to spend their own money for fallout shelters and it tied defense against nuclear war, at first, to defense against natural disasters such as floods and hurricanes, in order to make it more palatable. The Defense Civil Preparedness Agency (DCPA) had already undertaken such tasks as loaning generators and water-pumping equipment to cities fighting the aftereffects of storms and tornadoes. Such practices were continued until late 1976. A 110-page book, well illustrated and simply written—*Your Chance to Live*—gave citizens information on how to deal with forest fires, heat waves, tornadoes, thunderstorms, hurricanes, floods, earthquakes, tidal waves, technological failures, and environmental pollution. DCPA boasted that in Macon, Georgia, civil defense volunteers were running pistol classes for women and had directed traffic during a revival meeting, all to attract goodwill from the public. DCPA remained an orphan as far as the allocation of money was concerned—operating on an $92 million budget in fiscal 1976 and $71 million in fiscal 1977—but its role took on a new luster and evoked a new debate as to its utility.

Strictly speaking it was not a civil defense program so much as a program for developing a civil defense *capability*. "Our Civil Defense Program," said Schlesinger, "is, and has always been, an essential element of our overall strategic deterrence posture. Hence, one would expect that the recent shift in emphasis towards a more flexible strategic response policy . . . would be reflected in our Civil Defense Program." The Soviet Union, he continued, "for many years has given a great deal of attention to civil defense, including not only the construction of shelters and the training of civilians but also the preparation of plans for evacuation of the bulk of the population from its major cities in the event of a crisis." It has the option therefore to "evacuate the cities or to shelter the population in place," depending on its "assessment of the situation at the time." The United States must have a similar option "for two reasons: (1) to be able to respond in kind if the Soviet Union attempts to intimidate us in a time of crisis by evacuating the population from its cities; and (2) to reduce fatalities if an attack on our cities appears imminent." Note this strange equation between "defense" and "intimidation."

The Russians, Senator Howard Baker told the Senate (June 24, 1975), were spending ten times as much per capita on civil defense as we were, and were so well prepared that "an American strike would result in fatalities hardly amounting to four percent of their population . . ." This was an unhappy prospect because if the Soviets had the capability to come out of a nuclear war with "only" ten million dead, while we suffered many times that number, their "leaders might be tempted to resort to nuclear blackmail." What the United States needed, therefore, according to John E. Davis, former governor of North Dakota, who was the DCPA director, was "a crisis relocation *capability* . . . it would represent an *option* to be exercised during a severe crisis" (emphasis added).

"Crisis relocation" was to be the new magic. It would not replace "plans to protect the population in-place, in cities and elsewhere," such as community and private shelters, but would complement them and make it possible to save, under certain circumstances, all but 30 million of the American people. To the uninitiate Crisis Relocation (CR), or evacuation of 70 per cent of the nation's city population, might seem like a warmed-over turkey, but Davis insisted it was practical.

True, said Davis, the "tactical" evacuation plans of the 1950's in which urban areas were to be depopulated in the few hours it took for a bomber to reach the United States, had become obsolete with the advent of missiles. "The time between the detection and arrival of a barrage of incoming missiles would be far too short to permit people to move out of likely target cities. In fact, an attempt to evacuate cities under such circumstances would increase exposure to the effects of nuclear weapons [i.e., fallout] and increase the number of casualties." What then had changed? Nothing, really, Davis implied, except that CR would be implemented "during a period of international crisis" days or weeks before hostilities. While the diplomats were arguing and tensions were mounting, Americans by the tens of millions would be relocated to rural areas, mines, caves, where they would be immune not only to fallout but blast and fire as well. Davis did not explain why civil defense planners of the 1950's did not make the same assumption: that there would be days and weeks to evacuate during the prewar period; but that insight is the key to present strategy for Crisis Relocation.

In a long briefing, Ren F. Read, a top government planner in this field for a quarter of a century, rejected the notion that there wouldn't be time. "No," he said, "there would be plenty of time. Before actual hostilities there is bound to be a period of tension lasting at least a few days and perhaps weeks. We can relocate during that period." But wouldn't the Russians conclude that relocation meant the United States had given up all hope of a diplomatic solution, and was ready to unleash nuclear bombs at them? Wouldn't they be tempted by CR itself to beat us to the punch? "No," said Read, "because we wouldn't evacuate our cities unless they evacuated first."

The scenario for activating CR, as Carol H. Falk explained it in the *Wall Street Journal* (June 23, 1975), went something like this: "U.S. intelligence discovers that the Soviets have begun to evacuate their cities. The President takes to the airwaves and advises all Americans except essential workers to disperse from high-risk cities to previously designated small towns and rural areas. Once there, everyone pitches in to build or dig make-shift fallout shelters. The people of both countries then hunker down and wait while negotiators try to stave off nuclear war. . . . On the basis of Soviet plans they have seen, U.S. officials say the Russians figure they need 72 hours to evacuate their cities. That would allow fleeing U.S. city-dwellers enough time to reach 'host areas' in the hinterlands."

Another scenario might be for the same evacuation to take place *during* the initial exchange of bombs in Europe (or perhaps even Korea). The United States unleashes a bomb at a Soviet position, the Soviets retaliate, also with a single bomb, and both sides hold off further action while their diplomats talk. In the meantime Americans could, in "plenty of time," be relocated to rural areas and mines. DCPA director Davis admits there is a chance of "a nuclear accident, equipment malfunction or miscalculation" that might "cause a nuclear detonation in another's territory" without much warning. But he feels confident that "such a suddenly developing event would be identified for what it is in time to avoid a war." Anyway there would also be "in-place protection"—shelters in the cities—to mitigate the effects in case of accidental war, or "in other circumstances" where "city evacuation might seem too dangerous because of concern for how it might appear to the other side. . . . Evacuation might be taken as a sign of offensive intent, counter to efforts to reduce the crisis through diplomacy." Americans, however, would be protected in all circumstances, either in-place, or through Crisis Relocation, or both.

Like everything else in the arms race mythology the new civil defense style is presented as mathematically controllable, and the horror is minimized. Should the Soviets do the "rational" thing and limit their attack to fifty-five American missile sites, six million of the thirteen million people living nearby would normally die, according to DCPA's Ren Read. But with Crisis Relocation and fallout shelters, that figure can be pruned to one million—"at most." If the attack included cities—say on a ratio of one city-directed bomb against two directed against military targets—there was equal cause of optimism. A study called Ponast II, reminiscent of the cheery studies of *Life* and Dr. Teller in 1961, claimed that civil defense could decrease the number of fatalities from 46.2 per cent of the population to as little as 5.7 per cent.

If no more were done but to identify spaces so that people could take shelter where they were, said Ponast II, 109.4 million Americans would survive, approximately 95 million would perish. That would cost $9.83 per survivor (in 1971 prices) over a ten-year period. But if the nation bestirred itself and adopted plans for Crisis Relocation, fallout shelters, and even blast shelters, the number of survivors could be increased to 191.8 million, or 94.3 per cent of the population—"a loss roughly equivalent," said Senator Baker, "to the 4 percent estimated Soviet loss." That would still be "a serious catastrophe," he noted, "but an essential equalization of the potential American and Soviet losses would render nuclear blackmail unrealistic."

To achieve this state of "equalization" America had seven options, according to the Ponast II study. Four of them depended on Crisis Relocation and three on improved shelters. For instance, Posture E-1, "is an exact mirror of the Soviet evacuation—70 percent of the population of metropolitan areas over 100,000 evacuated and sheltered in expedient shelters at a fallout protection factor (PF) of 20." That means that if the radiation outside totaled 3,000 roentgens over a two-weeks period, the sheltered evacuees would receive a dose of 150 roentgens—serious enough to cause, according to the 1957 AEC study, vomiting, nausea, loss of hair, gangrene and bleeding gums, but not death. Posture E-1 would cost the nation $32.07 for each of its 174.4 million survivors. By increasing the protection factor and introducing blast shelters for those who remained in the cities—capable of resisting blasts up to 300 pounds per square inch (PSI)—the number of survivors could reach a maximum of 191.8 million. But the costs would range from $47.53 per survivor up to $171.67 (approximately $35 billion total). For three and a half billion a year, for each of ten years, Americans could be made relatively invulnerable to nuclear war.

The central element in this program—Crisis Relocation—had some new and dramatic features, such as sheltering tens of millions of people underground. According to DCPA researcher

George N. Sisson, "mines could shelter millions of Americans, especially in the densely populated northeast corridor." As of May 1975 the National Shelter Survey had already located space for six million people in 2,000 mines "25 miles from major cities" and beyond. "Our estimates now are that, under Crisis Relocation Planning criteria, there is a potential for sheltering 50 million people in level, dry, and readily accessible mines." Ren Read was more optimistic—he thought places could be found for 100 million people underground.

DCPA does not think such programs are bizarre. It points out that "in the Kansas City area, scores of freight cars are loaded and unloaded daily in underground mine warehouses. The limestone mines of Pennsylvania are centers for a large mushroom-growing industry." A single limestone mine near Pittsburgh, Sisson says, "could shelter the entire population of the metropolitan area," 2.4 million people. Seventy per cent of the people of Missouri "could be sheltered in mines and caves in the State." All that was needed was proper lighting and ventilation equipment—and that could be installed at a cost of one dollar per person (former estimates were fifty dollars per person, but Sisson considers that outlandishly high).

All of this obviously depends on getting people out of the cities into safe rural areas with "host" families, or into safe mines. Read was most optimistic on this score. Advanced research in such places as Colorado Springs, Great Falls, Montana, Duluth, Tucson, Oklahoma City, and four others indicate, he says, that it would all go smoothly. Inhabitants would be given specific instructions beforehand—such as: "All residents of City W with Zip Code xxxxx should proceed South on U.S. highway yy to the town of Z. More detailed instructions will be provided there." Read does not anticipate that there would be any highway jams; certain gas station owners would stay behind to fill empty gas tanks; hundreds of buses would pick up those without automobiles at designated places. Once in the rural areas Read felt there would be little problem with shopping, since studies have shown that "most supermarkets work only at one-fourth capacity until week-ends." Experience has indicated, he also said, that large numbers of people have been evacuated in natural disasters with little panic; for instance in the Gulf Coast area three quarters of a million were removed up to 300 miles away within a day or two.

DCPA was meticulously researching every detail of evacuation, Read pointed out. It had learned, for instance, that in Denver there were 150,000 people without cars; they could be accommodated by 300 school buses and 600 city buses, which would pick them up at specified places. It had learned also that the average gas tank carries ten gallons of fuel at any given moment; hence it is possible to calculate in advance how many gas stations should be kept open. The Research Triangle Institute of Durham, North Carolina, was researching health care problems in the evacuation area; another agency was working on law enforcement. Read was confident that if the Communists engaged in sabotage or disruption they would fail for lack of public support. Polls in Colorado Springs, he said, "have shown that people are receptive to evacuation, and would not be dissuaded by extremists." Read is certain that if the nation put its heart into it, plans to evacuate the people in 250 cities with populations over 50,000 and 150 other areas "of significant military-industrial-economic importance" could be completed in five to seven years.

Even Read, however, has a few misgivings. What would happen, Vernon A. Guidry, Jr., of the Washington *Star* asked him, "if 80,000 people were placed in the Kansas City mine and the lights went out?" He didn't have a ready answer. Nor was he sure that there was an adequate method to handle the "tremendous logistics problems associated with caring for 80,000 people in one confined space for up to two weeks." At the end of the interview, he told Guidry "We may never use mines."

There were many other problems, including all those brought to light by critics in the 1961–62 civil defense hysteria—where to find the necessary doctors, medical supplies, food (which ordinarily comes from town to city, not from city to town), law enforcement, how to evacuate the densely inhabited Northeast, where 50 million people live, what to do about the natural reluctance of people to leave their homes. William Murray, a local civil defense co-ordinator in Montana, reminded a *Wall Street Journal* reporter that in a 1964 flood "people wouldn't leave even when they were up to their hips in water."

Representative Les Aspin called Crisis Relocation "extremely dangerous nonsense," and Leslie Brown, director of the State Department's office of International Security Policy, noted that if it were put into effect it would "take on a somewhat irreversible character to those observing [on the other side] . . . It's a damn drastic thing to do." Even DCPA director Davis hinted that Crisis Relocation might spark the very war it was supposed to thwart. Under some circumstances, he conceded, CR "might seem too dangerous because of concern for how it might appear to the other side." The Russians might conclude, once the exodus began, that there was no hope for an understanding and shoot their bolt.

Parenthetically it should be stated that the one thing Crisis Relocation punctuated with trip-hammer force was the open contempt by the imperial presidency for the public it is supposed to serve. The Nixon and Ford administrations emphasized that under the new civil defense program, CR, there would be "plenty of time" —days, perhaps weeks—to move enormous numbers of people from the cities. Why wasn't it possible in those same days and weeks to conduct a debate and referendum as to whether the 215 million Americans affected wanted to go that route? Americans, given a choice, might opt for a modus vivendi with the Soviets rather than face the prospect of nuclear war. In a democracy truly pledged to "government by consent of the governed" they had that right; even, indeed, the right to surrender. It is for them to decide, not the President and a few dozen unelected secretaries and generals who serve him. But The Bomb, whose purpose was to have been the defense of "freedom," in the end demolishes that which it was supposed to defend. The imperial presidency had always argued that there was no time to consult the people. Now that it says there is "plenty of time" it simply disregards the Constitutional mandate to seek popular consent. There is perhaps no greater irony to the nuclear arms race. For even if all the projections were correct and 94.3 per cent of the American people could be saved and the Joint Chiefs could "win" a total war, 215 million U.S. citizens would have lost beforehand—indeed are in the process of losing—the very democracy which The Bomb and civil defense were supposed to make secure.

VI

It is difficult to understand, in reviewing the postwar history of civil defense, why so little is budgeted to implement it. The researchers, as already noted, claimed that with an expenditure of $3.5 billion a year over ten years—a small sum in the light of the 1977 $114 billion military budget and a gross national product of $1,600 to $1,700 billion—nineteen out of every twenty Americans could be saved from death. Yet only $91 million was allocated to cover fiscal 1976 requirements, less than half of it ($43 million) to aid state and local governments, only $8 million for the shelter program per se. And Secretary Rumsfeld, the following year, asked for a mere $71 million. If indeed, as the Ponast II study claims, there would be 82.4 million more survivors with an all-out civil defense program of blast shelters and improved fallout shelters, it would seem that the Pentagon is derelict in not demanding the extra $3.5 billion a year—with the same vigor it demands funds for Trident submarines or B-1 bombers.

Some observers have suggested that the reason for this strange reluctance is public apathy. "One of the biggest crosses civil defense has to bear," says civil defense official William Murray of Montana, "is that, looked at in the light of no perceptible threat, a lot of the plans look pretty paranoid." The horror of nuclear war becomes more graphic when a citizen realizes that he is scheduled for "relocation" to a limestone or mushroom mine a long way from home. Others have suggested that the civil defense program is retained as an option merely so that a small bureaucracy of a few hundred men in DCPA can find a niche for itself. The cost is negligible, and even if the program is unrealistic it may implant in some minds the idea that nuclear war is "thinkable" and "fightable." It is just possible, moreover, that the rhetoric of a civil defense "capability" may also convince Moscow that Washington is "determined."

With all that, however, civil defense must appear as a Strangelovian fantasy to those who seek a logical purpose for it—unless it is correlated to the driving "win syndrome" that is behind *every* aspect of American policy. "Anyone who saw *Dr. Strangelove* several years ago," writes Phil Stanford in *Parade* (June 15, 1975), "will probably remember the mine-shaft gap. *Dr. Strangelove*, of course, was the funny movie about blowing up everything in a nuclear war, and the mine-shaft gap was just another of its nutty jokes. In the film the United States was supposedly in grave danger of falling behind Russia in the number of mine shafts that could be used as fallout shelters." But if civil defense is correlated to the "win syndrome" it acquires a more serious character. It is part of a holding operation, until technology someway, somehow can provide the weaponry for "damage-limitation"—for destroying the Soviet Union while our own nation suffers minimally.

On that score, Secretary of State Henry Kissinger gives us a remarkable confirmation both of the dilemma the United States faces and its plans for circumventing it. In a confidential speech to American ambassadors stationed in Europe (December 1975), Kissinger stated the dilemma thus: "The problem of our age is how to manage the emergence of the Soviet Union as a superpower. In today's circumstances, neither side can gain a strategic advantage that can be translated into political utility." In simpler English: neither side can win an all-out nuclear war "in today's circumstances." Tomorrow things may be different. Nonetheless, even today, "the strategic balance provides increased opportunities for regional pressures." If we cannot yet win an all-out war, we can still use our military, political, and economic leverage to contain and roll back Soviet power on a limited scale—in the various regions of the world, Asia, Africa, parts of Europe, and of course our bastion, Latin America. The weight of Kissinger's speech was on measures to prevent local Communist Parties—in Italy, France, Portugal, Spain—from coming to power or sharing power; but that is not our concern here. Nor is the fact that the Secretary of State has a more pessimistic view of the future than some others—"The fact is that, with the Soviet Union as an emerging superpower, we are doomed to coexistence." What is significant is the judgment that there is a permanent war under way, and that it must be waged with whatever military, political, and economic weapons are at hand at the time. We do not give up our "strategic balance"—our nuclear arsenal for total war. We keep it on the theory that additions and modifications in the future will make it usable for victory.

It is in the same light that the strategists view civil defense. It may not be of much value today, but—who knows?—it may serve some purpose in the future. At the least it reinforces the fear psychology that is so essential to militarism.

8

National
Security State

The nuclear arms race, as stated often in these pages, is self-propelling—in the sense that it proceeds automatically under the pressure of forces more powerful than any single individual or group, no matter how well positioned. The President or Congress can effectively influence the decision whether or not to proceed with a particular program (e.g., the B-1 bomber), but even if they were so disposed they cannot, on their own, terminate the arms race itself. After a third of a century the decision-making process is institutionalized; the arms race has become the cornerstone not merely of a military edifice but of a new political and social *structure*. It has changed institutions and behavior patterns of the nation more drastically than anyone anticipated in 1945. The self-generating character of those changes is reflected in the flight from reality, described in the last chapter. More basic has been the consolidation of military-minded forces, and the refashioning of government into a National Security State, whose twin purpose has been to organize American power, while denying the American people the checks and balances to retard or abrogate the arms race on which that power was to be based. With the stifling of opposition through secrecy, loyalty oaths, security checks, McCarthyism, Cointelpro, and a dozen other devices peculiar to the National Security State, the barriers to rearmament have been removed, and the pressures of constituencies promoting it have to that extent been freed from restraint.

There was a brief period in the 1940's when all this might have been prevented—the structural change was not yet far advanced and there existed a faction in and out of government trying to prevent it.

On September 11, 1945, Secretary of War Stimson, in an expression of concern about how to deal with The Bomb, sent a memorandum to Truman urging a forthright offer of atomic partnership to the Russians, without strings attached. "I have become convinced that any demand by us for an internal change in Russia as a condition of sharing in the atomic weapon would be so resented that it would make the objective we have in view less probable." The memorandum pleaded that "unless the Soviets are voluntarily invited into the partnership upon a basis of cooperation and trust, we . . . will almost certainly stimulate feverish activity on the part of the Soviet [Union] toward the development of this bomb in what will in effect be a secret armament race of a rather desperate character."

Specifically, Stimson suggested that we "stop work" on The Bomb, impound the bombs we already had, and provide "for the exchange of benefits of future developments whereby atomic energy may be applied on a mutually satisfactory basis for commercial or humanitarian purposes." The arms race, Stimson felt, must be averted at all costs. "The chief lesson I have learned in a long life," he advised Truman, "is that the only way you can make a man trustworthy is to trust him; and the surest way to make him untrustworthy is to distrust him and show your distrust." Stimson's proposal was supported within the Truman Cabinet by Secretary of Commerce (and former Vice-President) Henry Wallace, by Secretary of Labor Lewis Schwellenbach, and by Postmaster General Robert Hannegan, but rejected by Truman and the rest of the Cabinet. Had Stimson carried the day the state of the nation (and the planet) would have been very much different from what it is today.

Wallace, who would soon be called a "Communist stooge" for his efforts, made a similar plea against the win syndrome. In a confidential letter to the President (July 23, 1946), he warned that other nations would inevitably see the United States as aggressive. He pointed to "concrete things like $13 billion for the War and Navy Departments, the Bikini tests of the atomic bomb and continued production of bombs, the plan to arm Latin America with our weapons, production of B-29's and planned production of B-36's and the effort to secure air bases spread over half the globe from which the other half of the globe can be bombed." Such behavior, he wrote, gave the impression that "we were only paying lip service to peace at the conference table." They "make it appear either (1) that we are preparing ourselves to win the war which we regard as inevitable or (2) that we are trying to build up a predominance of force to intimidate the rest of mankind."

How would it look to us, asked Wallace, if "Russia had the atomic bomb and we did not, if Russia had 10,000-mile bombers and air bases within 1,000 miles of our coastlines, and we did not?" He decried the "irrational fear" of Russia being built up in American minds. "The slogan," he said, "that Communism and Capitalism, regimentation and democracy, cannot continue to exist in the same world is, from a historical point of view, pure propaganda. . . . This country was for the first half of its national life a democratic island in a world dominated by absolutist governments." Wallace's prescription called for trade and loans, for cooling tensions, and for negotiating a settlement on atomic issues which did not force the Soviets into subservience.

Responding to a hypothetical question—"What's wrong with trying to build up a predominance of force?"—Wallace replied that "the flaw in this policy is simply that it will not work. In a world of atomic bombs and other revolutionary weapons, such as radioactive poison gases and biological warfare, a peace maintained by a predominance of force is no longer possible." His ideas were endorsed by thousands of liberals, but were never entertained by the Administration. The choice for America's future was whether to "coexist and disarm" or "confront and rearm"; Washington took the course of confrontation and rearmament, a policy that has not varied to this day. "In contrast to 1918 and 1919," wrote Blair Bolles in *Foreign Policy Reports* (October 1, 1946), "when . . . governments hoped to find lasting peace through limitation of national armaments, this time they hoped to avert war by remaining armed."

Once the opposition was sidetracked and the decision made to "confront and rearm," a train of events was set in motion that transformed the United States almost overnight. The nation:

1. Became a militarized society, under a National Security State.

2. Spawned a new arrangement of power, which Eisenhower would later call the Military-Industrial Complex.

3. Established a host of mechanisms for restricting dissent, manipulating the public, and undermining "government by consent of the governed."

4. Exported the arms race to every region of the globe, encouraging conflict and war between lesser nations, and between innumerable governments and their peoples.

5. Subverted negotiations for disarmament, so that they became in reality an appendage to the process of rearmament.

II

The United States has engaged in many military campaigns, major and minor, during its existence as an independent state (159 times between 1798 and 1945), but it has never been a militarist society. George Washington, the Continental Congress, and a considerable majority of the founders considered that large standing armies were the "destructive engines for establishing despotism" and "dangerous to the liberties of a country." On the eve of the Mexican War there were about 9,000 officers and men in the armed forces; as of 1904, only 53,000; and just before World War II, a mere 139,000.

The Bomb and the Cold War, however, turned matters around decisively. Prior to World War II Uncle Sam's overseas stations had been limited to Guam, Hawaii, the Philippines, and a few spots in the Western Hemisphere; as of September 1945, U.S. forces were ensconced in 434 installations all over the world, most of which remained under their control thereafter. As of 1969, according to former Senate majority leader Mike Mansfield, American forces were emplaced in 427 major and 2,295 minor bases in foreign countries. A Navy "second to none," far exceeding that of the British in their heyday, policed the seven seas. Three and a half million men were under arms, on foreign soil as well as in 470 major domestic bases, camps, and installations, and 5,000 lesser ones. Though the number is now substantially reduced, it is still fifteen times larger than it was before World War II, and incomparably stronger in firepower. In terms of wealth, the Department of Defense was the custodian, as of 1974, of $228 billion of property, making it far and away the richest institution in the world, with assets equal to those of the fifteen largest U.S. industrial corporations and the fifteen largest utilities combined.

An institution so immense could not help but leave its imprint on everything. It drew to itself functions never before exercised by the armed forces, and captured political power in pivotal sections of government. "Today," boasted the *Army and Navy Bulletin* of January 18, 1947, "the Army has virtual control of foreign affairs. . . . The chain of control in diplomatic hot spots, both in the execution of basic policy and in the formulation of ad hoc arrangements, lies almost totally in the hands of military authorities." The *Bulletin* was not wrong. General MacArthur ruled Japan, Lieutenant General Lucius D. Clay ruled the American sector of Germany, and Lieutenant General Geoffrey Keyes, the American sector of Austria. General of the Army George C. Marshall held the second most important post in government, Secretary of State, and ten of the twenty executive officers in the Department were transferees from the military services. Lieutenant General Walter Bedell Smith was ambassador to Moscow, Admiral Alan G. Kirk, ambassador to Belgium. As of 1953 nine Army generals and fifty-eight colonels, on leave or retired, were working for civilian agencies of government; and as of 1957, 200 generals and admirals, plus 1,300 colonels or Navy officers of similar rank, and 6,000 of lower grade. The military incursion into civilian politics subsequently became less visible, but its role in determining policy was no less important—exercised through the National Security Council (established in 1947), through partnership with the CIA in a host of ventures, through the atomic energy and space agencies, and through many interdepartmental committees.

As a barometer of the military's incursion into international affairs, the 1968 Defense Department budget called for $27 million for "foreign policy-oriented research and nearly $40 million on research in foreign countries." By contrast, the intelligence and research operations of the Department of State were funded with a mere $5 million. Among the items researched at DOD's expense were such esoteric subjects as "witchcraft, sorcery, magic, and other psychological phenomena" in the Congo; political influence of university students in Latin America; ideology and behavior; resettlement in Latin America; the political influence of students south of the Rio Grande. None of this appears to have relevance to waging war, but the Pentagon's vistas kept widening. It also acquired certain domestic functions which have always been considered the province of the FBI and the Justice Department, such as the operation of a multimillion-dollar "war room," 400 feet long by 250 feet wide, for the "dispatch and coordination of military troops in the event of urban riots"; surveillance over thousands of dissidents during the turbulent Vietnam years; and many community activities. According to a Defense Scientific Board panel in 1967: "The DOD mission now embraces problems and responsibilities which have not previously been assigned to a military establishment. It has been properly stated that the DOD must now wage not only warfare but 'peacefare' as well. Pacification assistance and the battle of ideas are major segments of the DOD responsibility."

An inevitable corollary to military expansion was still another innovation in the American way of life, a permanent "defense" industry. Never before in peacetime had the United States maintained a defense industry as such. When a war broke out certain segments of the economy shifted to the production of arms, and when the war was over shifted back to peaceful pursuits. Gunsmiths who made guns for hunting prior to the Revolution, made the same or similar weapons for Washington's army, then went back to supplying hunters and homeowners when the war ended. Manufacturers of blasting powder for the railroads, before the Civil War, fabricated gunpowder during that war, then converted back to peace production. Before and during World War I the government produced most of its own armaments in federal arsenals, leaving private industry free to continue traditional endeavors. (Even during the war, General Motors didn't miss a beat in the manufacture of automobiles, though it also did $35 million war work.) But World War II changed all that. Entire industries closed down normal operations to provide tanks and planes for the war effort. General Motors this time did $12 *billion* war work.

After V-J Day, contrary to past practice, much of the war plant remained in place—and expanded. By the late 1960's, three of every five workers in the aircraft industry were working on "defense" orders, two of three in the ordnance industry, and one of ten in manufacturing generally. Giant firms such as Lockheed, McDonnell Douglas, United Aircraft, General Dynamics, depended for survival on military orders, their civilian operations constituting barely more than a sideline; and almost every sizable manufacturing company was being plied with "defense" work ranging from a few thousand dollars a year to hundreds of millions in the case of such firms as General Electric, General Motors, American Telephone & Telegraph. All told there were 22,000 prime contractors and 100,000 subcontractors with a stake in defense procurement; and in five states, Georgia, New Mexico, Tennessee, Mississippi, and Louisiana, "defense" was the largest single employer. By 1974 the Pentagon was buying $40 billion worth of hardware and other supplies from private business, most of it from the fifty largest corporations in the country.

What Eisenhower called the Military-Industrial Complex was actually a soldering of the military establishment with the corporate, banking, academic, labor, and other establishments which share a common interest in the arms race. Its members move back and forth, from the corporate or academic world to the Pentagon, and vice versa, as if there were no line of demarcation, as indeed there isn't. "Between 1940 and 1967, when I stopped counting," writes Richard Barnet, "all the first- and second-level posts in a huge national security bureaucracy were held by fewer than 400 individuals who rotate through a variety of key posts." Military people established great pockets of power in civilian government, as already noted, and businessmen, financiers, and Wall Street lawyers—Forrestal, Charles E. Wilson (of General Electric), McElroy, McNamara, Clark Clifford, Robert A. Lovett, David Packard—assumed top positions in DOD. Retired officers took jobs with industry, e.g., General Lauris Norstad, former Supreme Allied Commander in Europe became president of Owens-Corning Fiberglas; Admiral William M. Fechteler, former Chief of Naval Operations, a consultant to a division of General Electric; Admiral Arleigh Burke, another Chief of Naval Operations, became a director of many corporations and head of a think-tank at Georgetown University; and scientists such as Herbert F. York, Harold Brown, and John S. Foster, Jr., became directors of Research and Engineering for the Pentagon after serving in similar capacities at the Livermore Laboratory. Hundreds of former military officers—sometimes more than a thousand—went to work for the large defense corporations, in many instances arranging for contracts with men in the Pentagon who were formerly their subordinates.

In all the Complex is a conglomerate of eight interlinked constituencies:

1. The Pentagon, which is the fountainhead though not the brain.

2. The large corporate contractors who do business with the Pentagon, a sort of Who's Who of American industry.

3. A select group of organizations that act as liaison between industry and the military, such as the American Ordnance Association or the National Security Industrial Association.

4. A host of DOD-subsidized research organizations popularly called "think-tanks," such as the RAND Corporation and the Institute for Defense Analysis (until the late 1960's a consortium of twelve universities). Some are headed by former defense officials—General Maxwell D. Taylor, for instance, once directed IDA.

5. A civilian-militarist faction in Congress. Many of the most influential figures in the national legislature hold officer ranks in the military forces—active, inactive, or retired; men such as Democratic Senator Howard Cannon of Nevada, Republican Senator Strom Thurmond of South Carolina, Republican Senator Barry Goldwater of Arizona. In addition scores of Representatives and Senators own stock in defense companies, and scores more, without investments or commissions, share a blind allegiance to the military.

6. The international affairs department of the AFL-CIO, which has engaged in innumerable clandestine activities together with or parallel to the CIA.

7. A considerable number of private research and educational organizations, such as the American Security Council, the Center for Strategic Studies, the American Enterprise Institute for Public Policy Research.

8. The academic community whose fate is tied to the Pentagon, including such prominent professors as Edward Teller, certain de-

partments at the Massachusetts Institute of Technology, Johns Hopkins, etc., and the "contract centers" run by elite universities.

"The institutions which support the Economy of Death," writes former ACDA official Barnet, "are impervious to ordinary logic or experience because they operate by their own inner logic. Each institutional component of the military-industrial complex has plausible reasons for continuing to exist and expand. Each promotes and protects its own interests and in so doing reinforces the interests of the others. That is what a 'complex' is—a set of integrated institutions that act to maximize their collective power."

The influence of the Complex on public opinion and Congress is impossible to exaggerate. The Complex sometimes must compromise or on occasion retreat from an objective, but its efforts are persistent and far-reaching. During the 1948 campaign for universal military training the War Department enlisted the aid of 370 national organizations, according to a subcommittee of the Committee of Expenditures in the Executive Departments, "including the U.S. Chamber of Commerce and the American Legion; it . . . contacted 351 mayors in the principal cities of the land; it . . . promoted at least 591 articles and editorials in the press." The Boy Scouts were prevailed on to distribute fact sheets and the American Legion was induced to print 600,000 copies of a brochure titled "You and the Army Reserve." The congressional subcommittee branded all this a violation of "section 201, title 18 of the United States code" and charged that the War Department was "using government funds in an improper manner for propaganda purposes." But such activity continues nonetheless.

Senator Proxmire once charged that the Pentagon employed 339 full-time lobbyists to plead its case in Congress. A staff of at least 6,000 educates the public in the latest military styles and ideas. Hundreds of radio stations, innumerable books and articles with a "defense" slant, movies made with the Pentagon's help, trips and seminars for "opinion makers"—all this adds up to the greatest propaganda machine in American history. In the words of ex-Senator Fulbright, "There is something basically unwise and undemocratic about a system which taxes the public to finance a propaganda campaign aimed at persuading the same taxpayers that they must spend more tax dollars to subvert their independent judgement." And it is supplemented by thousands of documents, press releases, brochures, "educational" films, books, that pour like torrents from think-tanks and other research groups, winding up eventually as news stories or newspaper columns.

Dr. Ralph McDonald of the National Education Association said many years ago that there were two ways to destroy freedom —through concentration camps or "through influencing public opinion." By constantly "scaring the hell out of them"—the citizenry—the Military-Industrial Complex blankets the nation in fear and timidity, vulnerable to secrecy and to government decisions without the "consent of the governed."

III

The Military-Industrial Complex represents an informal rearrangement of political power, an unwritten compact, as it were, between many groups and individuals with a monetary or ideological investment in The Bomb and the arms race. It has no headquarters, no constitution, no president, no membership cards. But the militarization of America includes, in addition, formal changes in American institutions. The old ones were inadequate because the secrets to be withheld from the public had to be given *legal* sanction; the probing of loyalty had to be placed on a less haphazard basis than congressional "investigations" by such committees as the House Committee on Un-American Activities (HUAC); the three armed services had to be unified; and the innumerable activities that constituted the Cold War had to be centrally co-ordinated so that the State Department, the CIA, the military, the Commerce Department, and others could act in concert.

The armed forces, for instance, could not be allowed to establish military bases or negotiate the two score secret executive pacts they eventually entered into, if the countries they were dealing with were deemed hostile or unstable by State. The three services had to be informed what each was doing, to avoid duplication in research and procurement. State needed to know what the CIA was doing, the CIA had to be sure its actions did not conflict with State Department policy. Business needed firmer ties with the Defense Department to know its needs, the direction of its research, its long-term plans—especially since the new weapons were so complex and sophisticated they needed six to eight years lead time.

Economic aid had to mesh with military aid to foreign countries, domestic policy with foreign policy. Public opinion had to be shaped to government action, since public opinion itself was a factor in the equation of "deterrence." Not merely those directly involved in the military effort but a whole nation had to be mobilized for Cold War, just as it had been mobilized for Hot War.

To meet all these needs, a National Security State—or what Fred J. Cook terms a Warfare State—was superimposed on the prewar social structure. America did not turn fascist, as some thought it would in the early days after World War II, but it became—in the words of author Alan Wolfe—a "dual state," one part of it "democratic, highly visible and generally open; the other . . . covert, lean and ready to operate where it had to."

Though there was as yet no coherent plan in 1945, the institutional rearrangement of the state began almost at once. Truman's first concern, as we have seen, was to retain the monopoly of The Bomb, and for that purpose he created an Atomic Energy Commission to continue research and production. Though it was nominally controlled by civilians, more than 95 per cent of its functions were on behalf of the military, and it operated under a militarist way of life that former Marine Corps Commandant David M. Shoup describes as "secretive, devious, and misleading in its plans and operations."

The second brick in the edifice was to have been universal military training (UMT), a proposal that the President made in the fall of 1945, and which was justified by a commission he subsequently appointed on the grounds that "by making war universal, devastating, and immediate in its impact, the atomic bomb and new developments in warfare had created a need for trained men in every city and town who would be available at once in an emergency." This too was a stern departure from national tradition. Except for the Civil War and World Wars I and II, the United States had never conscripted men into the armed forces, let alone subjected them to universal military training in peacetime. Under UMT, service in the armed forces would no longer be *selective,* with men deferred for a variety of reasons, but *total*—all youth reaching the age of eighteen, except the physically handicapped, would be required to take military training for a period of years and then be placed in the reserves to continue training a few nights each month and every summer.

Many members of Congress could not understand why we needed so many troops when we had atom bombs that could kill 75,000 people at one fell blow. But as Major General F. O. Bowman, a commander at Fort Knox, explained later, there was more than a direct military purpose involved: "We have these young people while they are young and fresh. Their minds have not been cluttered up by worldliness. They make wonderful subjects for Army training." The implication was that civilian schools do not offer youth the right approach to citizenship. As Assistant Secretary of Defense Anna Rosenberg explained it in 1952, "a large part of the training as envisaged . . . is citizenship training, literary training, training in morale, and training in the type of things that young people ought to have." The military's idea of good citizenship was attested to by the armed forces security questionnaire, which draftees were required to fill out to show they were "reliable, trustworthy, of good character, and of complete unswerving loyalty to the United States." They were asked to state that they were not now or had ever been members of any one of 200 organizations on the Attorney General's subversive list, including of course the Communist Party, and such esoteric groups as People's Drama, Inc., and the Chopin Cultural Center.

The military did not win its fight for UMT; Congress, on one of the few occasions when it showed signs of resistance, rejected it. But it did win a second-best alternative, selective service, the right to draft young men nineteen to twenty-six for a specified period. This was to be fundamental to the militarization of the nation for the next quarter of a century. "It is the draft," Professor John M. Swomley, Jr., wrote in March 1967, "which makes it possible for the President to send 400,000 troops into Vietnam without a declaration of war. Each step of escalation was possible only because the Joint Chiefs of Staff and the President knew they could draw on hundreds of thousands of American youth without going to Congress for such authority. If the President had had to ask Congress either for a draft or a declaration of war he would have faced a national debate over his policies."

In addition to ready-made military manpower the National Security State required a command and operations structure suitable for worldwide confrontation. The most comprehensive step in that direction was the passage in 1947 of the National Security Act, the handiwork in large part of Ferdinand Eberstadt, a friend and former partner of Navy Secretary James Forrestal, in the Wall Street investment firm, Dillon, Read. On the military side, there was a general consensus for unifying the armed services, so as to eliminate overlap, duplication, and other malfunctions that had become grossly apparent during World War II. President Truman noted a small example in his memoirs: "I found immense air installations side by side at various points, in this country and Panama, where the Navy could not land on the Army's airfield, and vice versa. A silly procedure, if ever I saw one." The 1947 bill created a "National Military Establishment" under a single civilian Secretary of Defense and gave legal sanction to the Joint Chiefs of Staff. Under this unified structure, rearmament and intervention, it was hoped, could be more effectively systematized.

On the civilian side, the 1947 "security" act fashioned the most wide-ranging command institution in American history, the National Security Council, which was in essence a dual state—covert, secretive, removed from popular controls; together with the changes in the military command, this was, as C. Wright Mills put it, a "military definition of reality." The Council was charged with co-ordinating "domestic, foreign, and military policies." Composed of four statutory members, the President, Vice-President, and the Secretaries of State and Defense, plus others designated by the President such as the Director of Central Intelligence and the chairman of the Joint Chiefs, it formulated long-term policy and sanctioned, as Senator Frank Church's committee reported in 1976, literally thousands of covert undertakings around the world —a coup d'état in Brazil, the financing of friendly political parties in Italy, the disruption of a union movement in France, and so on. All of these were acts of war or internal interferences outlawed by Article 2 Section 4 of the UN charter and dozens of treaties to the same effect, or outright violations of Article 1 Section 8 of the U. S. Constitution, which places in Congress—and Congress only— the right to declare war. Since the whole procedure, moreover, was under the direction of the President, it in effect was the legal basis for the imperial presidency. Whether or not it was so understood in 1947 the fact is that a vast area of government functions was cut adrift from public or congressional review.

By way of example two classified documents of the National Security Council (NSC), set the specific goals of the United States for decades to come, though they were never discussed in Congress or by the citizenry at large; they were not even made public for a quarter of a century. NSC 20/4 elaborated a six-point program for confronting the Soviets and rearming the United States:

"a. Develop a level of military readiness which can be maintained as long as possible . . ." This was the mandate for an ultimate expenditure of a trillion and two thirds dollars on arms; for spreading a network of bases around the world; and for maintaining the largest military peacetime force in U.S. history.

"b. Assure the internal security of the United States against dangers of sabotage, subversion, and espionage." This was the mandate for loyalty programs, security checks (and discharges), secrecy, the Counter Intelligence Program (Cointelpro) by the FBI (to disrupt dissident groups), and Nixon's "plumbers" and the Tom Charles Huston plan.

"c. Maximize our economic potential, including the strengthening of our peacetime economy and the establishment of essential reserves readily available in the event of war." This was a mandate to build up an armaments industry through various forms of subsidy and blandishments, and to procure a reserve stockpile of raw materials.

"d. Strengthen the orientation towards the United States of the non-Soviet states; and help such of these nations as are able and willing to make an important contribution to U.S. security to increase their economic and political stability and their military capability." This was a mandate to form NATO, CENTO, SEATO, OAS, and other alliances, to arm and train foreign armies, to enter into secret executive agreements with forty-odd countries to defend their governments against their people, to use the CIA, bribery, and military support to keep such governments in power—or overthrow those inimical to "American interests."

"e. Place the maximum strain on the Soviet structure and power , . ." This was a mandate to deny aid and loans to a World War II ally, and isolate it economically, politically, and militarily.

Before the end of World War II the State Department under Cordell Hull was prepared to grant Moscow a postwar credit of $10 billion at 2 per cent a year interest, provided the Kremlin committed itself to supply strategic raw materials to the United States and to "normalize" economic relations. But after Roosevelt's death, on May 8, 1945, Truman abruptly cut off lend-lease, and refused the Soviets any further loans or grants to take its place. This policy was extended under the Marshall Plan to include pressure by U.S. allies; each month those receiving American aid had to certify that they had not exported to the Soviet Union or the other Communist countries, any arms, strategic material, or goods on which the United States had placed an embargo. Even the export of technological know-how was subsequently included in the *verboten* list.

"f. Keep the U.S. public fully informed and cognizant of the threats to our national security . . ." This was a mandate for intensified anti-Communist propaganda. "Led by Acheson and Forrestal," Robert Borosage writes, "the leaders of the postwar state viewed the public and Congress as objects to be manipulated in pursuit of their goals."

NSC-68, a secret 1950 report, contains a four-page section that states Washington's attitude towards negotiations with Moscow. "It is still argued by many people here and abroad," the document says, "that equitable agreements with the Soviet Union are possible, and this view will gain force if the Soviet Union begins to show signs of accommodation . . . The free countries must always, therefore, be prepared to negotiate . . ." Negotiation, however, "is not a possible separate course of action but rather a means of gaining support for a program of building strength . . ." In other words, by posing conditions which appear reasonable but which the Russians could not accept without "a change in the Soviet system," the United States would mobilize public support for an armament policy. And if somehow the Russians did concur with our conditions for disarmament, including "the withdrawal of Soviet influence from the satellites" the United States would withdraw its own proposal. "If," says NSC-68, "contrary to our expectations, the Soviet Union should accept agreements promising effective control of atomic energy and conventional armaments, without any other changes in Soviet policies, *we would have to consider very carefully whether we could accept such agreements*" (emphasis added). This in fact was what happened in the mid-1950's—as we shall see in Chapter 9—when the Kremlin approved an offer made by the West, only to have the United States change its mind.

Never in the past had any institution of the government committed the nation to so broad-ranging a program for so long a time, without an opportunity by the public to discuss or debate it. Had the decisions been made openly, at least certain portions would have been disavowed. Certainly the electorate would not have endorsed a policy of negotiations deliberately designed to fail, or an "internal security" policy so patently illegal.

IV

On the operational side, the National Security Act created a Munitions Board under the Defense Secretary to orchestrate and evaluate military procurement; and a Research and Development Board to perform a similar function in the scientific and engineering field. Under another bill passed the same year, the Armed Services Procurement Act, the acquisition of armaments was effectively freed from bidding. If any one of sixteen "exceptions" obtained, as was the case in the overwhelming majority of cases, the Pentagon did not have to advertise for bids or give the work to the lowest bidder, but could contract directly with the corporation of its choice. This of course had the effect of consolidating the military-industrial and the military-academic relationship, and producing what Professor Irving Louis Horowitz called a class of "civilian militarists."

A particularly ominous aspect of the dual state was the provision in the 1947 law for a Central Intelligence Agency, whose purpose, according to its first Director, Allen Dulles, was not only to cope with the Soviet "menace," but "the *internal conflicts* within the countries of Europe, Asia, and South America" (emphasis added). It was ominous because it empowered the CIA, under NSC direction, to initiate coups d'état, to embroil other nations in civil wars, and to ignite "little" wars.

The United States was not exactly a novice at interfering in the internal affairs of other states. American leaders had conspired to uproot governments of other countries all the way back to the naval war with Tripoli (1801–5). But there was little of this sort of activity outside the Western Hemisphere, and even there the accepted technique was to send in the Marines—as, for instance, in December 1914, when Marines landed at Port-au-Prince, Haiti.

But during World War II, when action behind the lines was often as important as the front-line war itself, Major General William J. (Wild Bill) Donovan collected a blue-ribbon group of scholars (Arthur Schlesinger, Herbert Marcuse, Carl Kaysen), business leaders (e.g., David Bruce, Andrew Mellon's son-in-law), political leaders (e.g., William Vanderbilt, former governor of Rhode Island), and adventurers—all told, about 30,000 people—to spy and evaluate information, infiltrate resistance movements, conduct psychological warfare, engage in paramilitary activities, distribute counterfeit currency, form guerrilla forces where feasible. This was to be the prototype of the CIA, and many members of Donovan's Office of Strategic Services (OSS) were enlisted in the new agency.

No institution of the National Security State revealed the tendency to enlarge its area of activity more than the CIA. The law, for instance, carried no explicit directive for covert action overseas, and it specifically excluded domestic functions. But a catchphrase in the bill—"perform such other functions and duties . . . as the National Security Council may from time to time direct"—was taken as a mandate for activity far beyond intelligence gathering. A secret directive in December 1947, NSC-4-A ordered the Director of Central Intelligence to engage in covert psychological warfare. NSC 10/2 authorized him to "conduct political and paramilitary operations," such as sabotage, guerrilla-type operations and other black activities. From here it was only a matter of time before CIA would be engaging in black activities at home.

For the first time in U.S. history a federal agency was permitted by law to keep its budget secret from the public, open only to four small subcommittees of the Armed Services and Appropriations committees. Its activities too were removed from effective scrutiny. "As a matter of fact," writes Harry Howe Ransom, a Harvard specialist on intelligence, "the real operating constitution of the CIA is probably not so much the statutory authority given by Congress in 1947 and 1949, but about a score of super-secret National Security Council Intelligence Directives which probably only a few high government officials have ever seen."

The CIA formed alliances and associations, and did things that were not anticipated when it was first created. To provide cover for its agents, and services for paramilitary activities, for instance, the CIA established or took over dozens of companies—with assets of $57.3 million. Included were such successful businesses as Air America, an insurance complex, and Intermountain Aviation, Inc. The CIA subsidized the publication of hundreds of books which were sold at home as if they were the works of disinterested scholars, and entered into arrangements with giant corporations such as ITT both for cover and information.

Thus in many instances a partnership evolved between CIA and big business, again reinforcing each other and above all reinforcing the militarist spirit. Tad Szulc, in an article for the *New Republic* (April 10, 1976), gives some idea of how insidious this process can become. Szulc reveals that Yoshio Kodama, a rightist Japanese who took millions of dollars in bribes to influence his government to buy Lockheed planes, "had a working relationship with the CIA from the time he was released from a Japanese prison in 1948 after serving a three-year term as a war criminal." The money Kodama received was transferred to him through Deak & Co., a firm with twenty international offices dealing in foreign currency. Nicholas Deak, head of the firm, was a wartime employee of OSS and has handled large sums of CIA money—according to "reliable sources"—for its activities in Iran, Vietnam, and elsewhere.

Anthony Sampson, in his book *The Sovereign State of ITT*, tells how John McCone, a director of this vast multinational firm and a former CIA director, remained a consultant to CIA while serving ITT. McCone told Congress, according to Sampson, "how he discussed the Chilean elections with his successor as CIA director, Richard Helms, and had later seen Helms and Kissinger to offer help to stop [Salvador] Allende . . ." A corporation with large investments in Chile uses one of its directors, with links to CIA and government, to press the Administration for covert and overt action that would help his company. Multiply this sort of thing a hundredfold and it is difficult to tell the line of demarcation between CIA and other government agencies on the one hand, and business on the other.

Similarly, the CIA has a viable partnership with the leadership of labor—George Meany and his international affairs officials. Through the years the intelligence agency has financed activities by AFL officials such as Irving Brown to split the trade union movements of France and Italy; isolate Communist union leaders in Germany; finance a general strike in Guyana in an attempt to bring down the Cheddi Jagan government; pay the expenses of former East European unionists who engaged in intelligence work; break a strike in Marseilles, France, when dockmen refused to unload American ships with arms; give support to synthetic unions in Vietnam, the Dominican Republic, Chile, Brazil, and elsewhere who either helped bring down governments the United States didn't like or sustained governments Washington did like; and train many thousands of unionists in "anti-Communism," through a host of "educational" programs conducted by AFL-CIO official-dom overseas. Not a few of these trainees became functioning CIA agents.

In its totality, then, the National Security State became the operative structure for an imperial presidency that acted in thousands of instances without either the advice or consent of Congress, and usually without even its knowledge. "Within the branches of government," writes Robert Borosage, "a realignment of power took place. The executive pre-empted many of the legislative functions. In the area of national security, the executive became sovereign; the legislature, except for its powerful committee heads, who are satraps of the security bureaucracies, was rendered impotent."

The executive entered into treaties with forty-two countries—called "executive agreements"—without bothering to secure the approval of the Senate, as required by the Constitution. Neither Congress nor the public, for instance, was informed in 1960 of an agreement by which the United States committed itself to give military assistance to a 40,000-man Ethiopian army and to intervene more directly, as it later did, if the Haile Selassie government were in danger. Executive agreements with Spain, similarly, were never submitted to Congress, though they explicitly pledged to help the Franco regime fight off a revolt, and though U.S. and Spanish armed forces engaged in joint war exercises for that purpose. Deals with Thailand, Korea, the Philippines, and many others, a congressional committee reported in December 1970, remained classified. "If the Executive Branch," said the committee, "actually believes it has the authority to undertake this kind of arrangement, it also must believe that certain portions of the Constitution can be abrogated by acts of the Executive."

The presidency in addition took unto itself the right to make war without congressional sanction. When Truman sent troops to Korea in 1950—presenting the nation with a *fait accompli* before it could be discussed or voted on in Congress—Secretary of State Acheson argued that the President's "authority may not be interfered with by the Congress . . ."

There is no law on the books which delegates this authority to the President, and the Constitution itself in Article 1 Section 8 specifically confers the right to declare war on the Congress. But in the erosion of checks and balances that was the essence of the National Security State, the President became supreme. Congress itself rubber-stamped this state of affairs when a joint committee of the Senate Foreign Relations and Armed Services committees in February 1951 agreed that the President's powers as commander-in-chief conferred such prerogatives on him, and pointed to 125 incidents since the republic was founded in which a President, without congressional approval, had "ordered the Armed Forces to take action or maintain positions abroad." But most of these were minor police matters, such as rescuing a ship or a citizen held captive. Subsequently Congress had a change of heart, and realized that the presidential duties and rights were being expanded far beyond the intent of the founders. "Already possessing vast power over the country's foreign relations," said the Foreign Relations Committee, "the executive, by acquiring the authority to commit the country to war, now exercises something approaching absolute power over the life or death of every living American—to say nothing of millions of other people all over the world." Until its sovereign rights are restored, the American public, according to the committee, "will be threatened with tyranny or disaster."

V

Since thousands of the actions of the National Security State were by their very nature covert and violated innumerable existing treaties and standards of international behavior, they had to be kept secret not only from people overseas but the public at home.

You could not state openly that you were contributing $8 million or $10 million to the election funds of Christian Democrats in Italy or attempting to overthrow Jacobo Arbenz in Guatemala or Mohammed Mossadegh in Iran, because such acts flaunted the UN Charter, the treaties of the Organization of American States, and many similar international understandings. Hence these acts, plus details of the many new military innovations, plus the intelligence activities (spying) had to be concealed from the American people as well. The second purpose of the National Security State, therefore, was to reverse the traditional relationship by which the public restrains the government through checks and balances, into a relationship by which the government restrained its electorate through secrecy and repression.

Nothing in American history remotely approached in scope this present effort to remove the public from the decision-making process. The Alien and Sedition Acts, passed during another cold war —with France in 1798—endured for only two or three years. The Alien Act, little enforced, empowered the President in the interests of "public safety" to expel or imprison aliens (such as the Irish) in times of war or emergency. The Sedition Act, enforced with greater vigor, imposed jail sentences and fines on anyone penning malicious statements against the government. The National Security State achieved the same objectives in part through the blacklisting which followed in the wake of hysterical charges by HUAC or Senator Joseph McCarthy, but much more (a) by withholding from the public vital information it was entitled to; (b) by intimidating potential dissidents through loyalty checks; (c) by illegal surveillance and disruption practiced by the FBI, CIA, Army and other agencies, and (d) by outright lying and deception. "Information," said a former Assistant Defense Secretary, Arthur Sylvester, "is power. In the beginning was the word. It is more powerful than the bomb and the gun." On December 6, 1962, in the wake of the October missile crisis, Sylvester made the startling claim that "it's inherent in the Government's right, if necessary, to lie, to save itself when it's going up into a nuclear war. This seems to me to be basic."

One of the first manifestations of the National Security State, the Atomic Energy Act, showed where the nation was headed. In a message to Congress less than two months after Hiroshima, on

October 3, 1945, Truman proposed creation of an Atomic Energy Commission which would continue operations at the "two vast industrial plants in Washington [State] and Tennessee" where nuclear fuel was being produced, and take over general direction of research and production of nuclear weapons. This was obviously vital if America was to brandish the atomic stick. And precisely because it was so vital the AEC, Truman urged, "should be authorized to establish security regulations governing the handling of all information, material, and equipment under its jurisdiction. Suitable penalties should be prescribed for violating the security regulations . . ."

The regulations that were subsequently embodied in the McMahon-Douglas Atomic Energy Act of 1946 contained punitive sections more severe than even the Espionage Act, operative *during* hostilities. Under the latter the death penalty could be imposed only in time of war, but the Atomic Energy Act provided for the ultimate punishment in peacetime as well, if in the opinion of a jury the theft of an atomic "secret" was done with the deliberate intent of injuring "defense." Indeed the act was so sweeping it punished even carelessness and indiscretion, as well as the dissemination of "restricted data" that a scientist might discover independently in his own laboratory, without government aid. The effect, wrote Alan Barth, an editorial writer of the Washington *Post,* was "to make perilous the very interchange of ideas and information indispensable to scientific progress." As of 1949 the AEC had 308,000 reports in its file, all but 10 per cent of them marked secret. To indicate how far afield this protective tendency went, on one occasion AEC ordered General Electric to refuse collective bargaining rights at an atomic energy installation to the United Electrical Workers Union (UE), on the grounds that its leaders were suspect and might betray secrets.

That there were spies afoot who passed atomic information secrets to the Russians—the most notable being Klaus Fuchs, a scientist who worked at Los Alamos and was arrested by the British in 1950—was undeniable. But whether the cure was worse than the disease is another matter. The "secret" that was to be safeguarded was not as impenetrable as most Americans believed. The Russians were only a few steps behind in atomic research, having begun their efforts in the late 1920's and having separated ura-

nium 235 (the material for bombs) from ordinary uranium in
1942. According to Leneice N. Wu of the Library of Congress, in
a report for the House Committee on Foreign Affairs (August
1972), "Soviet development of atomic energy had proceeded quite
well until World War II. In terms of the quality of research, the
Soviet capability at that point has been estimated to have been on
a par with that of the United States . . ." But the Soviets were so
preoccupied with the Nazi attack after June 1941 that they abandoned the "calculated gamble" of developing an atomic bomb.
When they resumed in 1944 they made headway almost as rapidly
as the United States had done: by late 1947 they had a nuclear reactor in operation and by 1949 a bomb. "Secrecy," Wu points out,
"cannot long delay the independent acquisition of scientific and
technological information."

Nonetheless secrecy became an obsession in the United States,
used as a tool not only against the Russians (whom it inhibited
minimally) but mostly against the people of the United States. To
guard the mounting heap of alleged secrets, the government instituted "loyalty" and "security" programs of dubious consti-
tutionality; and, as with so many other aspects of the National Security State, did so by executive order, not legislation. Three
months after the Atomic Energy Act became law Truman issued
Executive Order No. 9835, calling for investigation of the "loyalty" of "every person entering the civilian employment of any department or agency of the executive branch of the Federal Government." Before 1939 a federal employee took an oath to defend
the Constitution, and that was deemed an adequate test of his loyalty. A civil service rule, going all the way back to 1884, prohibited the government from asking employees or prospective employees about their "political or religious opinions or affiliations."

Beginning with the Hatch Act of 1939, however, the government breached this rule, and with Truman's Executive Order
9835, demolished it. A whole machinery was put into place, with
the FBI as its linchpin, to inquire into the "loyalty" of applicants
for federal jobs, and loyalty was defined in terms of beliefs and associations—not actions. A man who believed that it was necessary
to overthrow the government by force and violence or belonged to
an organization that so believed, would not be hired, and if already employed would be fired. The Attorney General prepared a

list of what he considered "totalitarian, fascist, communist, or subversive organizations," and anyone who appeared to be linked to
one of them was punishable. Under the order he was given an opportunity to appeal, but the government did not have to produce
the informer and the victim had no opportunity to confront his ac-
cuser. Thus, without trial, with no chance to defend himself, and
simply for *believing* in a set of ideas—not *doing* anything illegal—a
man might be denied employment with the government; and worse
still would probably be blacklisted elsewhere. (The loyalty questions on federal job forms survived until mid-1976, when the
American Civil Liberties Union won two court decisions to remove them.)

In the first five years after Truman's order the FBI, according to
J. Edgar Hoover, investigated and processed four million applica-
tions for government jobs. The sweeping aspect of the loyalty program, in retrospect, seems ludicrous. James Kutcher, a war veteran
who had lost both his legs in the 1943 Battle of San Pietro in
Italy, was fired from a clerk's job in the Newark office of the Veterans Administration because he was a declared member of the
Socialist Workers Party, a small group that followed the teachings
of Leon Trotsky. A minor clerk in the Veterans Administration
obviously had no access to "secrets" that would do the Russians
or anyone else any good, but the object of the loyalty program, it
became apparent, was not so much to protect secrets as to impose
conformity and inhibit dissent.

The Attorney General of the United States, Francis Biddle, prepared a list of 200 "subversive" organizations, many defunct, as a
guide to checking the loyalty of federal employees; and when the
Dies Committee (HUAC) made that list public it became the
"bible" for ferreting out subversives in private occupations as well.
Soon there was a cascade of measures to check "loyalty" everywhere, even in federal housing projects. A million tenants in gov-
ernment-financed homes had to sign loyalty oaths that they were
not Communists. Some were evicted for failing to comply. Lieutenant Milo J. Radulovich, whose own loyalty was impeccable,
was discharged from the Air Force Reserve because his *father*
read a Slavic-language newspaper which was pro-Communist, and
his sister associated with "Communist-fronts." Before long loyalty
oaths were being required of teachers in public schools and profes-

sors at universities, maritime workers and workers in defense factories. In Indiana, prizefighters and wrestlers had to sign loyalty affidavits to fight or wrestle. Under the Taft-Hartley Act of 1947 union officials were required to swear they were not members of subversive organizations, in order to earn the right for their unions to use the facilities of the National Labor Relations Board.

"It is the essence of the institutions of liberty," the 1912 presidential candidate and later Supreme Court Chief Justice Charles Evans Hughes had stated, "that it be recognized that guilt is personal and cannot be attributed to the holding of opinion or to mere intent in the absence of overt acts . . ." The loyalty program mocked this definition of democratic right; but in an era of hysteria even that was not enough. To supplement it, the Army had already instituted what was called a "security risk" program in 1940; and in 1947, State, the AEC, and the CIA followed suit.

"It is necessary," said Representative Richard Nixon on January 30, 1950, "that we completely overhaul our system of checking the loyalty of federal employees . . . placing the program on a security risk basis. In this way, where there is any doubt about an individual who has access to confidential information, that doubt can be resolved in favor of the government *without the necessity of proving disloyalty . . .*" (emphasis added). The government's decision, in other words, was final, not subject to review. The person to be discharged need not actually be disloyal, but if his superiors and the FBI considered that he might be indiscreet or a "risk" because he was, say, a homosexual, that was enough. Not only was there no appeal but the "risk" usually feared to make the fact publicly known lest it lead to reprisals of a dozen other types. How much the five loyalty-security programs dampened the spirit of dissent amongst millions of scientists, soldiers, workers, civil servants and DOD employees has never been measured. But it is safe to assume that with a sword hanging over their heads innumerable persons were constrained to be silent on controversial issues in order to protect their jobs. As a consequence there was still another widening of the "power gap"—greater prerogatives for an elite at the top, sterner manipulation of the great mass at the bottom, and the removal of controls—checks and balances—on those who furthered the nuclear arms race.

Perhaps the most unwholesome aspect of the National Security

State was that at a time when the public needed to know more about what its government was doing and thinking, the government withheld information on an unmatched scale. "Secrecy," notes a report prepared by the Library of Congress for the Senate Foreign Relations Committee in December 1971, "has been a factor in making foreign policy since the first days of the nation's history. . . . It is only in the period since the Second World War, however, that the problem of classified information has grown to its present dimensions." The Atomic Energy Act, of course, cut off one big source of government activity from public purview. It was followed by the National Security Act of 1947, the Internal Security Act of 1950, and a number of executive orders, culminating in Eisenhower's famous Executive Order 10501, which gave thirty federal departments and agencies the right to "classify" government documents as secret, top secret, confidential, classified, etc. Millions of documents were thereby kept from the public, not because they would feed valuable intelligence to the Soviets, but because they would either reflect negatively on America's officialdom or cause problems for it.

Ridiculous as it sounds, the menu for a dinner tendered Queen Frederika of Greece at an American military base was stamped "classified" lest reporters comment on how lavish it was. A "secret" label was attached to newspaper clippings about a Navy communications project in Wisconsin. The cost of chemical and biological weapons was, according to Army testimony before Congress, "hidden and scattered throughout the defense budget for years." The National Security Agency, which the Church Committee report of 1976 called "the most secret of all U.S. intelligence agencies," was established by an executive order—not a law —on November 4, 1952, and its very existence was not acknowledged until five years later.

How far afield secrecy has taken the nation is illustrated by an incident prior to the Bay of Pigs invasion of Cuba. In 1960 the CIA arranged for Cuban opponents of Fidel Castro to train at a remote coffee plantation in Retalhuleu, Guatemala. Americans did not know about this training station, let alone the decision to sponsor an invasion. To add a bizarre touch, however, on November 13, 1960, a section of the Guatemalan Army rebelled against President Miguel Ydigoras and captured a banana port on the Caribbean, Puerto Barrios. Washington was faced with a dilemma. To permit the rebels to continue their uprising might have "blown the cover" for the impending Bay of Pigs expedition. It was decided, therefore, that to sustain one illegal intervention, the CIA would have to engage in another: it ordered Cuban exile pilots at Retalhuleu to use American C-46 and B-26 planes to bombard the base held by the Guatemala dissidents. The American public didn't know about this either until two reporters, David Wise and Thomas B. Ross published their book *The Invisible Government* in 1964.

Even Congress is denied facts it needs to approve budgets or pass new legislation. A subcommittee of the Foreign Relations Committee looking into American commitments abroad, for instance, ruefully reported in December 1970 that the executive branch refused to enlighten it about tactical nuclear weapons because the "subject is of such high classification it could not be discussed before the Foreign Relations Committee under any circumstances."

VI

The founders and many subsequent leaders of the United States understood clearly that a militarized society must veer towards totalitarianism. "You know, my fellow citizens," Woodrow Wilson told a Kansas City audience not long after World War I, "what armaments mean: great standing armies, great stores of war materials. . . . So soon as you have a military class, it does not make any difference what your form of government is; if you are determined to be armed to the teeth, you must obey the orders and directions of the only men who can control the great machinery of war. Elections are of minor importance."

These warnings all came true in the nuclear age. Secrecy, loyalty, security programs, and a pervasive fear deliberately spread over the land by the militarist elites, had the chilling effect of muting dissent and opposition, of inhibiting intelligent discussion. More, it released agencies such as the CIA, FBI, NSA, the Pentagon, and others from public restraint to the point where these agencies became in a real sense a second state, immune not only to popular control but to the legal system itself.

The reports of the Senate Select Committee on Intelligence Activities released in April 1976 showed that the government itself was the worst lawbreaker in the nation. According to the report, the CIA, in violation of its mandate under the 1947 National Security Act, indexed 300,000 American citizens and kept files on 100 domestic groups from 1947 to 1973, under what it called Operation CHAOS. Between 1953 and 1973 it opened and photographed "nearly a quarter of a million first class letters . . . producing a CIA computerized index of nearly one and a half million names." The NSA, created under executive—not legislative—fiat, arranged with three telegraph companies to obtain and read millions of private cables from 1947 to 1975. The FBI headquarters alone investigated a half million domestic groups and individuals, spent twice as much money on political informers as on criminal informers, and at one time prepared a list of 26,000 people who were "to be rounded up in the event of a 'national emergency.'" Army Intelligence collected files on 100,000 Americans between the mid-1960's and 1971, including files on such figures as Senator Adlai Stevenson and Representative Abner Mikva. The Internal Revenue Service, under President Nixon, created a file on 11,000 individuals the Administration felt were hostile to its purposes and started tax investigations on them "on the basis of political rather than tax criteria."

Worse still, these organs of government engaged in illegal harassments that only a totalitarian society would countenance. The FBI and others "frequently wiretapped and bugged American citizens without the benefit of judicial warrant," including hotel rooms occupied by a legendary black leader, the late Martin Luther King, Jr. They not only investigated groups they admitted had never acted illegally—the National Association for the Advancement of Colored People, for instance, or the Socialist Workers Party—they sent derogatory anonymous letters to wives and employers to break up marriages and cost the members of such groups their jobs. They manipulated the media by planting derogatory information to discredit organizations they didn't approve. During the 1960's alone the FBI "conducted hundreds of break-ins" against individuals and domestic organizations either to plant microphones or steal membership files, and continued them as late as 1976, after FBI Director Clarence Kelley asserted they had stopped.

So far removed were these agencies from checks and balances that even when the Administration pledged to eliminate certain practices, the CIA and FBI continued them anyway, under new forms. Thus, when *Ramparts* magazine in February 1967 exposed the fact that the CIA had subsidized the National Student Association, President Johnson ordered discontinuance of such activities; but they went on nonetheless. Millions of dollars formerly allocated through the CIA itself were subsequently funneled through the Agency for International Development. CIA-financed groups moved headquarters overseas and continued to receive money from the same source, on the theory they were now "foreign" rather than domestic organizations. The flight from legality was so rampant that under the Nixon administration a plan was formulated—the Tom Charles Huston plan—whereby a half dozen agencies would co-ordinate activities that the plan itself stated were beyond the law. The Administration even contemplated kidnapping anti-war opponents at San Diego or Miami during the Republican Party convention of 1972.

The theory behind democracy is that leaders, even great ones, are fallible, and must therefore be subject to constant corrective action by the citizenry they govern. Unlike a totalitarian society, where the administration and the state are considered one and the same—so that to criticize one is to be treasonous to both—the democratic society sternly distinguishes between the state and its leaders. To be critical of the leadership is not only a privilege, but a duty—otherwise corrective actions, the checks and balances, are inoperative. It was in that spirit that the liberal tradition in America has always held that the state is prohibited from punishing anyone for his *ideas,* no matter how antagonistic they are to the state itself, no matter how revolutionary.

But the democratic principle was very much at odds with the course that the American Government set for itself at the onset of the nuclear age. An atmosphere of permanent emergency was indispensable for militarism and its huge budgets. "Our government," noted General Douglas MacArthur in the mid-1950's, "has kept us in a perpetual state of fear—kept us in a continuous stampede of patriotic fervor—with the cry of a grave national emergency. Always there has been some terrible evil at home or some monstrous foreign power that was going to gobble us up if we did not blindly rally behind it by furnishing the exorbitant funds demanded." In a permanent Cold War, and a permanent war economy, ideas were a central factor; the Communist idea was the enemy, the anti-Communist idea, a means of mobilizing the American nation against that enemy. Unlike Britain, which at the peak of its imperialist reign talked of a "balance of power," the United States—in the words of Dean Acheson—talked of "an unbridgeable *ideological* chasm." Without homogeneity on the anti-Communist issue the United States could not be rallied to the spirit of crusade required for large military budgets, or to accept without question the many illegal activities being committed abroad. To impose that homogeneity on the American populace was a logical conclusion from the policy of "confront and rearm." Men like Joseph McCarthy, J. Edgar Hoover, Richard Helms were merely acting out that logic, and if they frequently trespassed beyond the bounds of legality they justified it to themselves on the grounds they were fulfilling a higher purpose.

The sum total, however, was to remove the American people from the decision-making process on the arms race, and as a corollary to magnify the power of the Military-Industrial Complex and the imperial presidency. The self-propelling character of the arms race was, thereby, institutionalized.

9

Re-arm
Versus Dis-arm

Exactly as predicted by the critics of 1945–46, The Bomb hatched an arms race, and, as happens with arms races, reproduced generations of offspring. The contest between two superpowers was a military decathlon, encompassing first nuclear weapons, then conventional weapons; first, Washington and Moscow alone, soon almost every nation on earth; first, a few billions annually, and as of 1975 some $280 billion. The National Security State in America found itself, for a variety of reasons, attending to the "security" of dozens of allies and satellites as well. It became the operating agency for a web of what George Washington called "entangling alliances," and the exporter not merely of arms but of arms races. Once the tap was opened no one seemed to know how to make the water flow backwards. Literally thousands of meetings were held, in what is surely the grandest hoax in all history, to discuss "disarmament" or "arms control," but the self-propulsion of the arms race could not be deflected by their lofty protestations.

Here again the nuclear age has a singular quality. In the century or two that Britain dominated the world, she tried to discourage the acquisition of arms by all but a handful of close allies, such as France. Except when she subsidized revolts against the Turkish, Chinese, Moghul, Spanish, or other empires she withheld military hardware from the peoples of Eastern Europe, Asia, Africa, and Latin America. The arms races of that era, therefore, were delimited to the so-called great powers. But the United States, given its postwar determination to "confront and rearm," of necessity pursued an opposite course. It has given and sold scores of billions in weaponry to friendly states on every continent, and it has encouraged the development of armaments industries by its colleagues in the Cold War, including its World War II enemies. In a sense it spread the matches to six continents, which help to ignite local wars but may in time also ignite the global war.

It is doubtful that a single leader deliberately chose this singular strategy. MacArthur, it may be recalled, insisted that the Japanese write into their constitution a prohibition against future rearmament; and the Big Three—Roosevelt, Churchill and Stalin—agreed during the war that Germany should be permanently disarmed. There were two factors, however, working against their wishes. First was a desire to maintain a monoploy of The Bomb, and if that was not possible, a near monopoly. Washington looked askance at British or French attempts to achieve nuclear independence. But if its allies—like the Soviet allies—were to be self-deprived, those allies could not escape the fact that they lived under the nuclear threat and required protection from it. Hitherto, as James Schlesinger pointed out in a perceptive paper for RAND, "a full-fledged nation-state has been presumed . . . to have control over the forces necessary for its own protection." That is no longer the case. Though the NATO alliance was conceived as a partnership "between sovereign and (juridically) equal nations, the reality has become the overwhelming dominance by a single major partner—though to maintain the customary fiction, a number of charades continue to be performed." Circumstances dictated, therefore, that great states such as Britain, Germany, and Japan, had to yield part of their sovereignty and seek shelter under the American nuclear umbrella, while America had no choice but to compensate them accordingly. The result was a new arrangement of alliances in which the United States provided arms for "protection" and gave aid to rebuild ravaged economies, but demanded in return that allies join the confrontation against the Soviets.

A second reason for the extension of the big arms race into

lesser arms races elsewhere was that the military revolution symbolized by The Bomb was accompanied by an equally compelling social revolution. The atom came onto the stage of history at an unfortunate moment for those who espoused the status quo. The threat to world order and stability stemmed, after World War II, not so much from a conflict *between* great powers but *within* scores of nations threatened with or soon consumed by national and social revolution. In an earlier day, during the era of Pax Britannica, this was of minor account; the conquest of weak nations took place over decades and involved small numbers of troops and weaponry. France defeated Algeria in 1830 with only 37,000 men and the great subcontinent of India was finally crushed in the 1850's by the British with 50,000 soldiers. But in the post-World War II period France was required to deploy a half million troops against 45,000 Algerian guerrillas, spend $3 million a day, $1 billion a year, for seven and a half years—but was unable to defeat its adversary and had to grant it independence. In Vietnam, the United States and its allies, after 1965, were to command 1.5 million troops and spend as much as $30 billion a year against a vastly inferior numerical force of a quarter of a million North and South Vietnamese troops and guerrillas, but could not achieve victory.

In circumstances such as these The Bomb was irrelevant. The United States found itself in the anomalous situation that it could produce an exceedingly cheap kill-weapon, but in most situations it was of little use. A 20-kiloton bomb, somewhat more potent than the Hiroshima bomb and capable of killing at least 100,000 people in a medium-sized city, cost—according to a figure once released by the AEC—$380,000. For another hundred thousand—according to *Science News* (July 8, 1967)—AEC could produce a fusion bomb of 200 kilotons, and for still another $120,000, a two-megaton bomb. No combination of rifles, machine guns, artillery or other conventional means could approach The Bomb in price per death. A Russian military writer, A. A. Sidorenko, estimates it would take 18,000 122-millimeter shells to neutralize enemy personnel on 100 hectares of land six miles away, while a single atom bomb "of a certain yield" could do the job in one blast. But what good was an atom bomb in suppressing a civil war in Greece or preventing one in Italy, or emplacing the "right" government in Brazil? In point of fact the United States not only had to give economic aid to buttress such governments but saturate them with arms and military advisors. There could be no American "security" without "mutual security," which is another way of saying that the "big" arms race of necessity seeded many "little" ones.

Consider the situation in Greece. For four years during World War II the Communist-inspired EAM and its military arm, ELAS, had fought with vigor against the Nazis and Fascists, but at the end of hostilities British troops drove ELAS out of Athens after sixty-three days of machine-gun terror—and reinvested in power a discredited monarchy. The predictable result was a civil war, with one side supported from neighboring Yugoslavia and the other from Britain. But in 1947 Britain advised the United States that it was too enervated to continue aid for Greek rightists. Here was a grave problem for the Truman administration, for if the Mediterranean bastion were to fall into Communist hands it would seriously affect America's control of the world's waterways. It would also torpedo a plan making the rounds of the State Department to erect a "Greek-Turkey-Iran barrier" against Soviet penetration of the Middle East. Washington felt it had to intervene. But since it could not intimidate the guerrillas with atom bombs or occupy Greece—an idea whose time had passed—the only option was an "entangling alliance." Under the heralded Truman Doctrine of 1947 Washington supplied Greece (and Turkey, which was also felt to be on weak ground) with $400 million in aid. Seventy-four thousand tons of artillery, dive bombers, napalm, etc., were shipped to Greece in the last five months of 1947 alone, and 250 military advisors, under General James A. Van Fleet, were dispatched to train and direct its enlarged army.

Once cemented, that alliance endured even after the guerrillas were defeated in 1949. Greece was recruited into the ranks of the North Atlantic Treaty Organization and received in the next quarter of a century almost $2 billion of American military hardware (nine tenths of it in non-repayable grants). Turkey, second link in the Greece-Turkey-Iran barrier, was rewarded with $3 billion, and Iran, through 1973, approximately $2.25 billion (more than half, however, in arms purchases).

The weapons supplied these three nations were put to interesting use. In Greece they helped a group of military figures, headed by Colonel George Papadopoulos, to execute a coup d'état and impose a cruel dictatorship that lasted the better part of a decade. Turkey applied its weaponry to a dispute with Greece over Cyprus, invaded the island and sliced away a piece of it—all with U.S. arms. Had Greece taken the challenge there would have been a fair-sized war with Turkey, both sides shooting at each other with made-in-America arms. Furthermore, the bases which the United States had established in Greece and Turkey as part of the quid pro quo for the grants and sales of arms, contained hundreds of nuclear weapons. In the July 1974 crisis over Cyprus the Pentagon was duly alarmed at the possibility that either or both of these nations might seize those weapons and use them for their own purposes. According to a New York *Times* dispatch of September 9, 1974, the Sixth Fleet was ordered "to be prepared to send in a Marine detachment aboard helicopters to recover the atomic warheads." What began as the export of a few hundred million dollars in arms to put down a force of guerrillas thus posed the possibility twenty-seven years later of a limited nuclear exchange between two American allies.

Iran applied its American guns and planes to suppress its opposition at home, to exacerbate tensions with neighboring Iraq over the Kurdish problem, and to help a reactionary sheik in Oman conduct a campaign against guerrillas. There seems to be little doubt that, with American support, Iran expects to become the dominant power in the Persian Gulf. Bloated with petroleum profits, its military purchases from the United States from 1972 to mid-1976 totaled $10.4 billion, according to the calculations of a Senate Foreign Relations Subcommittee—plus another $4 or $5 billion from Western nations other than the United States. For a nation with only 34 million people—half to two thirds illiterate—this is an impressive sum, but whether it will bring "peace" to that part of the world (where Saudi Arabia, Kuwait, Yemen, and Jordan have also been buying weapons at an accelerated pace) is doubtful.

Among the items purchased from the United States were 160 F-16 planes at a cost of $3 billion, a half dozen Lockheed P-3 sea reconnaissance aircraft, 80 Grumman F-14 Tomcat fighters, 300 McDonnell Douglas F-4 fighter-bombers and Northrop F-5 fighters, 500 Bell military helicopters, Tang-class submarines, Spruance-class advanced destroyers, a top-secret communications monitoring installation called Project Ibex, and many others. Clearly all of this is far too sophisticated for the purpose of maintaining "internal order"—for suppressing student demonstrations or guerrilla movements—and it is far from adequate to resist a Soviet attack along the 1,250-mile common border. Its purpose is to consolidate an American-Iranian center of power in the Persian Gulf, where most of the world's known oil reserves are concentrated— 356 billion barrels, as against 311 billion barrels for all other areas. A powerful Iran in league with the United States could cut the supply of petroleum at the narrow Strait of Hormuz, through which flows most Western European and 80 per cent of the Japanese needs.

The arming of Iran thus has multiple purposes: to establish one of Washington's closest allies as the supreme power in the Persian Gulf, especially against a Soviet ally, Iraq; to use that ally to maintain the political status quo in the Persian Gulf sheikdoms, where guerrilla war is now under way in Oman and may soon spread elsewhere; to give the United States leverage against friendly nations such as Japan; to consolidate the Gulf as a Western sphere of influence, relatively immune to Soviet pressure. A 1976 cartoon published in a Turkish newspaper indicates the tenor of the Iranian-American objectives: it shows the Shah perched on an ammunition box, pointing to a new map of Iran that includes the whole Middle East as well as the Indian subcontinent. Another barometer of the common purpose between Teheran and Washington is the fact that, as of early 1977, the third highest official of the U. S. Embassy, Eric F. von Marbod, is ensconced in an office in Iranian headquarters down the hall from General Hassan Toufanian, chief of military procurement for the Shah.

The burgeoning acquisition of armaments by Iran will certainly inspire neighbors in the area—Iraq and Pakistan, for instance—to increase their tempo of rearmament. It may also speed acquisition of *nuclear* arms, because many of the "conventional" planes and missiles being bought by Iran have the capability to deliver nuclear warheads. Since Iran will have the capacity to produce The Bomb within a few years, anxiety will run high amongst potential adversaries, despite assurances by the Shah of Iran that he will live up to commitments under the Non-Proliferation Treaty. (According to Admiral Gene R. LaRocque [ret.], director of the Center for Defense Information, 18,000 missiles, ships, and aircraft sold or given away by the United States to various nations can carry nuclear warheads.)

The history of postwar arms transfers is not reassuring. As *Newsweek* observes (September 6, 1976), "in the 1965 India-Pakistan war, both sides used U.S. weapons, increasing the violence and extending what otherwise might have been a brief and primitive skirmish." Similarly, *Newsweek*'s Arnaud de Borchgrave reports that "arms from a dozen countries have clandestinely poured into Lebanon in recent months, escalating the conflict there. And now that both the Soviet Union and the U.S. are arming their respective allies in Africa, there is increased danger that a new arms race could trigger a war there, too."

Should the Persian Gulf arms race explode into warfare in that area there is a strong possibility that the United States itself will be embroiled—as in Vietnam. The Senate Foreign Relations subcommittee report estimates that there are 24,000 American administrators and advisors (including their families) in Iran now and that the number will grow to 50,000 or 60,000 by 1980. "If the Shah wanted to start a war . . . or if someone started one with him," writes Tom Wicker, New York *Times* columnist, "Iranian forces would be as dependent on their American advisers . . . as on their American weapons. Or if, in the event of war, Washington pulled the Americans out, the Shah's forces would be left all but helpless." For all practical purposes the Americans on the scene are "hostages" and their safety could easily promote U.S. involvement.

Many members of Congress, and others, are justly disturbed about this prospect. "I am particularly concerned by our nation's role as the world's leading arms salesman . . ." Jimmy Carter told the Foreign Policy Association (June 23, 1976). "Sometimes we try to justify this unsavory business on the cynical ground that by rationing out the means of violence we can somehow control the world's violence. The fact is that we can not have it both ways." Presidential candidate Carter's formula for change is to "work with our allies, some of whom are also selling arms, and also seek to work with the Soviets, to increase the emphasis on peace and to reduce the commerce in weapons of war." Though this would be a step in the right direction, it is not likely to be enough; as long as *some* sales are permitted, the pressures of competition between the great powers for military markets is bound to increase the level of procurement. That in fact is how the present state of affairs came about.

Clearly, American gifts and sales have not brought "security" either to the Eastern Mediterranean or to the Persian Gulf; they simply predispose that when hostilities do break out they will be much bloodier.

II

The sickness of Europe in 1947 was not confined to Greece and Turkey. If British citizens were to enjoy 1939 living standards, the country's exports would have to rise by 75 per cent; in fact they had fallen by two thirds. Each day Britain was losing precious dollars to the United States, and the dollar gap threatened her with bankruptcy. Conditions elsewhere were even worse. France was producing only half as much iron and steel as before the war. Germany lay in rubble, its major cities—Cologne, Essen, Berlin, Frankfurt, Hamburg, Munich, Mannheim—immobilized. Food was scarce; money, almost worthless. As Dean Acheson, Undersecretary of State at the time, summarized the economic facts of life, "the world needed and should receive in 1947 exports from the United States—the only source—of sixteen billion dollars (four times our prewar exports), and could find imports to the United States with which to pay for them of only half that sum." To save Europe for the American system, Secretary of State Marshall formulated a plan for massive economic aid—originally $17 billion over a four-year period, but in actual expenditures somewhat less, $12.3 billion. Without that assistance, said Undersecretary of State William Clayton, "the Iron Curtain would . . . move westward at least to the English Channel."

Given this danger—that Communism might seize the heartland of Western Civilization—the United States decided to fortify economic aid with *physical* security. The North Atlantic Pact, conceived in late 1947 but formally consummated in April 1949, was the embodiment of that design. Contrary to the general belief,

however, that the pact's primary concern was attack from the outside, the true order of priorities was stated otherwise by the interdepartmental foreign military assistance co-ordinating committee:
"First, to protect the free North Atlantic Pact countries *against internal aggression* inspired from abroad" (emphasis added), only
secondly to "deter aggression" by foreign forces. A statement by
Dean Acheson confirms this point: "The danger from Communist
elements reached its peak before the moderate governments
proved themselves capable of overcoming internal threats to their
security." Economic recovery, as it turned out, undercut revolutionary potential; but there was a charge for the American service.

Having enticed the nations of Western Europe (and Japan) into
an alliance and meshed their economies with the American economy—through a host of quid pro quos, such as acceptance of the
dollar as the international medium of exchange—the United States
also incorporated them into the arms race. From April 3, 1948, to
June 30, 1954, it launched them on the new militarism with more
than $14 billion in military assistance (including a billion and a
half for Germany, previously slated for permanent disarmament),
plus another $14 billion for "economic and technical assistance,
defense support, and direct forces support." More, it supplied
them with machinery to fabricate their own weapons. According to
a statement by the interdepartmental committee, $155 million in
aid of this type made it possible for the pact nations to produce
$700 million in homemade armament. The United States, with un-
subtle severity, made it clear that aid and arms were conditional
on the recipients' status as disciplined, even supine, members of a
military alliance.

A few months after the Korean War began, the State Department advised Marshall Plan beneficiaries that help would be forthcoming to the extent they contributed to the common defense
effort. Similarly, in December 1953 Dulles warned that unless the
allies accepted an American version of the European Defense
Community, Washington would make an "agonizing reappraisal"
of its aid program. By such devices, then, the United States was
able to station a permanent force of hundreds of thousands of its
own troops in Europe and Japan, flush against the Soviet empire,
as well as draw fifteen other nations plus Canada into the militarist
syndrome. In time there were 7,000 tactical American nuclear

weapons in eighty depots, 3,000 French and British nuclear weapons, and many billions of dollars in conventional weapons on European soil. By any measuring rod this was the most colossal export of an arms race in human history.

Assuming the validity of a program to preserve the old status quo, it is indisputable that the twin Marshall Plan-NATO program saved the cornerstone of the Western World from social upheaval. Its long-term effects, however, are another matter. The rearmament of Europe made possible a host of futile forays by the colonial powers against their wards. Some of the arms supplied by the United States helped Britain make war against the guerrillas of Malaya and the so-called Mau Mau of Kenya; helped the French to fight the Algerians and Indochinese; helped the Portuguese to challenge the nationalist movements of Angola and Mozambique; helped Britain and France (and Israel) to invade the Suez in 1956. To be sure, it probably also helped the former great powers to retain neo-colonial status over such countries as Morocco and Ivory Coast, and it certainly offered the United States an opportunity to extend its influence to segments of the globe it had never penetrated before. But the ancient empires disintegrated anyway, and there can be no question that the travail of the people in many places—Vietnam, Iraq, Algeria, the Belgian Congo, to name four—would have been much eased if Britain, France, Belgium, and other nations had not been rearmed from Pentagon stockpiles.

Another facet of "mutual security" which served to export the arms race was what became known as the "forward strategy." Early in the 1950's the "free world" allies came face to face with the paradox that the more they armed—at least up to a point—the less they were prepared. By expanding military horizons they found there were just too many bastions to cover. Thus when the Korean War broke out in 1950, a half year after the first Soviet nuclear explosion, analysts at the Pentagon, State Department, and elsewhere speculated feverishly as to whether the war was a limited engagement or a Soviet demarche to deflect attention from an impending attack on Europe. As it happened there were no such Soviet plans, but the United States and NATO had no choice but to prepare for all contingencies. General Eisenhower therefore was appointed Supreme Allied Commander in Europe to shore up its defense.

The problem apparently was that NATO lacked the conventional power to resist a possible Soviet march westward—it had under arms only twelve poorly trained divisions; and an atomic defense offered little comfort. To rely on nuclear bombs for liberation of Western Europe after it had been overrun by the Warsaw Pact states was like committing suicide in order to avoid being killed. The only alternative seemed to be a "forward strategy"—to augment the conventional forces facing Soviet troops at the Elbe, in the hopes they would delay the Russians long enough for the United States to devastate Russia with The Bomb. "Forward strategy" demanded, in NATO's judgment, a sharp increase in troops— from twelve to ninety-six divisions, with at least thirty-five to forty divisions ready by the time hostilities began. It also demanded that the alliance renege on the solemn pledge by wartime leaders to divest Germany of military potential. If every inch of Reich territory were to be defended as long as possible, it was logical to require that Germany be asked to contribute troops and other accouterments of war for the common objective.

"Forward strategy" drew the knot tighter around the Soviets and recruited other states into the arms race. It also exacerbated tensions, which in turn created pressures for more armaments. The Russians had already responded to Secretary Byrnes's warning in 1946 that "security forces will probably have to remain in Germany for a long period," and to the 1948 plan for establishing a separate government in West Germany, with a 324-day Berlin blockade. It was something of a miracle that world war was avoided at that time. Now, with the prospect of West German rearmament, the Soviet position vis-à-vis East Germany hardened further, and in due course led to the erection of the Berlin wall and other measures that attenuated the division between East and West.

III

The formula of aid and arms was applied to every continent. Washington built an edifice of alliances, bases, and satellite armies which had the effect of extending a "vertical" arms race, between two superpowers, "horizontally." It implanted the military seed where none existed or where it would otherwise have had difficulty taking root. In the short period from 1947 to 1955 the United States entered into nine security agreements—with twenty Latin American nations in 1947 (the Rio Pact), with fourteen Western European countries and Canada in 1949 (the North Atlantic Pact), with Japan in 1951, with the Philippines the same year, with Australia and New Zealand (the ANZUS Pact) also in 1951, with South Korea in 1953, with Spain in 1953, with "Nationalist China" in 1954, and with seven other nations (only three of them in Asia) for the defense of Southeast Asia (SEATO) also in 1954. In addition the United States became an associate member of the Baghdad Pact (later called the Central Treaty Organization—CENTO), which included Britain, Turkey, Pakistan, Iraq, and Iran. All the treaties included language to the effect that an attack on one would be considered an attack on all, requiring each to come to the aid of the others; and virtually all underscored America's commitment to help allied governments against native revolutionaries. The security treaty with Japan, for instance, provided for the United States, when so requested, to use its troops "to put down large-scale riots and disturbances in Japan, caused through instigation or intervention by an outside power or powers [i.e., the Russians or Chinese Communists]."

This system of "mutual security" not only primed the United States for intervention anywhere, from its thousands of bases and installations overseas, but it had the effect, as political analyst Amaury de Riencourt has observed, of "bringing to the Pentagon satellite military establishments in Latin America, the Far East and Europe . . ." The United States assumed a "protectorate" over "more than 40 nations covering some 15 million square miles with populations amounting to over 600 million human beings." The satellite armies became an adjunct to the American empire—making it unnecessary to *occupy* countries in order to dominate them—and in many respects were preferable to U.S. troops. "Military assistance," McNamara told the Foreign Relations Committee in 1966, "provides essential arms, training, and related support to five million men in allied and other friendly forces. . . . These men are critical to our forward strategy." More, they are cheaper. McNamara boasted that while it cost—at the time—$4,500 to maintain a U.S. soldier, the five million men "critical to our forward strategy" could be supported on $540 a year. "We get eight soldiers to one for our money," was the derisive comment of Senator Joseph Clark.

By 1964, the United States was supplying weapons to sixty-nine nations, almost half the sovereign states in the world, and though this figure has been drastically cut in recent years it indicates how massive has been the horizontal transfer of the arms race. From the end of the war through 1975, the United States furnished, according to the House Committee on International Relations, $67 billion in "security assistance to friendly foreign countries and international organizations." Much of it unfortunately was shipped to areas where tensions were already at the explosive point, and usually in cadence with rising tension, as—for instance—in the Middle East. As of mid-1976 the Middle East nations, with an average per capita income of $845 a year, was spending $135 per capita on armaments—a sixth of their gross national product. As often as not, American guns went to dictators who could not have remained in power without them—in Jordan, Paraguay, Bolivia, Brazil, Taiwan. Section 502(B) of the International Security Assistance Act prohibits military aid to "any foreign government which engages in a consistent pattern of gross violations of internationally recognized human rights"—which is defined as "torture or cruel, inhuman, or degrading treatment or punishment, prolonged detention without charges and trial, and other flagrant denial of the right to life, liberty and the security of person." By these criteria most of the recipients would be ineligible, but the law is seldom observed—Washington invariably places "security" above humanity.

Supplementing the security assistance programs has been a very sizable growth in military sales to foreign nations by the U. S. Government—rising, according to official figures, from $1 billion in 1969 to $9.5 billion in 1975. To make matters worse, the armament industry has grown in the other industrialized countries, the result being that world trade in non-nuclear weapons skyrocketed from $300 million in 1952 to $18 billion in 1975. A hundred and thirteen nations were buying; fifty-seven were selling. The United States accounted for 51 per cent of total exports from 1964 to 1973, but Russia was not too far behind, accounting for 27 per cent, and France—which ranked third—had orders in 1973 for $3.2 billion, and was delivering at the rate of $1.8 billion a year. Britain, Poland, Czechoslovakia, Germany, China were similarly selling the instruments of death wherever they could find politically suitable customers. "Not surprisingly," writes Edward C. Luck of the United Nations Association, "the economically developed countries have supplied the bulk of the arms trade, accounting for some 96 percent of world arms exports from 1963 to 1973." What is surprising is the immense expenditure by weak and developing countries: as of 1973 they were purchasing more than four fifths of the war matériel on sale.

The exporters, it should be stressed, were no longer private companies (the so-called merchants of death) for the most part, but governments. And what they were giving away or selling was not old, obsolete weapons but the most sophisticated hardware—tanks, fighter-bombers, surface-to-surface missiles such as the American Pershing (scheduled for sale to Israel), or Scud missiles (already sent to Syria and Egypt by the Soviets), which can deliver nuclear warheads. "What the supplying nations are offering their clients now," writes Ann Hessing Cahn of Harvard, "are the most technologically advanced weapons, hot off the design tables. For instance, the Bell AH-1J gunship helicopter, ordered by the Shah of Iran, can fire cannon, rockets and antitank missiles and is more advanced than any now used by the U. S. Army. This whirlybird will be delivered to the Iranians at the same time it is introduced into the American armed forces." Just how sophisticated was the hardware provided developing nations is indicated by the weapons toll during the three-week Middle East war of 1973; the defensive weapons were so modern that one airplane was shot down every hour, one tank every fifteen minutes. As the United Nations Association notes in an April 1976 report, "whether or not advanced weapons increase the likelihood of conflict, they do expand the potential destructiveness of modern war."

When and how these weapons transfers will ignite other sparks of war no one can tell, but in the words of veteran diplomat Charles Yost, writing in the *Christian Science Monitor,* "we learned to our cost in Vietnam" that "arms supplies may be the first slope on a long toboggan ride. Recipients have to be trained in the use of American arms. This means advisers and military missions. It is often difficult for advisers to avoid becoming involved in local politics. If war breaks out, they may be asked to

give advice in this field, to pilot planes, to fire rockets. At the end
of the toboggan slide the United States may find itself embroiled in
a prolonged war or drawn into another confrontation with the Soviet Union."

Each little step leads to the next. First come the tanks, planes,
and missiles, either as gifts or sales, then the American military
advisors to explain how to use them and what to use them for. As
of 1974 the United States was spending $70 million to finance mil-
itary assistance advisory groups (MAAG) in forty-nine countries.
Fifty-four men, for example, were dispatched to Iran to support
procurement of F-4 aircraft and 131 other teams were roaming the
world performing similar functions. Pentagon and private organizations, in addition, were training military personnel in thirty-four
countries under contracts totaling $727 million. Vinnell Corpora-
tion of Los Angeles entered into an arrangement—with Washington's blessings—to train Saudi Arabian troops in the art of war,
though it is not very clear whom the Saudi Arabian Government
intends to fight unless it be its own people. All told, 21,981 foreign
officers were receiving instruction on the operation of American
hardware and the intricacies of counterinsurgency wars, under a
variety of U.S. programs. The Administration argued that these
efforts were necessary for five good reasons: that they supplied allies who could not supply themselves, that they were "a useful
mechanism for correcting our balance of payments and to help pay
for oil," that they allowed the United States "to maintain influence
over the recipient governments," that they helped "maintain internal security," and finally that "if we didn't do it someone else
would."

But the sum total was a vast proliferation of armaments and a
plethora of arms races, which made the world a tinderbox and dis-
torted its priorities. Worldwide expenditures on arms in 1975 were
a staggering $280 billion—ten billion more than the year before—
and rising. Within a decade and a half the outlay had jumped by
45 per cent—in constant dollars. On every soldier the world was
spending $12,330; on every school-age child, $219. Sixty-five
cents of the research and development dollar went for military and
space programs, as against ten cents for health. On a planet with
four billion people, 1.3 billion had incomes of less than four dollars a week, 1.5 billion lacked effective medical care, 700 million

adults were illiterate, and 500 million were severely malnourished; but the nations of the world, consumed by an arms race, were diverting their monies to guns in ever greater amounts.

American leaders may call this "security," but it is the kind of "security" which breeds instability, revolution, and war. Worse still, there is no telling which of these unstabilizing events will burgeon, by an inherent tendency towards escalation, into Dooms-day.

IV

In an address to the National Strategy Seminar for Reserve Officers, back in 1959, Dean Acheson told of a visit by "some earnest people" who asked him to help promote an educational campaign for disarmament. "You need not carry the doctrine of disarmament," he told them, "to the American public. Everybody in the United States is desperately eager to get rid of the burden of armaments. You need to carry this message to the very places which are closed to you, namely, the Soviet Union." This is the conventional wisdom, expressed in a hundred different styles, by which the arms race—horizontal and vertical—is justified. "We" would like to disarm—so goes the argument—but "they" force us to continue our military program. "They" refuse to listen to reason; when "they" use the word "peace" they really mean world domination; "we" have no choice therefore but to be armed and strong; the only language "they" understand is force.

Every President since 1945 has expressed an urgent desire for "peace," for settlement of differences through "negotiations"—none more so than those who conducted wars. "It has been the purpose of this Administration," Richard Nixon told Congress in his foreign policy report of February 9, 1972, "to transform the U.S.-Soviet relationship so that a mutual search for a stable peace and security becomes its dominant feature and driving force." But comforting as are such speeches, they do not explain why in more than three decades the United States has never worked out a single agreement with Moscow to freeze the arms race, let alone reverse it. The term "peace" has been used in the sense that Sir Solly Zuckerman expressed—the peace of surrender—and the term "negotiations," in the sense that Lyndon Johnson did during his many offers of "withdrawal"—if North Vietnam and the National Liberation Front would get out first and give America six months to remain. Negotiations are definitely not meant as a means of accommodation, but rather as a crowning of victory, or at the least, as NSC-68 put it originally, a device for "building strength." Negotiations, the record shows irrefutably, have been part of the process of rearmament.

Since 1945, American and other diplomats have met at least 6,000 times to discuss "disarmament" and "arms control." Washington points to this long and fruitless chronicle as proof that it has been trying to contain the arms race, but has been frustrated by the Kremlin. In point of fact, however, "arms control" like "deterrence" has been a hoax. The record shows that there never was any intention to disarm, and that all the jousting has been designed simply to quiet public opinion. Whatever agreements have been reached were minor, none having the effect of slowing the race, and indeed the SALT I talks and the Vladivostok understanding, which still awaits codification into a formal pact, have served to augment the nuclear potential of both superpowers.

As for negotiations to reduce conventional forces, the record is so melancholy that writers on "arms control" seldom mention it. From 1946 to 1948 the UN Commission for Conventional Armaments bogged down on talks to establish a world police force (as envisioned in Article 47 of the Charter), which was expected to lessen the need, or at least the size, of national armies. Before the Soviets began to produce nuclear weapons they proposed that the great powers slash their armies by a third. In the mid-1950's, when nuclear negotiations were proceeding desultorily, they made another suggestion—force levels of one and a half million men each for themselves, the United States, and China, and 650,000 each for France and Britain. This suggestion had originally come from London and Paris, as part of a package that included cutbacks in atomic weapons, but it was turned down. In 1965 Malta proposed that arms transfers be widely publicized so that the glare of world attention might inhibit proliferation. Denmark, in 1968, urged the UN Secretary-General to look into the feasibility of such a plan. The United States itself, in 1967, asked that limits be placed on grants and sales to the Middle East. Nothing came of any of this, perhaps because it didn't make much sense to contain conventional contrivances while nothing was being achieved to curb the nuclear race.

The Bomb, of course, was another matter. On this score there was always *some* public pressure, both here and abroad, to "do something"; and the pressure doubtless will continue because no one can think of the subject with equanimity. Hence the 6,000 meetings. The true purpose of negotiations, insofar as the United States was concerned, however, was stated in NSC-68 as one of building up military power while laying the blame on Soviet obduracy. The dialogues at the bargaining table were meant to score debaters' points with the U.S. citizenry, not to reverse the arms race; indeed if the Soviets were to accept an American or Western offer, NSC-68 called on the United States to withdraw it. There can be no question in reading this document—still official policy— that American policy makers always intended to place the emphasis on rearming not disarming, and that their commitment to "disarmament" or "arms control" was simply a device to neutralize the American people so they wouldn't object to *continuation* of the arms race.

The first manifestation of this strategy was the Baruch Plan. One must recall its background to understand its significance. In September 1945 Stimson had sent two memoranda pleading with Truman voluntarily to invite the Soviet Union into a "partnership upon a basis of cooperation and trust" so that they might jointly "arrive at a satisfactory international arrangement" to "control and limit the use of the atomic bomb . . ." A number of cabinet members sided with Stimson (and Henry Wallace) in favor of a forthright approach to Moscow rather than the prevailing view of holding on to "the secret" at all costs. There is no doubt that Stimson reflected the overwhelming world sentiment; tens of millions had seen their lands twice devastated and their fathers and brothers killed in a single generation. He also expressed the anxieties of a sizable element at home, whose fears for the future outweighed their pride in America's technological achievement. The subject came up at the Moscow conference in December that year, where the three world leaders decided to establish a UN commission on atomic energy. Under the circumstances it would have been impolitic, and perhaps dangerous to Truman's political longevity, not to take some action.

In January 1946 Truman appointed a committee under Dean Acheson to elaborate a plan, and Acheson in turn selected a Board of Consultants, headed by David Lilienthal, to advise on technological matters. Their joint product, the Acheson-Lilienthal report, sketched out a scheme for placing uranium mines and all nuclear production facilities in the hands of an international agency. That was an idea previously espoused by many scientists, but the Acheson-Lilienthal report introduced an irremediable flaw. It required the Soviet Union and other nations to turn over control of their uranium mines, and open their doors to geological surveys immediately—whereas the United States would not have to end its bomb production or divest itself of its hoard until some vague point in the future. Even so, the Acheson-Lilienthal proposal might have been negotiable—especially since it specifically excluded the need for inspectors on Russian soil—but by the time Bernard Baruch got through modifying it there was nothing to negotiate. Baruch, a prestigious financier, was designated by Truman —along with John Hancock of Lehman Brothers, Ferdinand Eberstadt of Dillon, Read, Fred Searls of Newmont Mining, and others of hawkish bent—to present the plan before the United Nations Atomic Energy Commission.

As submitted to the twelve-nation Commission on June 14, 1946, the plan provided for an International Atomic Development Authority which would assume "various forms of ownership, dominion, licenses, operation, inspection, research, and management" of everything associated with atomic energy throughout the world. As with the proposals Washington would make for many years thereafter, the difficulty was that Baruch's blueprint was long on inspection but short on disarmament. Before the United States would be required to scrap a single atomic device or communicate its secret to the international authority, the machinery for inspection and control would have to be in place and functioning throughout the world. It was only at the end of what promised to be a long process that the United States would terminate its research and manufacture, and destroy its stockpile.

In the Soviet view everything in the Baruch Plan was patterned to reinforce the American monopoly, while barring the door for Moscow to enter the nuclear club. The United States would be able to continue nuclear operations, while the Soviet Union would have to scuttle research and development forthwith. "In other words," Henry Wallace wrote to Truman (July 23, 1946), "we are telling the Russians that if they are 'good boys' we may eventually turn over our knowledge of atomic energy to them and to other nations."

In the Russian view the deck was stacked. The authority—in effect an embryonic world government—would be staffed, under the Baruch Plan, by men of "proven competence"—those, in other words, who had had experience with nuclear bombs, namely Americans, Britons, Canadians, and perhaps a handful of others. Nations that violated the decisions of these men of "proven competence" would be subject to what Baruch called "condign punishment" by the UN Security Council. Since the UN was then safely in the American pocket (typical votes in the General Assembly were 40 to 6), and since the United States demanded that Moscow be deprived of veto power on atomic issues such as "condign punishment," the Kremlin would be at Washington's mercy. America would retain all the chips for nuclear blackmail, whereas the Soviets would be prevented from continuing its catch-up program, and if it did something distasteful to the international authority, might be subject—with UN blessings—to nuclear attack. The very terms "condign punishment" or "swift and sure punishment," as Acheson, who differed with Baruch's toughness, noted, were "dangerous words that added nothing to a treaty and were almost certain to wreck any possibility of Russian acceptance of one." The Baruch Plan as proposed, said Acheson, would "be interpreted in Moscow only as an attempt to turn the United Nations into an alliance to support a United States threat of war against the U.S.S.R. unless it ceased its [nuclear] efforts, for only the United States could conceivably administer 'swift and sure' punishment of the Soviet Union."

The Baruch Plan was clearly a propaganda ploy rather than a serious basis for negotiations, and everyone in high places knew it. The Russian response, by a young diplomat, Andrei Gromyko, omitted reference to a world authority, called for disarmament without inspection, for destruction of existing bombs within three months, and a prohibition against further production. Only after these measures were taken would Gromyko discuss methods of control and inspection. A year later Gromyko agreed to periodic inspection at designated facilities, but it was not enough to satisfy American negotiators. By 1948 an impasse had been reached and by 1949 a new factor had been added to the equation—the Soviets had exploded their first device. By 1950, when the Korean War broke out, disarmament talks languished.

"Nevertheless," records William C. Frye of the *Christian Science Monitor,* "the following year, war-weariness began to set in, especially in Western Europe, and there was increasing reluctance to endure the continued hardships—inflation, goods scarcities, high taxes, conscription—necessary to hold the West's position. The United States, Britain, and France felt it wise to dramatize the Soviet Union's responsibility for the arms race by offering a disarmament plan and *letting Moscow knock it down*" (emphasis added). The 1951 plan provided for the "regulation, limitation, and balanced reduction of all armed forces and armaments," and hinted that some changes might be made in the Baruch Plan. Moscow's response seemed to concede two points to the West: inspection would be continuous, not periodic, and controls and disarmament would be put into effect simultaneously. Somehow, however, the positions were never reconciled, perhaps because both superpowers were about to explode their first hydrogen bombs.

v

The most promising moment for nuclear disarmament came in 1954–55. Stalin had died in March 1953, and his successor, Malenkov, seemed to be a man of moderation. Public opinion again demanded that steps be taken to shelve The Bomb, and in Washington the mood seemed favorable toward a settlement. Eisenhower had finally ended the war in Korea, had formally presented his atoms-for-peace plan to the UN, and proclaimed, after the H-bomb was detonated, that "there is no longer any alternative to peace." In obeisance to all these factors Britain and France took a major step in May 1954 to puncture the impasse. Their memorandum sketched out a step-by-step plan, first prohibiting the use of nuclear weapons "except for defense against aggression," then moving to reduction of armed forces (1,000,000 to 1,500,000 for the United States, the Soviet Union, and China; 650,000 each for Britain and France), termination of manufacture of nuclear weapons after the first half of the conventional arms scale-down had been completed, and "the establishment of a control organ . . . adequate to guarantee the effective observance of the agreed prohibitions and reductions." These control measures were to be emplaced stage by stage, in accordance with the level of disarmament. Eisenhower softened the American position by eliminating the demand for "condign punishment" and dropping the idea of a world authority to own and manage nuclear facilities.

Moscow accepted this plan as a "basis" for talks, and on May 10, 1955, surprised the whole world by introducing a treaty which virtually accepted the British-French scheme. British Nobel prize winner Philip Noel-Baker, then in his eighties and long an advocate of disarmament, called this the "moment of hope." Jules Moch, one of the French spokesmen, exuberantly observed that "the whole thing looks too good to be true." The British delegate expressed pleasure that the Western "policy of patience" had "now achieved this welcome dividend." Western proposals, he said, "have now been largely, and in some cases entirely, adopted by the Soviet Union." Even the U.S. delegate to the disarmament talks said he was "gratified" that Moscow had finally accepted "in a large measure" concepts "which we have put forward over a considerable period of time." The Russians added to the spirit of accommodation, agreeing to paced cutbacks in manufacture and stockpiles of "weapons of mass destruction," and to the international control organ that the West had always insisted was indispensable. The inspectors, under the Russian treaty, would live permanently in the countries they were investigating and would have "unimpeded access at all times to all objects of control," as well as "unimpeded access to records relating to the budgetary appropriations of States for military needs."

At this juncture, with everything moving smoothly, the United States astonished the world by rejecting the West's own proposal. Eisenhower's Special Assistant for Cold War Strategy, Nelson Rockefeller, had caught the President's interest with an elaborate scheme for "open skies." Thereupon, Eisenhower in a meeting with Khrushchev and Bulganin in Geneva, proposed "an arrangement, very quickly, as between ourselves—immediately," by which the two nations would, as the President expressed it, "give each other a complete blueprint of our military establishments, from beginning to end" and "provide within our countries facilities for aerial reconnaissance to the other country . . . where you can make all the pictures you choose." Khrushchev rejected the idea as "nothing more than a bald espionage plot against the U.S.S.R."

A month later, in August 1955, the new U.S. delegate to the disarmament negotiations, Harold Stassen, officially withdrew all previous proposals made by the United States, leaving on the table only this imaginative but unworthy plan for "open skies." "For years," journalist I. F. Stone subsequently observed, "we had accused the Russians of proposing disarmament without inspection. Now it looked as if we were proposing inspection without disarmament. Though it was presented as a way to prevent surprise attack, it would obviously have provided the Strategic Air Command with exactly the maps its bombers needed."

There were a number of reasons for the turnabout, one of them being that the Pentagon had recalculated and found that a million and a half men were inadequate to operate overseas bases along with other responsibilities; hence it would lose, at least to an extent, the cherished capability to use atomic bombs, deliverable at the time only by airplanes, preferably close up. Truman, it seems, had offered that figure—a ceiling of 1,000,000 to 1,500,000 troops —in 1952, confident the Soviets would never accept it. When they did, Washington rejected its own offer. Another reason was that the May 10 proposals would have scuttled the American-sponsored rearmament of Germany, which already had 460,000 men under arms. It was simply too horrifying for the Pentagon to contemplate: no German Army—or at best a small one; no bases; no NATO; and little if any nuclear deterrent.

Insofar as prohibition of nuclear weapons was concerned "it seemed to Stassen illogical and indeed dishonest," writes Frye, "to go on proposing something which no one genuinely intended to carry out. Western-sponsored plans had always contained an escape clause: no disarmament obligation would come into effect until the control organization was ready to verify the steps envisaged. And of course no control organ would ever be in a position to verify bomb elimination, short of a major technological breakthrough."

To Moscow's credit, it ultimately tried to appease Eisenhower on both the "open skies" issue and force levels. In November

1956 it acceded to the U.S. position of two and a half million troops for the American, Russian, and Chinese military establishments, and some months later offered the United States continuing aerial inspection over more than seven million kilometers of its territory. Stassen was encouraged. He flew back from Europe to win Eisenhower's approval for further exploration, but even the latest concessions were to no avail—everyone from Admiral Arthur W. Radford to German Chancellor Konrad Adenauer picked the plan to pieces.

International talks continued throughout the Eisenhower years, causing cycles of joy and disappointment amongst political doves, but came to an inglorious end when the Russians shot down an American U-2 spy plane flying over their territory in May 1960—on the eve of a Khrushchev-Eisenhower summit meeting. Except for the inconsequential Antarctic Treaty of 1959, designating that frigid area a nuclear-free zone, the record for fifteen years of disarmament negotiations was zero. It is impossible to read that record without concluding that there simply was no will on the part of the United States to defuse the arms race. Negotiations were a necessary evil to allay public opinion, nothing more.

When Kennedy took office the focal point of negotiations narrowed perceptibly. The new President paid the necessary homage to the rhetoric of disarmament, and his special disarmament advisor, Wall Street lawyer John J. McCloy, drafted a shiny statement of principles with Soviet Deputy Foreign Minister V. A. Zorin, which talked of "disbanding armed forces," closing foreign military bases, ending arms production, "eliminating of all stockpiles of nuclear, chemical, bacteriological and other weapons of mass destruction"—and so on. But the true direction of "the best and the brightest" was marked out in a campaign book by one of Kennedy's aides, historian Arthur Schlesinger, Jr.: "Only by showing that we can stay in the arms race as long as they, can we convince the Russians of the imperative need for arms control. But *we will arm in order to disarm*" (emphasis added). Even that of course was a fiction, testifying only to the excellent prose of Kennedy's speech-writers. For in fact the policy pursued was to "arm in order to arm." Under the prodding of General Maxwell Taylor conventional forces were built up to fight limited, brush-fire wars; and for no discernible reason other than that the Air Force wanted 3,000 missiles, it was agreed to build a force of 1,000. The Kennedyites themselves had to admit that the "missile gap" issue they had raised during the campaign was a fiction. The Soviets didn't have 600 to 800 ballistic missiles, as claimed, but a mere 50 to 100. Nonetheless the program went forward.

All that came out of the Kennedy years by way of "arms control" (the term "disarmament," it should be noted, slowly dropped from the international lexicon in favor of "arms control," which is hardly the same thing) was a "hot line" agreement to string a telephone between the White House and the Kremlin, and a test ban treaty of questionable value. It took almost a decade of world pressures before the United States would accept a ban on testing of any kind. The Indian prime minister, Nehru, urged a "stand-still agreement" on tests in 1954, followed by the Burmese, who made a more specific suggestion. The Russians included it in their May 10, 1955, disarmament proposal and subsequently offered a test ban treaty as a separate agreement, an offer repeated two years later. In April 1958 Khrushchev announced a unilateral cessation of tests and urged Eisenhower to follow suit. Each time, however, Washington argued that a test ban must be tied to a full disarmament pact and made the usual point about the need for "adequate inspection."

Meantime there was a general alarm, here as well as abroad, over the dangers of radiation. Scientists claimed that innumerable children would be stillborn or malformed from the strontium 90, cesium 137, and other radioactive elements released into the atmosphere by nuclear testing. Under the leadership of Nobel laureate Linus Pauling, nine thousand of the most famous scientists in forty-three countries signed a petition calling for "an international agreement to stop the testing of nuclear bombs," and presented it to UN Secretary-General Dag Hammarskjöld in January 1958. Finally a moratorium was agreed to by the superpowers in late 1958, and remained in effect for two years until the Soviets resumed testing in September 1961. (France in the meantime joined the nuclear club, exploding its first atomic device in February 1960.)

From April 18, 1961, to August 5, 1963, when an agreement was finally signed, the United States, Britain, and the Soviet Union went through a charade, debating whether there should be twelve to twenty on-site inspections a year to verify violations, or only two or three. It was all irrelevant because, as one group of scientists after another testified, there was adequate means of detection by modern seismology. In any case, the pact (eventually signed by 106 nations, but not by China and France), contained a giant loophole. It banned tests in the atmosphere, outer space, and underwater—but not underground.

The Russians had repeatedly insisted on including underground tests—and according to a top American negotiator, Adrian Fisher, in an interview, were sincere about it—but the Pentagon, in a confidential memo to Kennedy, had demanded a "safeguard." The Joint Chiefs of Staff informed the President that it was absolutely essential to conduct "comprehensive, aggressive and continuing underground nuclear test programs designed to add to our knowledge and improve our weapons in all areas of significance to our military posture for the future." The Joint Chiefs were right, for if *all* tests had been banned it would have been next to impossible to develop most of the new glamor weapons conceived by scientists and engineers. It would have, in effect, ended, or severely slowed down the whole competitive effort. Nations entering the nuclear club today do not necessarily have to test small nuclear bombs whose feasibility has long been confirmed; but the sophisticated weapons being worked on in the Pentagon (and the Soviet equivalent of the Pentagon) are another matter. In America's own interest, notes William Epstein, the former Secretary of the UN Disarmament Commission, it would have been wise "to freeze the situation on the existing basis" because the United States was far ahead in 1963. Moreover, "Had a comprehensive test ban been agreed upon at the time . . . the problem of preventing the spread of nuclear weapons might have become easily manageable." The Pentagon and Washington generally, however, were not impressed by such arguments.

The results of the so-called test ban, or lack thereof, are attested to by the statistics: in the 19 years from 1945 through 1963 the Soviets conducted 164 tests (3 underground) and the United States, 282 tests (89 underground); in the ten years from August 1963 to June 1973, the Soviets carried out 121 tests, the United States, 259—a rate 33 per cent and 65 per cent, respectively, higher than in the pre-treaty period. Thirteen years after the 1963 pact was signed, and after innumerable further talks, it was still impossible for the superpowers to outlaw all tests; the most they would agree to, during the administrations of Richard Nixon and Gerald Ford, was to limit underground tests to 150 kilotons— eleven times the firepower of the Hiroshima bomb and even that had a loophole, allowing for tests of greater firepower for "peaceful" purposes.

VI

Negotiations in the thirteen years after the partial test ban treaty were monotonously and uniformly unproductive. Talks continued, agreements were signed, but the results were pyrrhic. No one gave up anything important, not a single nuclear weapon was destroyed, the level of armaments—especially the qualitative level—spiraled upward. Multilateral pacts were concluded, for instance, on prohibiting nuclear weapons in outer space, in Latin America, on the seabeds; and bilateral pacts were entered into between the United States and Russia to consult each other if there was an accidental explosion. But none of these were of great moment. The three understandings that did have substance—the Non-Proliferation Treaty of 1968, the SALT I (Strategic Arms Limitation Talks) treaties of 1972, and the SALT II agreement "in principle" arrived at in Vladivostok in late 1974, are for all practical purposes dead letters.

The Non-Proliferation Treaty (NPT), signed in 1968 and ratified by almost 100 nations since then, has been an exercise in futility. NPT, as the name suggests, is a compact not to spread nuclear weapons beyond the five nations that had them in 1968. The nuclear states (United States, Soviet Union, Britain, France, and China) pledge not to transfer nuclear weapons, or the capability to make them, to non-nuclear states. The non-nuclear states pledge they won't produce or purchase their own and in return the "haves" commit themselves "to pursue negotiations in good faith" for "cessation of the nuclear arms race at an early date," as well as for nuclear and total disarmament "under strict and effective international control."

Had all the nations of the world endorsed NPT and had the nuclear states kept their word to pursue disarmament "in good faith," this might have changed the course of history. But it was apparent immediately that NPT was a flaccid and porous arrangement. Two of the five nuclear states (France and China) refused to sign. India, which would explode a bomb in 1974, also held out. So did a host of nations which did not have The Bomb but had the potential for producing it, some immediately—West Germany, Japan, Israel, Spain, Portugal, South Africa, Brazil, Chile, North Korea, South Korea, Italy, Libya, and so on. All told, sixty-one nations either refused to sign or failed to ratify NPT; and while the number has been pared since then, numerous nations remain uncommitted. The treaty, moreover, included a number of loopholes —such as an exemption by which signers might conduct nuclear explosions for "peaceful" purposes, e.g., digging a canal ditch; and enforcement, unlike the "condign punishment" plank in the Baruch Plan twenty-two years earlier, was loose and ineffective.

In May 1975 a Review Conference was held in Geneva to assess NPT's goals and prospects, but it had evidently become so meaningless that only fifty-seven of the ninety-six nations that acceded to the treaty were present. The rest couldn't be bothered. Those who did come argued rancorously about the fact that the "have" nations had failed to carry out their promise "in good faith" to negotiate nuclear disarmament. The three "have" nations present (United States, Soviet Union, Britain), however, showed little disposition to meet that obligation, making it certain that additional "have nots" will join the nuclear club progressively in coming years—on the same justification as the "have" nations have given, "deterrence." "If we had known in 1968," a prominent former diplomat from a non-nuclear state told an unofficial conference in September 1974, "how little the nuclear powers would do over the next six years to meet their end of the NPT bargain by controlling their arms race, I would have advised my government not to sign the Treaty."

The Strategic Arms Limitation Talks (SALT) were another illustration of how noble ideas are subverted in the militarist machine. In 1964, with prospects for general disarmament dim, the thought occurred to some UN arms discussants that perhaps something more limited had a chance of approval, say a "freeze" on strategic (though not necessarily tactical) nuclear weapons. Lyndon Johnson picked up the idea, adding the word "verified" to freeze, as testimony to the enduring preoccupation of the United States with inspection.

The Soviets, far behind in the race, refused to consider the proposal unless it was linked to "reduction"—freeze and reduce simultaneously. There the matter stood for a number of years, during which both nations became concerned about the anti-ballistic missile and the unimpeded thrust of the technological revolution. Finally, during the mellow ceremonies accompanying signature of the Non-Proliferation Treaty, Johnson in Washington and Kosygin in Moscow agreed to try their hand at "arms limitation." The Soviet invasion of Czechoslovakia in August delayed matters until the presidency of Richard Nixon, but at long last, in November 1969, two and a half years after the talks began as to whether to hold talks, the negotiators came together in Helsinki.

It was the better part of another three years (and after 434 days at the bargaining table) before Henry Kissinger and Soviet Foreign Minister Gromyko hammered out a set of agreements, and Nixon affixed his signature amidst great fanfare during his meetings with Brezhnev in Moscow. One pact limited the two superpowers to two ABM sites and a total of 100 ABM launchers. As noted elsewhere in these pages this was an empty exercise since anti-ballistic missiles provided no real defense, and indeed might be counterproductive. Both parties agreed subsequently to cut back to one site each, and even that was dispensed with by President Ford without any loss of military potential to either side.

The second pact, the Interim Agreement, did not provide for cutbacks in weaponry, but set limits on how far they could be increased *quantitatively*. The United States, by its terms, was allowed to expand the number of nuclear submarines from 41 to 44, with 710 missiles, and the Kremlin to build up from its existing 30 to 62 with 950 missiles. On land, the United States was allowed 1,000 ICBM's, the Soviet Union, 1,410. It was sound without substance, however, for not only were the total numbers higher than what each side then had, but nothing was done to curb *quality* improvements. Notably missing was a curb on the Pentagon's obsession of the moment, the MIRV, which carries three, four, or more warheads and can target each one independently. The United States had already announced it would place Poseidon missiles on 31 of its 41 submarines, each with 10 to 14 warheads, each capable of striking an independent target; and that it would MIRV 550 of its land-based missiles. But no effort was made to check this major escalation (or a similar one on the Russian side).

As with the partial test ban, the in-house bargaining between President, Pentagon, and State Department raised the numbers so that in the end arms "control" became arms "escalation." "To agree to support SALT I agreements," writes Jack Ruina, former president of the Institute for Defense Analysis, "the Joint Chiefs of Staff insisted on assurances that the U.S. would pursue 'aggressive improvements and modernization programs' to 'maximize strategic capabilities.' " They also demanded research and development programs to "maintain . . . technological superiority." The posture of "bargaining from strength," Ruina points out, "calls for arms programs that can serve as 'bargaining chips' to trade for concessions that the other side might not otherwise make." Even as you undertake "arms control," it seems, you must produce more weapons than you need so that you can bargain them away; and once you have concluded negotiations, you must produce still more so that you can bargain them away in the next round. The "net consequence," writes Ruina, "has been that, since SALT, existing strategic programs have actually intensified and many new developments started." In the words of Herbert Scoville, "arms control negotiations are rapidly becoming the best excuse for escalating, rather than toning down the arms race."

Both Washington and Moscow gave up nothing of importance; they simply agreed to escalate their efforts in tandem, concentrating on what each side considered most productive. The ink was hardly dry on the SALT agreements, moreover, when Dr. John S. Foster, Jr., Director of Defense Research and Engineering, made a plea to Congress, with the support of Secretary Laird and the Joint Chiefs, for a host of weapons still on the drawing boards. In a convoluted argument, he asserted that the "full success of SALT depends on sustained U.S. strength and . . . programs necessary to sustain that strength must go forward if the viability of the agreements is to be assured." One would think this was a time to hold back, but Foster called instead for speeding up the development of the Trident submarine (which has a ten times better chance of survival than a Polaris submarine), the undersea long-range-missile system (ULMS) submarine, the B-1 bomber, cruise missiles, mobile ICBM's, and communication improvements.

A year after the first SALT agreements were approved, Washington and Moscow signed another pact at the Washington Summit Conference of June 1973 to "continue active negotiations." Why this was necessary is not clear, except perhaps to enhance the importance of summit meetings. In any event Kissinger followed up with further meetings with the Russians, climaxed in November 1974 by the "agreement in principle" at Vladivostok between a new President, Gerald Ford, and Leonid Brezhnev. By this time, William Epstein points out, "it was estimated by American government officials that the total U.S. strategic nuclear arsenal was sufficient to drop 36 bombs on each of the 218 Soviet cities with a population of 100,000 or more. The U.S.S.R. had 11 nuclear weapons for each comparably sized American city." Yet, though the original purpose of SALT was to "freeze" strategic weapons production, Vladivostok increased them immensely. Each side is permitted 2,400 missiles, more than half of them, 1,320, MIRV'ed—with three, four, five, or more warheads each, instead of one.

The effect of this "control" is to augment by a factor of two or three times the present number of deliverable strategic warheads. Barry Schneider, former researcher for the Center for Defense Information, estimates that Vladivostok will result in an increase of American strategic weapons from 8,500 to 21,000. As this is written the SALT II talks are in limbo, the two sides reportedly at odds over the American cruise missile and the Russian Backfire bomber. Should cruise missiles, which can be manufactured easily and can be deployed in vast numbers on jumbo planes, be exempted from the SALT II agreement, the escalation will be staggering. And this does not take into account the Trident submarine, mobile missiles, the new generations of high-accuracy weapons such as the MARV, and research and development on many others now in the exploratory stage—none of which is prohibited under SALT II.

As Dr. Bernard Feld, MIT physicist, observes, "the rule until now seems to be that only those weapons or activities can be eliminated or banned that are of *no* interest to any substantial fraction of the military in the United States or in the Soviet Union." Why "after 30 years of intensive efforts in this direction," he asks, "are we nowhere? Indeed, we are even behind where we started, with numbers, types, forms, strengths, and all other destructive aspects of nuclear arms expanding almost unhindered . . ."

More biting is the look-back by historian Henry Steele Commager from some hypothetical time in the future: "A new security bureaucracy . . . lent their great talents not to devising ways of reducing tensions and avoiding war, but to ways of exacerbating tensions and preparing for war, and—when it didn't come fast enough—making war. With so much going for war it inevitably came, and thus the security managers were triumphantly vindicated in their apprehensions and prophecies. . . . For in this Alice-in-Wonderland bureaucratic world you achieve peace through war, order through chaos, security through violence, the reign of law through lawlessness . . ."

Lest anyone conclude that academics like Feld and Commager are too pessimistic and that the men of power in Washington will save us from our fate, let it be recorded that in January 1939 Lloyds of London, with the strongest connections to Downing Street, was giving odds of thirty-two to one that war would not break out that year.

10

The Second
Nuclear Age

The first nuclear age, roughly spanning three decades, was marked by an atomic race generally confined to two superpowers, the United States and the Soviet Union. The possibility of atomic war was horrifying, but at least there was a certain limit to the number of fingers that might push the fatal button. Membership in the so-called "nuclear club" was limited by the fact that it was impossible for all but a very few nations to obtain enriched uranium or plutonium—without which neither fission nor fusion bombs can be made. Gradually the club lost some of its exclusivity as Britain, France, China, then India (and perhaps Israel, which the CIA claims has secretly produced an arsenal of ten to twenty A-bombs), joined the nuclear-have nations. The button problem thereby became less manageable, but not yet out of control.

We have now entered the second nuclear age, superimposed on the first one. What distinguishes it is that the material for producing atomic warheads, especially plutonium, is becoming available to *dozens* of nations as a by-product of the worldwide spread of nuclear reactors for generating electricity. Added to the six (or seven) nations that now possess atomic explosives, said President Ford in July 1976, there are twenty others with the technical competence and the material to make them, and by 1985 the figure will be approximately forty. "A world of many nuclear weapons states," he noted, "could become extremely unstable and dangerous."

"In twenty years," asserts the Committee for Economic Development (CED), a prestigious group of business leaders, "100 countries will possess the raw materials and the knowledge necessary to produce nuclear bombs." By the year 2000, it says, "the total plutonium expected to have been produced as a by-product of nuclear power would be equivalent in explosive potential to one million bombs of the size that destroyed Nagasaki." The supply of plutonium, growing by almost geometric progression, changes all calculations of the past. In addition to the present danger of nuclear war between the two superpowers, the world faces in the very near future the danger of nuclear war between lesser powers, say in the Middle East or the Persian Gulf or around the Indian subcontinent or even in Latin America—as well as the potential of nuclear terrorism by both governments and individuals.

"Nuclear military threats between governments," says the CED report, "may take on many of the characteristics of terrorist threats"—such as the blowing up of a single city or a nuclear reactor by an agent smuggled into enemy territory. "Moreover, the technical knowledge to assemble a nuclear explosive device will not be confined to national armed services. The theft or capture of nuclear materials (in storage or in transit) by revolutionaries, terrorists, criminals, or even armed forces during a civil war or a coup d'état will be a frightening possibility." Representative Pete Stark (D-Calif.) may be overly pessimistic when he says that "unless the arms race and proliferation of nuclear weapons is stopped soon, the industrialized nations of the world, including the U.S., are likely to be destroyed within fifteen years." But it is obvious that within five, ten, or fifteen years the problem of containing the atom will be infinitely more difficult than at present, necessitating *international* measures more far-reaching than any currently contemplated, to prevent nuclear war, and *domestic measures of a police-state nature* to prevent gangsters and lunatics from practicing private nuclear terror.

These are consummations which American leaders devoutly did not wish, and certainly do not relish. Kennedy said a decade and a half ago that he was haunted by "the possibility in the 1970's of the President of the United States having to face a world in which fifteen or twenty nations may have these weapons. I regard that as the greatest possible danger." More recently, Fred C. Ikle, Director of the Arms Control and Disarmament Agency, has been punctuating what is surely a collective concern with even greater urgency. In a speech to the City Club of Cleveland, February 7, 1975, he said: "Up to this point I've been talking about arms control matters between ourselves and the Soviet Union . . . But this relationship may not always pose the greatest danger. The nuclear age—from the very first day—confronted us with a more distant danger—a danger that may make us look back on the present as a safe and easy time by comparison. I refer to the possible risks involved in the inevitable worldwide spread of nuclear technology." On another occasion he observed that "we are basically defenseless against threats of nuclear attack that could come from a great many different sources rather than from one or two principal adversaries." We are also defenseless, of course, against a nuclear attack by our principal adversary, Moscow, but it is clear that the problem is compounded with proliferation, and sizable numbers of legislators and administrators in Washington are poignantly aware of it. Summarizing those anxieties, the New York *Times* of June 9, 1975, observed that "the world now stands on the brink of a major breakdown in the long struggle to halt the spread of nuclear weapons." There are men who argue—Jerome H. Kahan, formerly of Brookings, then a key aide to Kissinger, for instance—that it doesn't really matter if Moscow and Washington increase spending on nuclear arms, so long as it is done in tandem, giving neither side additional advantages. But even the advocates of *"stable* deterrence" share misgivings that proliferation will de-stabilize matters.

Had it been in Washington's power, even its allies, Britain and France (let alone the Soviets), would have been excluded from the distinguished nuclear club. The impersonal element that seems to have given the arms race its self-reinforcing character, however, evidently was at work here as well. Washington stood by impotent as the Soviet Union exploded its first device in 1949, Britain in 1952, France in 1960, China in 1964, India in 1974. Russia had to be permitted into the club because it couldn't be stopped, Britain because it had been a partner in the development of nuclear energy, France because it refused to be excluded, and China and India for approximately the same reasons. The club is obviously expanding, and threatens within a few years to lose all semblance of rationality.

II

Oddly enough, the major impulse for the second nuclear age comes from the much heralded spin-off of Bomb technology—the peaceful atom that generates electricity. "It is ironic," Senator Stuart Symington told Congress (March 13, 1975), "that the United States, which in the first instance sought to limit membership in the nuclear weapons club, has made possible through its sharing of atomic technology, additional membership in that fearsome club."

Given the Yankee instinct for trade and the large investment made by the government in atomic science and atomic fuel plants, American leaders felt it would be a pity if other nations capitalized on U.S. pioneering efforts to line their own pockets. The sale of reactors for research and for generating electricity therefore was bound to be big business. Some years ago the AEC had hopes that 3,000 would be in operation worldwide by the year 2000. That figure was later cut back to half, then in 1974 to 1,090, an estimate that doubtless will be further reduced because of public protest in the United States and Europe. Even so, at today's prices of about a billion dollars for a 1,000-megawatt reactor it could come to hundreds of billions of dollars for reactors alone, not to mention the sale of nuclear fuel, the reprocessing of waste, and other supplements to the industry. This was not the sort of thing that corporations or their friendly allies in Congress were likely to overlook.

The formal debut of "atoms for peace" goes back to Eisenhower's speech before the UN on December 8, 1953. In his memoirs the late President records that in "draft after draft" of his intended talk "the exposition left the listener with only a new terror, not a new hope." The world had been shocked by the October 1952 detonation of a hydrogen bomb by the United States and a similar explosion by the Soviets in August 1953. No ordinary citizen on either side of the Cold War had been aware that development of a weapon of such magnitude was under way; sudden knowledge of a nuclear device a thousand times more powerful than the already frightening ones of only seven or eight years before, caused a new sense of alarm in many places—and demanded appeasement. Eisenhower provided the appeasement with a program for *peaceful* development of nuclear energy.

According to Steven J. Baker of Cornell's Center for International Studies, "the atoms for peace proposal helped to render politically acceptable in America and the world the government's decision to go ahead with the H-bomb." As a propaganda coup, it was immensely successful. After listing all the steps the United States and its allies had taken for "peace"—"let no one say that we shun the conference table"—Eisenhower proposed that the three nuclear powers (including Britain) "make joint contributions from their stockpiles of normal uranium and fissionable materials to an International Atomic Energy Agency" to "serve the peaceful pursuits of mankind. . . . A special purpose would be to provide abundant electrical energy in the power-starved areas of the world. Thus the contributing powers would be dedicating some of their strength to serve the needs rather than the fears of mankind."

The Russians, as expected, did not join the program because they were not interested in "atoms for peace" so long as there was no cap on "atoms for war." But the United States went ahead with commercialization of the atom anyway; a market, estimated at $30 billion in the mid-1950's, was too alluring to disregard. Indeed, if the United States had not taken the initiative, Britain might have captured the bulk of the business. "With more pressing energy needs than the United States," writes Baker, "Great Britain specialized earlier and gained initial successes with its natural uranium fuel reactor type. By 1952–53 the British seemed a step ahead of the American nuclear industry—and were aggressively seeking commercial outlets overseas."

Ironically, American corporations had been diffident about nuclear power because they saw little prospect for its use at home, where coal and oil were much cheaper than in foreign nations that had to import their fuels. The government, however, had a special interest in civilian uses of nuclear power, since research in that field furthered military development as well. Washington therefore encouraged its corporate friends by supplying large sums for R & D facilities—e.g., a $10-million commitment to build and equip a research plant for General Electric in Schenectady, N.Y. With the atoms-for-peace program the United States took the additional step of turning over to private enterprise the commercial business which federally financed science had made possible. Laws were passed breaching government's monopoly, and a new industry with enormous potential was born.

The doggedness with which the Eisenhower and succeeding administrations joined the nuclear power crusade—heedless of the problem of weapons proliferation or the intricacies of safety—is remarkable. Foreign utilities might have preferred the British reactor because it operated on natural uranium (U-238)—easily available on the world market—and therefore relieved the purchasing nation of dependence on America for reactor fuels. The American lightwater reactor, an adaptation of one developed for nuclear submarines, relied, by contrast, on an isotope, U-235, which was not only scarce but had to be enriched through an expensive chemical process. Any nation which bought the light-water reactor would be dependent on American nuclear fuel for decades—until it could develop its own enrichment facilities or invent a cheaper technique.

To overcome that handicap, the United States subsidized the customers of its corporations—at home and abroad—in a variety of ways. Foreign utilities that contracted for research reactors, for instance, were given an outright gift of half the selling price (up to $350,000), plus financing for the other half through the Export-Import Bank. Handsome terms were also offered to Euratom (a consortium of nine European nations), such as low-cost Import-Export Bank financing; and domestic customers were plied with a host of inducements, such as absorption of the expense of research and development (many billions), supplying enriched uranium at less than market value, disposing of the radioactive waste (a problem no one as yet has solved), and assuming the burden for most of the security measures and most of the insurance.

A barometer of the importance of these items in promoting atoms for peace is the last one, insurance. In 1957, when the industry was cranking up, a study financed by the AEC and conducted at the Brookhaven National Laboratory in Long Island, estimated that in the most serious type of accident (a meltdown of a reactor core) the average number of casualties would be 3,400 dead, 43,000 sick from radiation, and $7 billion in property damage. And this was for a relatively small reactor by today's standards, 200 megawatts. (An update of this report seven years later— for a larger reactor—estimated 45,000 deaths and $17 billion in property damage, the area of contamination being approximately the size of Pennsylvania.) The insurance industry in 1957, however, was unwilling to write policies for more than $60 million liability for each reactor. Congress therefore came to the rescue with the Price-Anderson Act (recently renewed). Under this act the utility company buys $95 million coverage from private insurance companies and $465 million directly from the federal government (AEC) at vastly reduced rates. An example of the relative costs is given by the Ford Foundation Energy Project, which showed that one licensed nuclear power plant was paying $250,000 a year premium on its private insurance, and only $73,500 for AEC insurance that provided five times as much coverage. Moreover, no matter how severe the accident, liability ceases, under the act, at $560 million. This is a form of private socialism: the government takes the risk, private industry reaps the profits; but without it, it is fair to say, there would have been no reactor business in the United States. Even industry spokesmen concede (as reported by *Nucleonics Week,* November 28, 1974) that "in the absence of Price-Anderson protection both utilities and the architect-engineers would get out of the nuclear business."

If the government was zealous about promoting "atoms for peace" commercially, it was not nearly so zealous about imposing safeguards so that recipient nations would be unable to convert nuclear material into bombs. It wasn't unmindful of the pitfalls, but its instinct for trade seems to have overwhelmed its instinct for security. The dangers were apparent even as Eisenhower made his offer: the enriched uranium sold as fuel for reactors, could be enriched further for bomb-grade quality, and the plutonium used in research reactors or extractable from the "waste" in power reactors could be fabricated with little additional effort directly into bombs. Yet the safeguards designed to check diversion of uranium and plutonium were unbelievably lax.

The Baruch Plan, it will be recalled, provided for both rigid inspection and "condign punishment." Eisenhower in 1953 repeated the demand for stringent inspection. But the International Atomic

Energy Agency (IAEA), established in 1957, was impotent from the start and grew progressively more so. The first problem was with Washington's closest allies—the six countries of the European Common Market that decided to pool their nuclear energy activities, and formed an agency of their own, Euratom, which refused either American or international inspection. The United States, faced with the choice of losing customers or granting the right of self-inspection (rather than international inspection) agreed to the latter. "This was a politically important concession," writes Steven J. Baker, "that rendered the IAEA stillborn."

The United States entered into bilateral agreements with forty-three nations between 1955 and 1958 to supply them with reactors, personnel, and fuel—some of it of bomb-grade quality. To be sure, Washington always attached provisos that none of the material be diverted to bomb production, and that the "waste," which contains plutonium, be sent back to the United States or a third country for reprocessing. There is no question that America's concern was genuine. But in the absence of international unity and with competitors breathing down its neck for the business, the United States yielded to a toothless program. IAEA inspectors roam the world auditing records and examining reactor sites to ascertain that no nuclear material is missing. But if they find uranium or plutonium unaccounted for there is little they can do about it other than report the matter to the UN Security Council, where the dereliction is usually buried and forgotten. Moreover, the staff is so small (only sixty-seven inspectors as of 1975) and the budget so minuscule ($29.6 million, most of which goes for other activities such as publishing 30,000 pages of scientific texts and operating laboratories and a center for theoretical physics) that the inspectors miss many violations, some of them serious. According to a *Newsweek* story (July 7, 1975), for instance, "U.S. intelligence sources reported last week that, *without IAEA detection,* Argentina recently removed 50 kilograms of plutonium waste from its Atucha station—potentially enough for five atomic bombs" (emphasis added). What made this incident so ominous was that Argentina was then seeking to acquire a reprocessing plant to separate plutonium from the waste, and would therefore soon have the capability to manufacture nuclear warheads from the diverted material. Yet even after the revelation no action was taken by the international community, nor could it be under present circumstances.

The sale of a nuclear reactor, either for research or electricity, is fraught with problems never encountered before. The more plentiful isotope of uranium, U-238, presents few difficulties because it cannot be fabricated into nuclear warheads. But in every hundred pounds of natural uranium there is seven tenths of a pound of a fissionable and radioactive isotope, U-235. To be usable in light-water reactors, that seven tenths of 1 per cent must be "enriched" by a complicated and sophisticated chemical process, so that U-235 constitutes 3 or 4 per cent of the uranium in the fuel rods. And to be applicable to bomb manufacture it must be "enriched" further, to as much as 90 per cent. This is no simple matter, since present enrichment plants (costing one, two, or more billion dollars each), demand a high degree of technological skill. As of January 1975 there were only seven uranium enrichment facilities in the world, three in the United States (at Oak Ridge, Tennessee, Portsmouth, Ohio, and Paducah, Kentucky), and one each in the Soviet Union, China, Britain, and France.

Nonetheless, like everything else in the nuclear drama, enrichment plants also tend to multiply. Frank Barnaby of the Stockholm International Peace Research Institute (SIPRI), reported in July 1974 that while the United States and the Soviet Union "show no real willingness to share the secrets of their enrichment processes with others . . . the proliferation of enrichment plants to non-nuclear weapons states is either underway (South Africa and the Netherlands) or anticipated (Japan, India and possibly Brazil)." There are on the horizon, moreover, a number of new techniques for enrichment which will be cheaper and more simple —the centrifuge process, for instance, and a process which depends on lasers. South Africa, using its own engineering methods, has built a pilot enrichment plant at Pelindaba; and while Washington, to be consistent, should have frowned on this development, a Massachusetts firm—with the approval of the State Department—provided two large computers to help operate the facility (Pretoria also may receive two reactors from General Electric, which has applied for the necessary license). Thus South Africa, which has a large supply of uranium (260,000 assured tons), will be able to produce atomic bombs, and in considerable number, when it sees fit. What that bodes for the future of Africa is not difficult to envision. The acquisition of enrichment plants by other states in the coming years promises to de-stabilize relationships on every other continent, for it can no longer be stopped by IAEA, the Non-Proliferation Treaty, or traditional diplomacy.

Of greater urgency than even the growing availability of uranium enrichment facilities, at the moment, is the prospect that dozens of nations will soon have access to uncontrolled supplies of plutonium. Unlike U-235, plutonium does not have to be enriched; nine pounds of pure plutonium 239 (or seventeen pounds of plutonium extracted from reactor waste, or twenty-two pounds of plutonium oxide), can be fabricated into a nuclear bomb without further modification, and there are thousands of people in the world who now have the basic know-how to do it. "I fear," says Nobel laureate James D. Watson, "that when the history of this century is written, that the greatest debacle of our nation will be seen not to be our tragic involvement in Southeast Asia, but our creation of vast armadas of plutonium, whose safe containment will represent a major precondition for human survival, not for a few decades or hundreds of years, but for thousands of years more than human civilization has so far existed." Plutonium is the primary material for most fission bombs, as well as for the "trigger" in hydrogen bombs. Unlike uranium, which appears in nature, element number 94 is a human invention: scientists, among them Glenn Seaborg, developed a process by which neutrons from the fission of U-235 are absorbed by U-238 atoms to form neptunium, then plutonium. During the war the federal government built a huge complex of three plutonium-producing reactors at Hanford, Washington, and in the 1950's added another complex of five reactors on the Savannah River in South Carolina. So long as the manufacture of this element was under AEC or military control, and the supplies relatively modest, there was little danger that other nations would acquire the necessary amounts to make atomic bombs.

The commercialization of nuclear power, however, has changed all that. Plutonium is now obtainable, or potentially obtainable, by foreign nations in four ways. Over the last fifteen years the United States has exported 814 pounds to Germany, 275 pounds to Italy, 330 pounds to Japan, 858 pounds to France, and smaller amounts to six other countries—enough to manufacture hundreds of bombs. Plutonium can also be produced in research reactors, already operating in more than fifty countries; and in "fast-breeder" reactors, which are expected to replace or supplement the light-water reactors a decade or two from now. The "breeder"—which France hopes to produce commercially by 1982—will multiply the problem by geometric progression because it "breeds" twice as much plutonium every ten years as is put into it. Most of all, the dread element can be extracted from the "waste" of burned-out fuel rods in the present reactors. All it needs is a "reprocessing" plant to separate the plutonium from other waste material—and that is a technology much less complicated than uranium enrichment and much cheaper. Small pilot plants can be built for a few million dollars, enough to provide plutonium for five, ten, or more bombs annually.

Symptomatic of how the nuclear barriers tend to break down is the fact that for thirty years the United States and other advanced countries refused to sell reprocessing equipment; West Germany and France broke this united front in 1975, and others will surely follow. According to Paul L. Leventhal, a special counsel to the Senate Subcommittee on Reorganization, Research and International Organizations, the nuclear power plants that President Ford agreed to sell Egypt will each be capable of providing 700 pounds of plutonium annually—after reprocessing—or enough to manufacture forty-one nuclear bombs. If we multiply this by a factor of a few hundred we have an idea of the dimension of the problem.

The peaceful reactor has run into some public opposition of late, but as of December 1975—according to the Energy Research and Development Administration (ERDA)—there were fifty-eight reactors in operation in the United States, eighty-seven more for which permits had been granted or authorized, and ninety-three in various stages of planning. Worldwide, the proliferation, since the first American reactor began to function at Shippingport, Pennsylvania, in 1953, has been equally awesome. The IAEA reported in 1974 that there were 170 reactors spread around 19 countries (producing 72,800 megawatts of electricity), and projected a figure of 393 reactors in 28 countries, producing 270,000 megawatts by 1980. In just six years capacity will have gone up about four times, and the plutonium extractable from the "waste," correspondingly. Though this figure may not be met, because of public resistance in many places, the wave is obviously swelling to tidal proportions.

Within the next few years at least ten nations will have the wherewithal to fabricate nuclear arms—Argentina, Brazil, Egypt, Israel (assuming it hasn't already done so), South Korea, Libya, Pakistan, South Africa, Spain, and Taiwan. Sixteen others are not far behind. Between them these twenty-six governments are either operating or building 274 power reactors, each with the implicit hazard that nuclear material will be diverted to bomb production. True, reprocessing has not yet started in earnest—the "waste" is either being "buried" or is accumulating on reactor sites, waiting for this end of the technology to catch up. American projects have run into technical difficulties (the reprocessing plant at West Valley, New York, had to be shut down in 1972; the one in Morris, Illinois, had to be abandoned because of faulty design, and the Barnwell plant in South Carolina is not yet finished).

But small reprocessing plants exist or are being built and larger ones are coming. What is more, they are being sold by "our so-called allies, France and West Germany"—as Senator Ribicoff scornfully calls them—to such countries as Brazil and Pakistan. The most sensational development along these lines has been the multi-billion-dollar deal between Germany and Brazil, by which the European nation will build eight atomic power stations, plus enrichment *and* reprocessing plants for its Latin American customer. Announcement of the pact came on the heels of a report that Brazil had made a discovery of "vast new uranium reserves." The separation of plutonium from reactor waste seems to be an idea whose time has come. In October 1975 Japan and Britain negotiated a one-billion-dollar ten-year agreement whereby the United Kingdom will import 4,000 tons of nuclear waste for reprocessing and Japan will build a new and bigger plant for the British to supplement their operations in Cumberland. France has a tentative arrangement to supply Pakistan with reprocessing technology.

It would be false to say that Washington welcomes these developments or has taken no measures to check them. In 1976, for instance, the State Department warned Pakistan that it would lose economic and military aid if it went ahead with the $150-million reprocessing plant project. It also urged France and other allies to agree to a system of *regional* reprocessing centers with multinational safeguards, so that no individual nation could siphon off plutonium from a facility of its own. Hints went out to France that if she didn't accept this program she might be deprived of the enriched uranium needed to run her own power reactors, currently supplied by the United States. But while Washington obviously has considerable leverage, France has evidently made it clear that she will accede only if she gets a "fair" share of the world's nuclear trade. Whether such agreements are possible in light of the fierce competition—and without Soviet participation—remains to be seen. As of the moment seven countries besides the United States are competing for the lucrative nuclear market in one or another field —the Soviet Union, Britain, France, Canada, Germany, Japan, Sweden—and that number is certain to grow.

The United States periodically castigates France, West Germany, and others for providing potential bomb capability to non-nuclear states. Yet when Senator Ribicoff suggested to Secretary of State Kissinger that the United States join with the Soviet Union to take stern action against proliferation, the Secretary replied that while "we are prepared to cooperate with the Soviet Union together with our allies . . . we are not prepared to cooperate with the Soviet Union against our allies." Dixie Lee Ray, former chairperson of the AEC, put the matter in more mundane terms: "I'm worried," she said, "about our industry losing potential nuclear contracts because we require more rigid conditions than the IAEA or other countries."

The United States is far from an innocent bystander in the proliferation of nuclear weaponry. It exports more than two thirds of the Western World's civilian nuclear technology, and thirteen of the twenty-nine countries to which it makes such sales have refused to ratify the Non-Proliferation Treaty. The United States is frequently as heedless of safeguards as its competitors. Germany, according to Senator Ribicoff, decided to sell enrichment and reprocessing facilities to Brazil only *after* it learned "that an American company was trying to sell Brazil an enrichment plant." The French and Germans, he says, "suspect that our warnings about weapons proliferation are a smokescreen for protecting our pre-eminent nuclear industry." There is no question that Washington intends to pyramid the production and sale of plutonium. In July 1974 the Atomic Energy Commission drafted a proposal for establishing a large *private* industry for recovering plutonium from waste. If AEC's plans mature—and they had the blessings of an administration harried by the oil shortage following the Yom Kippur war—a couple of dozen reprocessing plants will be recycling and selling 140 tons of plutonium by 1985 (enough to manufacture 16,500 Hiroshima-type bombs) and 1,700 tons annually by the year 2000 (enough to manufacture 200,000).

Assuming that these grandiose plans are aborted or modified somewhere along the way, domestic fabrication of plutonium for private use will still reach a million to two million pounds a year, according to Paul Leventhal. Worldwide, the expected avalanche is staggering: in 1970 by SIPRI's estimate, 4 tons of plutonium was being produced annually, by 1974 it was 18 tons, by 1990 it is expected to be 450 tons. The accumulated stockpile in 1970—in round figures—was 20 tons; in 1974, 85 tons; and by 1990 will register at 3,000 tons.

It is understandable therefore that the issue of proliferation is commanding growing and insistent attention even in the highest places. President Carter has suggested that the problem can be dealt with by withholding reprocessing facilities from individual nations and requiring that the separation of plutonium from nuclear waste be done exclusively by a multinational body outside the country where the waste is being accumulated. He proposed during the 1976 election campaign that the first site for multinational reprocessing be the Barnwell, South Carolina, plant now being constructed by Allied General Nuclear Services and expected to be in operation sometime between 1978 and 1983. The difficulty is that this would require a united front by all the industrialized nations that now have the capability of manufacturing power reactors, including the Soviet Union. No common action is possible, obviously, unless the nations competing for the world market come to an understanding on how to divide that market among themselves—and unless the developing nations are willing to remain indefinitely dependent on the industrialized states for their nuclear energy.

Michael Mandelbaum, a Harvard professor, states in an article for the *Bulletin of the Atomic Scientists* (January 1977), that "this market-sharing proposal gives more promise of retarding the drift towards a nuclear world than any of the others that have been put forward." It is an idea endorsed by Senator Ribicoff, one of the most concerned members of Congress on this subject. Yet even Mandelbaum agrees that the developing countries "can not be expected to look forward to such a state of affairs," any more than the industrial nations are "pleased about the hold that OPEC has over them."

Ribicoff and others—including President Carter evidently—feel that if "at least the enrichment, reprocessing, and waste storage" part of the nuclear fuel cycle were placed under "multinational authority," the danger of proliferation would be mitigated. "But to try to put the idea into practice immediately," notes Mandelbaum, "raises a number of questions: Where would these multinational facilities be located? Who would contribute what to them? How would decisions about operating them be made? And who would operate them?" Would France or Germany or India, for instance, agree that reprocessing plants be centered in the United States? Would the United States agree that the Soviet Union be given a major role in the cartel? What is involved, clearly, is the arrangement of world economic and political power. Short of ending the Cold War and using stern political measures to internationalize the atom, the prospects for united action by the nations of the world, therefore, seem destined to the same futility as the Non-Proliferation Treaty.

"The best that can be hoped for," says the Congressional Research Service of the Library of Congress in an "analytical report" for the Senate Committee on Government Operations (March 1976), "is to make further proliferation slow, difficult and undesirable." The Committee for Economic Development points out that Washington's reliance on NPT has proven to be hollow—not only because many nations have refused to adhere to it, but because it is possible to sign the treaty and still join the nuclear club. By establishing "mobilization bases" where the materials for bombs are stored separately—but not assembled—the nation involved is technically in compliance with the treaty. In time of emergency, however, it can assemble bombs within a matter of days.

CED still hopes that the United States can make the world so dependent on its uranium and other nuclear facilities, including reprocessing, that the nations will forgo proliferation. But even CED concedes that: "The many hazards associated with nuclear energy, especially with nuclear explosives, are enough to make any thoughtful person wonder whether, despite the world's need for new sources of energy, it might be better for mankind if nuclear technology could be suppressed and forgotten. A world economy charging towards a fuel shortage with no immediate relief in sight may be less frightening than a world economy powered by the fuel equivalent of millions of nuclear bombs. When the problem of radioactive wastes and the possibility of ordinary accidents are added, it is no wonder that concerned individuals are asking whether the world is obliged to imperil itself in this way." As far as the eye can see, under present circumstances, the prospects are not cheerful.

Scientist Bernard T. Feld judges that by 1980 developing nations will be able to make a thousand nuclear warheads annually, and by the end of the century, 30,000 (as much per year as the United States has accumulated in thirty years). The developed nations by then will have the capacity for 210,000 to 300,000 warheads annually. "There are many," says Feld, "who believe that we have already passed the point of no return, as far as nuclear weapons proliferation is concerned."

III

On May 18, 1974, to everyone's surprise, India conducted an underground explosion of a 12-kiloton nuclear device (approximately the equivalent of the Hiroshima bomb). It was made of plutonium recycled at its own Trombay reprocessing plant, from the waste of three power reactors, and from four research reactors. Though India is no fledgling in nuclear science, having opened its Tata Institute back in 1945, it had agreed to some inspection by the IAEA in 1971 and its Gandhian tradition seemed to militate against its joining the nuclear club. When it did, the reaction of the West was bitter; Canada, which had supplied some of the facilities, protested vigorously that there had been a breach of faith, a charge echoed in the American press almost unanimously. But the government of Indira Gandhi made a plausible—if not exactly palatable—rebuttal.

In the first place, it argued, it had no intention of making bombs for war; it was simply developing nuclear explosives for "peaceful" purposes such as leveling mountains or digging canals. As proof of this modest objective it pointed to the fact that the whole operation had cost a mere $400,000, including the charge for plutonium and readying the underground test site. Unfortunately, whether this claim is or is not made with tongue in cheek, the fact is that there is no difference between a "peaceful" nuclear explosive and a martial one; their utility is interchangeable. Interchangeable too is the rocket technology India claims is for civilian programs. By the 1980's the second most populous country in the world, says SIPRI, "may have a booster vehicle capable of putting a payload exceeding 1,000 kilograms into synchronous orbit. It could then produce a delivery system for nuclear weapons as a 'spin-off' from its civil space program." Its electronics industry by then will be producing advanced communications networks, radars, and real-time computers, that will give it a substantial nuclear capacity. Technology in India, as in the United States, it seems, has its own spiraling logic. And whether the "peaceful intentions" are true coin, or diplomatic counterfeit, the fact that India has joined the club has caused sufficient uneasiness in nearby Pakistan so that it too may soon apply for membership.

The second Indian rejoinder to the charge that it has been "irresponsible" is not so easily disposed of. "In this world," says K. Subrahmanyam, Director of the Institute of Defense Studies and Analyses in New Delhi, "you and I are asked to accept the credibility of the structure of peace built on 7,000 strategic nuclear warheads; in addition to another 7,000 tactical nuclear weapons capable of incinerating all of us on this globe many times over; the credibility of a Non-Proliferation Treaty since the signing of which nuclear weapons have quadrupled in number; the credibility of deterrence which means a non-stop arms race . . . Therefore, before we answer the question how credible India's [peaceful] declaration is, we have to ask for a definition of credibility in international politics." If America can do it, why can't we?—especially since our neighbor to the north, China, acquired The Bomb years ago. In fact, says Subrahmanyam, by developing its nuclear capability, India will "influence the arms control negotiations." For anyone who enjoys historical parallels this argument is not too different from that enigmatic Kennedy thesis—"arms to disarm."

The rationale for proliferation, it would appear, is a chain reaction as mystifying and invincible as fission itself. China needs The Bomb because America threatens the Asian continent; India needs it because China has it and once "penetrated . . . 70–80 miles of our territory"; Pakistan contracts with France to buy a plutonium extraction plant as a hedge against India. "The reason for the Pakistani interest in a reprocessing plant," says Fred C. Ikle of ACDA, "is the Indian development of nuclear explosives." Five days after India explodes its "peaceful" bomb, it signs a pact for "nuclear cooperation" with Argentina, which has anxieties about Brazil's "nuclear cooperation" with Germany.

An Argentine journalist, Mariana Grondona, expressed the psychology of proliferation aptly in a December 18, 1974, article for *La Opinión:* "Now with India the Atomic Powers are six in number. They would like to remain six. If we [Argentina] come to be the seventh, we would of course like to see no more than seven. The last one to arrive tries to close the door. That is only natural. But why should the door be closed in our face?" Similar thinking guides nations on the threshold elsewhere. Iran, which under the Shah has illusions of reconstituting the Persian empire, hopes to buy twenty to twenty-five reactors by 1985, which would give her the potential, according to ex-Senator Symington, of producing 800 to 1,000 atomic weapons a year. It, of course, has given all the requisite assurances that none of the U-235 or plutonium will be diverted to that purpose, but assurances between nations are never permanent—especially if Iran insists it is threatened by the Soviet Union or neighboring Iraq, or if the sheikdoms of the Persian Gulf, which Iran feels are its responsibility, are further menaced by guerrilla movements (as is Oman). There is no end to good reasons for joining the club—if plutonium or enriched uranium is accessible.

Thus the "peaceful" reactor, despite the best intentions of those who husbanded and nursed it in the hopes of solving humanity's urgent energy problems, takes us, it seems, a long way towards war. An augury of what proliferation bodes for the second nuclear age —if it is not choked off—is contained in an April 12, 1976, issue of *Time.* According to the newsweekly, "Israel possesses a nuclear arsenal of 13 atomic bombs, assembled, stored and ready to be dropped on enemy forces from specially equipped Kfir and Phantom fighters or Jericho missiles." The weapons are said to have a 20-kiloton yield. On the second day of the Yom Kippur war in 1973, says *Time,* these weapons were assembled and "sent to desert arsenals . . . ready for use." The Israelis were evidently hedging against the possibility they might not stem the Egyptian tide. Had Egypt had nuclear weapons, there is no telling what might have happened, with each side fearful of a "first strike" by the other. As it was—again according to *Time*—Moscow became fearful that its ally (at the time), Egypt, might be mercilessly mauled, and prepared for nuclear action of its own. "What is certain," writes the magazine, "is that on October 13, the Russians dispatched nuclear warheads from Nikolaev—the naval base at Odessa—to Alexandria, to be fitted on Russian Scud missiles already based in Egypt. The U.S., in turn, detected the Soviet warheads as the ship carrying them passed through the Bosphorous on October 15 and issued a warning to Moscow by means of a world military alert." The Israelis, it should be mentioned, denied the story and none of the other powers involved have commented. But it is a scenario that is plausible and destined to occur more frequently as the spread of nuclear capability continues unchecked.

It takes little imagination to visualize a dozen similar situations —though not quite so dire in all instances—between Pakistan and India, Iran and Iraq, Brazil and Argentina, and so on. What makes such prospects even more alarming is that in "limited" nuclear wars between the lesser nuclear states there is bound to be a greater pressure for a surprise attack—a first strike. The United States and Russia may be inhibited because each knows that the other side has a "second strike" capability; no matter how punishing the first blow, each will have enough bombs left to inflict Doomsday on the other. Rather than commit suicide, then, the two main adversaries try to avoid total confrontation—while they probe for technological breakthroughs for "damage-limitation." But with the lesser states there is unlikely to be a "balance of terror" at this stage, since neither side can have, as of now, enough weaponry for both a first *and* a second strike. The side that is losing a conventional war, therefore, must seriously consider putting its nuclear weapons to use at the earliest moment, lest it be forced to surrender; and the side that is winning must also contemplate first use for fear the enemy will do so and wipe it out as a viable society. Each would seek the propitious moment for surprise.

This circumstance makes the calculations of those who believe in "stable" deterrence—a real nuclear stalemate—inoperative. Could America stand idly by while its ally, say Iran, was being devastated by Iraqi atomic bombs? Could Russia stand idly by while its ally, say India, was being nuclearly devastated by Pakistan? It is not realistic to expect such forbearance.

The failure to end the arms race during the first nuclear age has led inexorably to a vast expansion of it, both horizontally and vertically. Nations that don't have nuclear bombs seek to obtain them; those that have, seek more and better ones. In 1974, for instance, Britain conducted its first nuclear test since 1965. The purpose was to improve the warheads on its four nuclear submarines. That number is small compared to the American or Russian armadas of forty-one and sixty-two submarines respectively, but the four British ships each carry 192 warheads with 200-kiloton firepower—enough to destroy virtually all the major population centers in either the United States or the Soviet Union. The impending chaos—and danger—from proliferation, obviously is unimaginable. "Soon the atom will have no secrets for anybody," observes President Qaddafi of Libya. "Some years ago we could hardly procure a fighter squadron. Tomorrow we will be able to buy an atom bomb and all its parts. The nuclear monopoly is about to be broken." The Defense Minister of Turkey, in a bellicose statement aimed at the United States because of its conventional arms embargo at the time, boasted early in 1975 that his country has "plans to manufacture atom bombs." The causes of World War III, to repeat C. Wright Mills's pungent observation, may very well be the preparations for it.

IV

The second nuclear age has elevated two other challenges to the level of immediacy.

One is the danger of weapons confiscation by America's own allies. Thousands of U.S.-owned bombs are presently mounted on planes or emplaced aboard ships operated by U.S. colleagues in

NATO. This fact is muted as much as possible by the Pentagon, but periodically it comes to public view. In August 1961 Deputy Defense Secretary Cyrus R. Vance stated that a "substantial percentage" of American weapons were deployed by West Europeans. In 1963 the Pentagon reported that two French fighter squadrons stationed in Germany were being armed with U.S. atomic weapons. In 1965, under persistent questioning by a New York *Times* correspondent, the Defense Department admitted that it had mounted nuclear weapons on planes belonging to nine allies. In addition thousands of bombs are stockpiled in depots manned by U.S. troops, many of them loosely secured. Jorma K. Miettinen, of the department of radiochemistry at Helsinki told a Harvard audience in May 1975, that America's 7,000 tactical nuclear weapons in Europe are held "in 80 depots, which are guarded by three to four men at a time; the whole guard force being only some 40 men per depot." Security may be improved as the number of depots is cut back, as expected, to sixty-five, but there are constant references in Congress to the "inadequate" protection of these weapons. One Representative is said to have visited a base not far from the border of East Germany, patrolled by 100 men working three shifts—twenty or twenty-five at a time. "Thus," notes Miettinen, "there is a possibility of seizure by terrorists even in peace time, seizure by allies in time of crisis, unauthorized use, and nuclear accidents. These risks increase exponentially in a crisis, as nuclear units with their weapons start moving around Europe."

While there is little incentive for Britain, say, to steal an American warhead, there are circumstances under which allies that do *not* have A-bombs or H-bombs may yield to temptation. The Pentagon tacitly concedes this point because it is constantly trying to improve its safeguards. An article by Victor K. McElheny in the New York *Times* of December 17, 1973, discloses, for instance, that the Defense Department "has begun a program to equip its tens of thousands of tactical nuclear weapons, maintained in foreign countries, with advanced electronic controls designed to prevent their misuse even if terrorists or hostile armies overrun an overseas base." The installation of electronic security devices, however, requires the virtual rebuilding of a weapon and is therefore, according to Major General Edward B. Giller of the Air Force, "a slow process." Even after the electronic "locks" or "keys" are put in place there is no guarantee that a foreign country (or a terrorist) won't be able to "unlock" them. Dr. Herbert Scoville, the former CIA and Defense official, who has considerable expertise in this area, says "it would be difficult, but it could be done—with the use of x-rays, for instance." Or the bomb, as General Giller says, could be melted down and its material refabricated into a new warhead. Admittedly this is a cumbersome process, but the possibility of confiscation periodically causes much anguish in high places.

During the Cyprus crisis of 1974, the Pentagon ordered a carrier of the Sixth Fleet to ready the landing of a Marine detachment to recover warheads in Greece or Turkey. "We are prepared," said a Defense Department official, "should certain contingencies arise, to remove the warheads." Within the two countries at the time were hundreds of atomic weapons with explosive power equivalent to millions of tons of TNT, some of them mounted or armed for detonation on Greek and Turkish planes. Such planes, despite Pentagon optimism, could not be disarmed even by Marine detachments—if they decided to take to the air.

The danger may not be overriding, but as retired Admiral Gene R. LaRocque observes, if a host country turned hostile to the United States "we couldn't get those weapons out and we might have to fight our way in to get control." Nuclear bombs stationed in South Korea (some of them only thirty-five miles from the North Korean border), as well as Italy, Germany, the Netherlands, and Belgium are certainly vulnerable to seizure. These weapons have what is called a "double key" system, which must be turned both by a member of the armed forces of the host country and an American. But it is not, in the opinion of many, a foolproof system —especially in a period of attenuated crisis.

v

Another worrisome form of proliferation in the second nuclear age, destined to become progressively more menacing, is the likelihood that plutonium will be stolen by individuals—say by foreign "CIA" agents bent on sabotage in the United States or elsewhere, and by terrorists, guerrillas, blackmailers, and cranks. In the military sense this is certainly not as serious as the proliferation of atomic capability to other *nations*. But as a *domestic* problem it threatens to erode or destroy the American democratic structure, as the government takes the necessary police-state measures to defend the nation's internal security.

It is one thing to sabotage a utility that generates elecricity from coal, quite another to sabotage a nuclear power reactor or the radioactive fuel "waste" presently stored in tanks or at reactor sites. Those who hijack a plane or a machine gun jeopardize at most a few dozen lives. But terrorism or blackmail with plutonium represents a quantum jump, in that thousands of lives are at stake. A crude nuclear bomb one half of 1 per cent as powerful as the Nagasaki bomb will kill, experts assert, 2,000 people (mostly from radiation) in a typical suburb, or 50,000 people if detonated under a very large skyscraper, and just about everyone in a big football stadium. Considering that there are sixty or seventy acts of international terror each year, such as the murder of Israeli athletes at the 1972 Olympic games, and many hundreds of bombings in the United States (1,439 in the first 11 months of 1976, for instance, causing 42 deaths and 193 injured, according to FBI data), the prospect of terrorists or guerrillas shifting from TNT bombs and blackmail to plutonium bombs and blackmail is frightening to say the least.

A report by CIA analyst David L. Milbank, declassified in June 1976, warns that the influx of foreign dignitaries during such events as the 1980 Winter Olympics "will inescapably afford a host of opportunities for dramatic terrorist action. . . . We should expect to witness steadily greater and more widespread sophistication in targeting, execution and weaponry"—including "weapons of mass destruction," i.e., nuclear bombs.

Part of the problem was already apparent in the first nuclear age. The reactors under AEC or Pentagon control that produced enriched uranium and plutonium for bombs also produced radioactive waste—including cesium 137 and strontium 90, with half-lives of about thirty years, thorium 230 with a half-life of 80,000 years, a number of transuranic elements such as neptunium, americium, and curium, as well as considerable amounts of plutonium. Plutonium has a half-life of 24,000 years (its radioactivity is diminished by half in the first 24,000 years, by half of the remaining half in the next 24,000 years, and so on), so that it will remain "fiendishly toxic"—in the words of one of its discoverers, Glenn Seaborg—for many times the history of civilization. Unless this amalgam can be isolated from the biosphere for hundreds of thousands of years it will cause death, illness, and genetic disorders to untold millions of people—far greater than any accident known in the whole human saga. That means that, as a minimum, the world will have to be ruled by stable governments or international agencies to supervise waste disposal and prevent sabotage, for a period of time no nation-state has as yet even remotely approached.

Unfortunately, until now, the AEC and its successor in the research field, the Energy Research and Development Administration (ERDA), have been unable to develop a feasible plan for a permanent storage site; and have limited themselves therefore to "interim" depositories which are described as "safe" for only thirty to a hundred years. The Hanford disposal site in the state of Washington, where three quarters of the waste from weapons production is stored in 140 huge tanks, each fifty feet high, has had eighteen known leaks. Five hundred thousand gallons of radioactive liquids have been discharged into the earth and nearby rivers. A "key AEC consultant" told the Los Angeles *Times* in 1973: "We are in a mess right now and what bothers the hell out of me is we are only on the toe of the nuclear age. We're sitting on a time bomb." There is more radioactivity in the Hanford storage site, reports correspondent Lee Dye, "than would be released during an entire nuclear war." What would happen if there were an earthquake in the area or if some terrorist or lunatic sabotaged Hanford? Gus Speth of the Natural Resources Defense Council reports that there were two unsuccessful attempts to blow up reactors in France during a six-month period in 1975. The Nuclear Regulatory Commission on May 27, 1976, sent a letter to the managers of fifty-eight nuclear plants advising of planned "intrusions" by two terrorist groups. "Information received in May," said the NRC note, "included threatened activities in Illinois . . . Washington and California. . . . Also during May, there were reports of persons, under suspicious circumstances, in the vicinity of two power plants in Connecticut. . . . In two separate instances in recent weeks the credentials of NRC inspectors have been stolen along with other personal belongings." Michael Flood, in an October 1976 article for the *Bulletin of the Atomic Scientists* on

"Nuclear Sabotage," reports that since September 1970 there have been at least nine attacks on nuclear facilities around the world—with pipe bombs, dynamite, incendiaries. Since 1969 there have been ninety-nine threats of violence against reactors, two instances of ransom demands (one for $10 million, one for $1 million), hundreds of cases of vandalism, sabotage, fuel rod theft, and security breaches.

Security and waste disposal are only part of the problem of the Plutonium Economy. Plutonium, according to Mason Willrich, former assistant general counsel of ACDA, and Theodore B. Taylor, former safeguards consultant to AEC, "is at least 20,000 times more toxic than cobra venom or potassium cyanide, and 1,000 times more toxic than heroin or modern nerve gases." It is probably less toxic than anthrax bacilli, but that is small comfort. A dose of between ten and a hundred micrograms (millionths of a gram—a gram is one twenty-eighth of an ounce) is enough to give lung cancer and ultimately kill an individual who inhales or receives it through the soft skin. A dozen milligrams (thousandths of a gram) is enough to cause fibrosis of the lung and kill the recipient within days. A lunatic who placed 100 grams of the right type of plutonium powder in an air-conditioner could jeopardize the lives or health of everyone in a sizable ten-story building. It is fearsome hazards such as these, in addition to easy access by would-be miscreants to bomb technology, that makes plutonium an "ideal" instrument for terrorism and blackmail.

A RAND expert, Brian Michael Jenkins, foresees the day, the Chicago *Tribune* reports, when terrorism "will render large standing armies practically useless." In the "not very distant future," he says, this sort of "warfare" may "virtually replace conventional war among nations." That seems hardly likely, unless by "terrorism" you refer to guerrilla warfare in certain countries. But it is technologically feasible even now for a group such as the Green Berets—of any country—to land in a foreign country and detonate small nuclear explosives. "Terrorism," writes *Tribune* correspondent Frank Starr (November 26, 1975), "has a future so significant that it may have a major long range impact on the current system of international order."

As things stand, both the material and the know-how are available. Deborah Shapley, in an article for *Science*, April 9, 1971, writes that "it takes only a very small bit of plutonium—about 5 kilograms or $50,000 worth—to make a bomb the size of the weapon that destroyed Nagasaki in August 1945. The technology and hardware are available—many sources recommend the *World Book* as a good text on atomic bomb-building." Speaking to an audience of the Atomic Industrial Forum in March 1972, E. M. Kinderman of the Stanford Research Institute noted that not only is "slow diversion" of plutonium "possible" today in considerable amounts, but "that a small group of technically trained people can, without massive support, create a few nuclear explosives of enormous destructive power." Testifying before the Joint Committee on Atomic Energy, Theodore Taylor stated that "nuclear weapons are relatively easy to make, assuming the requisite nuclear materials are available. All of the information, non-nuclear materials, and equipment that would be required to design and build a variety of types of fission explosives are readily available throughout the world. . . . Under conceivable circumstances, for example, a few persons, perhaps even one person working alone, who possessed about ten kilograms of plutonium or uranium 233 oxide or two dozen kilograms of highly enriched uranium oxide and a substantial amount of high explosive could, within several weeks, safely design and build a crude transportable fission bomb . . . with a yield equivalent to at least 100 tons of high explosive and that could be carried in an automobile." They need only follow directions in "publicly available documents" and "be reasonably inventive and adept at using laboratory equipment and tools of about the same complexity as those used by students in chemistry and physics laboratories and machine shops." There are experts who disagree with Taylor and his associate, Willrich, but there are many who don't. In any case it is certain that the job will become progressively easier in coming years, as the know-how is further disseminated and fertile minds find shortcuts to accomplish their task. Thousands can do it now—and many thousands more can conceptualize the design of a nuclear device.

Indeed, a twenty-year-old chemistry student, appearing on public television, showed how a functional nuclear bomb could be produced in six weeks. The AEC itself conducted an experiment with two physicists, just out of graduate school, to see if they could design an A-bomb based on the information available in public literature. The commission found to its dismay not only that they could, but that the weapon would explode with the yield the young men had predicted—give or take 10 per cent.

How universal this knowledge is can be gauged from a blackmail incident that occurred in Orlando, Florida. On October 27, 1970, a typewritten letter—in red ink—was delivered to the city hall, demanding a million dollars on pain of blowing up the city with a hydrogen bomb. Two days later, according to the Orlando police chief, a handwritten note was received repeating the demand and giving an address of a vacant house for reply. The first note contained a diagram of a workable bomb and stated that the required material had been pilfered from AEC shipments. It sounded convincing, because (a) a certain amount of plutonium and bomb-grade uranium is always missing and (b) because the bomb diagram was scientifically accurate. The authorities assembled the million dollars, and were prepared to pay the ransom, when luckily the culprit was apprehended. He turned out to be a fourteen-year-old high school honors student.

The major impediment to nuclear terrorism clearly has not been know-how but the availability of plutonium. As already indicated, however, the supply is about to increase astronomically. The U. S. Government, as late as 1974, still nurtured hopes there would be 1,000 nuclear power plants in the United States by the year 2000—producing 660,000 pounds of plutonium annually (assuming that the "breeder" reactors are then in operation)—and 2,000 reactors overseas—producing two million pounds of plutonium. Divide this by the ten pounds needed to fabricate a Nagasaki-type atom bomb, and you get a startling idea of the danger inherent in the second nuclear age. It is doubtful that this 3,000 figure will be reached—there was a marked slowdown, as previously noted, in the reactor manufacturing industry in 1975 and in 1976, due to safety problems and public pressures. It is also questionable as to whether the "breeder" reactor will reach those projections—indeed whether it will ever be put into operation if popular hostility to it continues to grow. But even if you cut the numbers to half or one quarter, there will still be between two thirds of a million pounds and a million and a third pounds accessible for theft and hijacking.

The diversion of plutonium into the hands of black marketeers, guerrillas, terrorists, and blackmailers is a virtual certainty—and there will be no lack of opportunity. It will be available in hundreds of places and during many thousands of shipments, by air, truck, railroad, and boat; at hundreds of reactor and reprocessing sites, and at the fifteen commercial fuel plants authorized by AEC —such as Kerr-McGee, Exxon Nuclear Company, Nuclear Fuels, Numec, United Nuclear Corporation. Consumer advocate Ralph Nader, testifying before the Senate Commerce Committee in June 1974, predicted on the basis of AEC projections of 1,000 reactors in operation by the year 2000, that there would be at that time 60,000 truck shipments of nuclear fuel, and 10,000 by barge, as well as 46,000 deliveries by truck and 10,000 by rail, of nuclear waste from the back end of the fuel cycle. All told, irradiated material would move across 100 million deadly miles a year. Fred Ikle, director of the ACDA, estimates that by 1995 the amount of fissionable material in transit in foreign countries alone, will be enough to fabricate 20,000 bombs a year.

It is not inconceivable that organized crime, which traffics in heroin, will take advantage of the opportunity for illicit traffic in plutonium, which Deborah Shapley estimated in 1971 cost $10,000 a kilogram—five times as much as uncut heroin and ten times as much as gold (before devaluation). An official of a company that was commissioned to study the threat of hijacking, Carmine Bellino, revealed an interesting statistic to a Los Alamos meeting: "on a list of 735 so-called Mafia members, 12 are or were owners of trucking firms, two are truck drivers, and at least nine were union officials." So far as is known none of the Mafioso have as yet entered this lucrative trade, but police, according to Bellino, would not exclude the possibility "that some foreign tyrant might offer a deal of some kind to any racketeer who would divert enriched uranium or plutonium. . . . In such a situation a truck carrying uranium or plutonium could be easily hijacked or the theft could occur at warehouse or dockside." And if organized crime is chary of this type of trade, there are, according to columnist Jack Anderson, "more than 40 foreign terrorist organizations that are considered a threat to the U.S.," not to mention domestic ones, which might not be so squeamish.

AEC Commissioner Clarence E. Larson predicted as far back as 1969 that "once special nuclear material is successfully stolen in small and possibly economically acceptable quantities, a supply-stimulated market for such illicit materials is bound to develop. And such a market can surely be expected to grow once a source of supply has been identified. As the market grows, the number and size of thefts can be expected to grow with it, and I fear such growth would be extremely rapid once it begins. Such a theft would quickly lead to serious economic burdens to the industry and a threat to national security."

Experts expect theft of nuclear material to be consummated in two forms—through holdup or hijacking, on the one hand, and slow but steady small-scale pilfering by workers in nuclear plants or power stations. Plutonium fuel, Ralph Lapp points out, is cased in small pellets the size of a thimble and weighing about a third of an ounce. Each pellet contains 0.05 ounces of plutonium, so that if a worker smuggled out twenty pellets a day from the twelve-foot rods in which they are emplaced—an ounce a day—he would have enough in less than a half year (160 days) to produce a bomb. Nuclear material, in fact, disappears constantly. Whether it is lost in vents, in scrap, in workers' gloves, in pipes, or through normal chemical reactions, no one knows; but between one fifth of 1 per cent and one half of 1 per cent vanishes without trace. Sometimes the loss is highly disturbing. According to Timothy H. Ingram (*Washington Monthly,* January 1973), a U.S. contractor reported in 1966 that over the previous six years, 220 pounds of U-235 was unaccounted for—enough to fabricate a number of Hiroshima bombs. A New York *Times* dispatch of December 29, 1974, asserts that "a highly placed official in the commission [AEC] said one of its plants was unable to account for 9,000 pounds of the highly enriched uranium it has produced since the plant began to operate." A scientist, the same article notes, says that the cumulative "MUF" (materials unaccounted for) of a gaseous diffusion plant ran into "tons." Kerr-McGee admitted its technicians periodically lost track of as much as sixty pounds of plutonium. The Nuclear Materials and Equipment Corporation was unable over a period of years to account for 220 pounds.

So far, little if any of the MUF seems to have been funneled into a black market or into a guerrilla group arsenal. But no one can be entirely sure, because the AEC (and its successor, the Nuclear Regulatory Agency) does not make such facts public. Even so, the New York *Times* drew from one official an admission that as of late 1974 there had been two instances when smugglers were caught trying to remove nuclear material. In Bradwell, England, two reactor employees tossed twenty fuel rods over the plant fence, either for confederates or themselves to pick up. The male-factors, in these instances, were caught, but there may have been some that weren't. Anyway, the idea of nuclear terrorism and threat is evidently occurring to a growing number of people: the AEC, in response to a December 1974 inquiry by a journalist, ad-mitted that government agencies had received seven plutonium bomb threats in the previous two years. Evidently they were the handiwork of cranks, but it is almost mathematically certain that the black art will become a frightening reality.

The government itself expects it and is preparing for it. A 1974 AEC report produced under the chairmanship of David M. Rosen-baum, argues that "the potential harm to the public from the ex-plosion of an illicitly made nuclear weapon is greater than from any plausible plant accident, including one which involves a core meltdown and subsequent breach of containment"—in other words, an accident which might kill thousands or tens of thousands of people. The Rosenbaum Report calls for stern measures to deal with this menace: "The first and one of the most important lines of defense against groups which might attempt to illegally acquire special nuclear materials to make a weapon, is timely and in-depth intelligence. Such intelligence may involve electronic and other means of surveillance, but its most important aspect is infiltration of the groups themselves."

Since there are already more than a million people trained in handling, moving, and operating nuclear weapons—and that num-ber will multiply considerably decade by decade—what Rosenbaum is actually proposing is surveillance, snooping, wiretapping, and infiltration on a scale that would make J. Edgar Hoover's Coin-telpro (counter-intelligence program) against Socialists, Commu-nists, the NAACP seem mild. The Rosenbaum Report doesn't ask the AEC to undertake this task itself, but to enlist all the in-telligence-gathering agencies of the United States Government, "including the FBI, CIA, and NSA." This is the essence of the Tom Charles Huston plan, which President Nixon originally ap-proved, then rescinded when Hoover refused to go along with it. The AEC also has asked for the formation of a federal police to offer protection and to provide a show of force against thieves, saboteurs, blackmailers.

"Fission energy is safe," Hannes Alfven wrote in the *Bulletin of the Atomic Scientists* (May 1972), "only if a number of critical devices work as they should, if a number of people in key positions follow all of their instructions, if there is no sabotage, no hijacking of transports, if no reactor fuel processing plant or waste repository anywhere in the world is situated in a region of riots, or guerrilla activity, and no revolution or war—even a 'conventional one'—takes place in these regions. The enormous quantities of extremely dangerous material must not get into the hands of ignorant people or desperados. No acts of God can be permitted."

Such problems are beginning to come into focus, but as yet have evoked little public discussion and, except for a few members of Congress (Ribicoff, Symington, etc.), no consideration of remedial measures. What would happen in a *conventional* war, say between Iran and Iraq, if each side blew up or sabotaged each other's power reactors? What would happen in the United States if a revolutionary or a reactionary placed a sufficiently powerful TNT bomb against the reactor in Zion, Illinois—not far from Chicago and Milwaukee? What would happen if a political blackmailer telephoned the press to advise the world that he has stolen a few pounds of plutonium and intended to use it? Thousands of police would have to break down thousands of doors, without benefit of warrant, seeking to find the dread cache. The quandaries of the second nuclear age are endless.

No wonder then that Dr. Alvin Weinberg, at the time Director of the AEC's Oak Ridge National Laboratory, felt constrained to write (in *Science,* July 7, 1972), that "we may have to modify our old—perhaps create new—social institutions if we are to live in harmony with the peaceful atom."

The atom bomb, which Harry Truman called "the greatest thing in history," was supposed to assure the survival of the United States and to defend democratic freedom against totalitarianism. What it has achieved is a steady propulsion towards Doomsday on the one hand, and—the final irony—towards a police state, which obliterates democracy and freedom, on the other.

11

The Obsolete
Institution

It is difficult to imagine a world without war, because war has been
central to the life of all societies, with the possible exception of
primitive ones, at least since the dawn of civilization. The threat of
war has been the mailed fist behind diplomacy; the implementation
of war, a primary means by which power and privilege have been
defended or extended. Despite humankind's much vaunted "rationality," war rather than reason has been the adjudicating instrument between organized nations or sub-nations. It "has served
from time immemorial," Walter Millis writes, "as the *ultima ratio*
of international society, the means of reaching and enforcing decision of those issues which, insusceptible to settlement in any other
way, yet had to be decided for good or ill if the great society was
to continue."

Leaving aside the moral question as to whether human beings
have a right to kill other human beings, war has been "useful" in
the sense that it offered the winner security and material advantages. The slave societies—Rome, for instance—were built by war,
the dukedoms of feudal days were consolidated into nations and
nations into empires through the institution of war. But war is lunacy when it cannot bring victory to either adversary. That is what
distinguishes the nuclear age from the past; it is the first time in

history that war cannot *decide*. In another day war decided between Rome and Carthage, between Britain and Spain, between
the Allies and the Axis; one nation or group of nations was the
winner, the other, the loser. The nuclear age has changed all that:
between the United States and the Soviet Union it is absolutely excluded that there can be a winner. This is a change of fundamental
importance, destined to affect profoundly every single aspect of
human existence, culture, religion, law, social organization, and of
course the institution of war itself.

Nuclear technology has robbed war of its essential ingredient,
the capacity to decide. Technology has always provided warriors,
General James M. Gavin reminds us, with "weapons of ever-
greater strength. Iron swords to break the bronze, animal sinews to
hurl weapons further than thrown stones. . . . Iron gave way to
steel, oil replaced coal, Greek fire was dwarfed by gunpowder,
gunpowder yielded to TNT." The theoretical limit of destructive
power was reached, however, when "scientists generated here on
earth the explosive power comparable to that taking place on the
sun itself." The scientific revolution of our day has sired a weapons system that can't be used because it fosters mutual suicide,
and can't be effectively threatened because everyone knows it can't
bring victory. That punctuates the end of a long human saga, and
opens the door—if the lessons can be absorbed—to a new one.

True, war can sometimes still be won at a less than all-out level.
But the very danger that it will escalate to total war dilutes the
prospect of victory here as well. That is why the Soviet Union and
the United States were forced to accept stalemate in the Berlin
crisis and the Korean War, and why the United States was defeated in Vietnam. In 1950 Washington muted its efforts in Korea
because it feared the Asian engagement might be a diversion to
cover a more fateful Soviet campaign in Western Europe. Though
there was a great din in some quarters to invade China or use tactical atomic explosives, the Truman administration held off for fear
that expansion of the conflict would lead to a worldwide explosion
which neither side could win. During the Vietnam War the unreconstructed hawks again demanded that Johnson bomb North Vietnam "into the stone age," but Johnson rejected such advice—not
because he was a "dove" or because he was pursuing a "no-win"

policy, but because the consequences were too shocking to contemplate.

Doris Kearns, Johnson's latest and most perceptive biographer, reports that he chose "step-by-step escalation" because it "would allow continuous monitoring of the reactions by China and Russia." In this way, he told Kearns, "I knew I could keep the control of the war in my hands. If China reacted to our slow escalation by threatening to retaliate, we'd have plenty of time to ease off the bombing. But this control—so essential for preventing World War III—would be lost the moment we unleashed a total assault on the North . . ." Obviously there were limits to what America could do even in a "small" war, since implicit in "small" wars was the possibility they might enlarge into total wars that were unwinnable. To that extent at least, war as the final arbiter between great nations has become obsolete, and will be much more so in future years as nuclear weapons proliferate here, there, and everywhere.

The splitting of the atom has caused a *qualitative* change in human affairs. "The unleashed power of the atom," said Albert Einstein early in the nuclear age, "has changed everything except our way of thinking. Thus we are drifting towards a catastrophe beyond conception." We face a "dilemma," observes Walter Millis, one of the great historians of war, "between the total abolition of the war institution and the total abolition of civilized society." The strategists in Washington try to escape this dilemma by recourse to theories of "limited war," but, as Millis observes, "the problem is unsolved . . . probably because it is insoluble."

The great discoveries of fission and fusion have changed *everything,* all the underlying principles by which human beings group together for protection and fulfillment—everything except "our way of thinking." The most far-reaching technological development of all time—outstripping in importance the discovery of fire, the domestication of animals, agriculture, the industrial revolution —has been treated by the men who engineered the arms race as if it were simply another, albeit grander, expression of human inventiveness. Disregarding the fact that a change of such dimensions has always had vast political and social consequences, American leaders elaborated policy as if the nuclear age were nothing more than a continuation of the pre-nuclear age. Little had been changed, they believed, except in quantitative terms. A blockbuster had the force of ten tons of TNT, a Hiroshima bomb, that of 13,000 tons, but this did not affect the fundamental assumptions on which Western civilization had been built. It merely meant that one weapon had 1,300 times the firepower of another, requiring certain modifications in tactics and strategy, little else.

Military might had been the essence of power for thousands of years; it was inconceivable to America's decision makers that this was no longer so. "In our ever-changing world," said Deputy Secretary of Defense William P. Clements, Jr., recently, "strength means military strength." "By power," said former Congresswoman and ambassador to Italy, Clare Boothe Luce, "I mean the military force that is needed to prevent war, or to win it if it cannot be prevented." Military might is the fulcrum of national security, and any reduction, it is argued, must lead to catastrophe. This is the prevailing thinking around Washington. "A major U.S.S.R. objective," General George S. Brown, Chairman of the Joint Chiefs, told Congress in his posture statement of January 20, 1976, "is to neutralize the U.S. military capability in order to gain economic and military advantage." Conversely, to offset Soviet strategy, "the principal interest of the United States" is to maintain both "adequate current military forces and the necessary long-term programs to sustain them." This is exactly the kind of talk one heard from British leaders during Pax Britannica, long before the atom bomb. Washington refuses to believe there is anything basically new.

War had been, in Karl von Clausewitz' famous dictum, the continuation of politics by other means; it was inconceivable that war could no longer decide which system, capitalism or communism, and which nation, the United States or the Soviet Union, would prevail. Policy makers subscribed to the slogan "There is no *substitute* for victory," when they should have been saying, "There is no *way* to victory." Another barren hypothesis inherited from the past was that the nation-state remains the supreme form of social organization, and that the enhancement of its security and influence is the prime objective of policy. Though the military and economic basis for the nation-state was eroding, it was assumed that nothing more was needed to hold the world in a relatively stable balance than a patchwork of alliances and the loose arrangements of the United Nations. It was simply unbelievable that these linchpins of a bygone day were about to outlive their usefulness.

The cardinal error of postwar Washington, then, has been its failure to recognize that the three axioms of prewar policy, relating to military might, war, and national sovereignty, were invalid for the nuclear age. A triple revolution had bisected history after 1945. The technological and military revolutions confirmed, as Stimson put it, a new relationship "between man and the universe," and hence the need to restructure human relationships as well. Coinciding with the technological and military revolutions, was a national and social revolution many times more extensive than anything in the past, and also demanding a new approach to world affairs. The American Revolution of 1776 had involved a mere three million people, yet its theme of "government by the consent of the governed" had influenced the course of events around the world. How much more profound would be a postwar revolution that would ultimately embrace two *billion* people in six dozen countries? Each of these revolutions, in addition to altering matters at home, de-stabilized relations between the two super-powers—at the very time that the military basis for "deciding" between them was becoming less and less feasible.

In this state of affairs the planet needed a *transition* from national forms of problem solving to international ones, if only because the war institution, which had lost its capacity to "decide," had gained the capacity to kill everyone on earth a dozen times over. But an American leadership, mired in three anachronistic axioms, elaborated a policy on the quicksand of national and bloc interest. In a situation demanding commonality and cohesion it exacerbated the tendencies towards embittered conflict and confrontation. It identified the enemy of its nation-state with undiscerning simplicity as "Soviet Communism," and the main instrument for subduing that enemy, The Bomb. Since the nuclear age was the *antithesis,* rather than the extension, of the pre-nuclear age, it was inevitable, therefore, that American strategy would suffer from myopic ineptitude.

Secretary Byrnes expected to drive the Russians from Eastern Europe by brandishing The Bomb. And when that didn't work, the Truman administration decided to go ahead with a bigger bomb, the Super. With that Super in the U.S. arsenal Secretary Dulles threatened massive retaliation unless the Soviets stayed on their side of the "Line." And when that didn't work and the Line was breached, the threats were modified in bewildering manner—counter-force, flexible response, limited nuclear war, selective response—all to no avail. The Soviet Union could not be waylaid, the world revolution and the disintegration of empire could not be stopped. Episodic victories could be won, especially at the lower rung of the military ladder in CIA coups or proxy wars, but the main battle was not and could not be resolved in America's favor.

Thus American strategy began to resemble a theology. In theology there are certain dogmas which cannot be questioned. The irreducible "truisms" of American strategy were that military might made the nation strong, and war or the threat of war would translate into political victory against the mortal enemy, Soviet Communism. That too was beyond question. Though it was no longer possible to "win" in the accepted sense of the pre-nuclear age, American decision makers formulated a win strategy that rearranged their institutions and behavior patterns in the image of militarism. Technology was given free rein with enormous infusions of money and the co-optation of the largest single segment of scientists and engineers to the military purpose. Since the scale of procurement was unprecedented and "lead time" for new weapons systems, six to eight years, a permanent "defense industry" was fostered and encouraged—and the military, business, bankers, labor leaders, academics, the media, and others who had a financial or ideological stake in that industry were forged into an informal alliance that Eisenhower would call the Military-Industrial Complex. Finally, since an enterprise so vast and foreign goals so all-inclusive required central co-ordination and secretive manipulation, the men of power superimposed on the federal government a second government, the National Security State.

The power of the public over foreign affairs was diminished, that of the Military-Industrial Complex allowed to grow unchecked. The power of Congress to advise and consent was whittled down (at times, as in Vietnam, to the vanishing point), the power of an imperial presidency was enlarged to totalitarian or near totalitarian dimensions. Over three decades, the premises of the Cold War and the nuclear race were ingested into the body politic. The ingestion included a steady dose of anti-Communism from the think-factories and the media, aligned to the Complex; and the steady assurances by men who knew better that since no nuclear war had occurred since 1945 we could go war-less unto eternity playing a game mislabeled "deterrence." Americans became immunized to the permanent emergency, the permanent war economy, the permanent National Security State—hardly realizing that they existed.

The leaders who performed this magic were not lunatics—on the contrary—yet what they set in motion was a lunatic *process,* in which all the participants were sane but all collectively were out of touch with reality. That psychotic process propelled itself; a mammoth constitutency and a grandiose new governmental structure gave it continuing and unending thrust; opponents were overwhelmed with synthetic anti-Communism; anti-Communism was the pretext for more armaments and the "mad momentum" of technology; technology spread the illusion of power; and the illusion reinforced an unrealistic win syndrome, so that the whole cycle repeated itself, with human beings in high places serving as almost impersonal puppets to its magnificent design.

II

The triple revolution of the nuclear age had decreed that humankind must alter its thinking about the values of militarism, war, and sovereignty. Just as the Americans of 1776 could not have made their revolution if they had clung to the old principle of the divine right of kings, so the world today cannot resolve the dilemma "between the total abolition of war and the total abolition of civilized society" without a reappraisal of basic axioms. Is there really such a thing as *national* security? Can *national* borders still be defended? Can the present technology be fitted to the contours of *national* interest? Experience has proven beyond question that the answer to all three is in the negative, yet the American society (and others) refuses to rethink them.

National borders are no longer defendable from chemical or biological agents, from new techniques for modifying weather, from missiles and nuclear warheads. Gas and viruses can cross borders with impunity, an artificial change in weather performed say over Cuba will change weather in other places as well, and a nuclear device that kills between 3.5 and 22 million people in the United States (under Schlesinger's "restrained counter-force" scenario) will also kill 800,000 people in Canada. An all-out war between the two superpowers will kill tens, hundreds of millions of people— or more—in the territory of the non-belligerents on every continent. *National* security and *national* sovereignty are eroding before our eyes, and will erode further as plutonium becomes universally available and a dozen or two dozen more nations join the nuclear club.

Technology, too—at least in its upper reaches—can no longer be reconciled with *national* interest. This is a bitter pill for twentieth-century communities to swallow, because technology has always been viewed as friend, not foe; it was the benevolent force which raised humankind from the insecurity of barbarism to a measure of conspicuous consumption. No one denied that technology has had destructive as well as constructive aspects: a gas flame boils water but can also burn a misplaced finger; a labor-saving machine fabricates ball-point pens, but can also sever a finger; dynamite helps mine coal, build buildings, move mountains to make way for highways, but is also the stuff used by murderers and terrorists. On balance, however, the constructive aspects have far outweighed the destructive ones. Humanity was willing to pay the price of thousands of annual accidents for an industrial system that turned out consumer goods in such torrents.

But with the splitting of the atom the detrimental features have finally overtaken the beneficial ones; and not by a factor of two to one or five to one, but by a factor of infinity to zero, because the survival of a whole species is at stake. It is folly to believe that the technology of nuclear weapons and nuclear energy can be contained within peaceful boundaries. It is a technology suited only— only—to a single world sovereignty. It cannot adjust to the interests, wishes, and behavior of 150 quarreling sovereignties. Sooner or later, this decade or next, or the one after that, someone—here, in Europe, in Asia, in Latin America, perhaps Africa—will put the match to the nuclear firecracker. It is not realistic to believe that two systems, capitalism and communism, or two nations, the United States and the Soviet Union, which have shown such passionate hostility towards each other can avoid a third military confrontation (as in 1918–20, when fourteen powers intervened against the Soviets, or 1941–45, when Germany and the Axis tried it) if they continue to place national interests above everything else. Nor is it realistic to assume that in a revolutionary era a hundred and one intranational crises can be contained, with exemplary discipline, to national or area-wide borders.

Given the present circumstances of a fragmented and bipolar world, the disputes that bedevil nations are bound to erupt into wars and ultimately to breach the firebreak between conventional and nuclear weapons. That, as so many scientists observed three decades ago, represents a basic change in the human condition, in the way people, classes, nations relate to each other, in the way they must adjudicate their differences. A long time ago, Rome defeated Carthage after three Punic Wars, destroying it forever as a viable society, but civilization itself survived, even flourished. The United States cannot destroy the Soviet Union today (or vice versa) and expect civilization to continue. Nor is there any possibility whatsoever that limited nuclear war will fail to graduate, either immediately or after a short period, to total nuclear war. It staggers the imagination to believe that national leaders can conduct a nuclear exchange in the orderly manner Kissinger proposed in his 1957 book, or in the orderly manner Schlesinger envisions in the latest installment of "limited nuclear war" strategy. What technology has provided, national leaders will ultimately use—unless technology, and its greatest accomplishment, The Bomb, are placed under international auspices.

Not only energy and arms proliferation but a host of other functions today demand internationalist solutions. What has become known as the "four P's"—proliferation, pollution, poverty, and population—are problems which cannot be remedied within the national framework. The shortage of food as population mounts worldwide, the pollution of international waterways and air, the endemic poverty of a Third World, which has not yet realized the benefits of its revolution, the impending competition for the rich minerals of the sea, the quest for new raw material sources —all this commands both internationalist collaboration and institutional forms to carry out that collaboration. If the "four P's," on the other hand, remain part of the calculus of Cold War, with each superpower trying to play on adversity for its own purpose, the result can only be the ignition of revolutions and military conflicts in endless profusion.

"I do not wish to seem overdramatic," the late UN Secretary-

General, U Thant, said in 1969, "but I can only conclude . . . that the Members of the United Nations have perhaps ten years left in which to subordinate their ancient quarrels and launch a global partnership to curb the arms race, to improve the human environment, to defuse the population explosion, and to supply the required momentum to development efforts. If such a global partnership is not forged within the next decade, then I very much fear that the problems I have mentioned will have reached such staggering proportions that they will be beyond our capacity to control." U Thant may or may not have judged the timetable correctly—it may take longer than he expected, or it may already be too late— but it is certain that unless these overriding problems are suitably dealt with soon the much cherished status quo, around which American policy has been built, will collapse no matter how many bombs are in the SAC arsenal.

III

Unfortunately, both the theorists of capitalism and those of communism have been unwilling to do the kind of rethinking that Einstein—and many others—suggested was indispensable for the nuclear age. National "security" remains the focus of their concerns.

Henry Kissinger, perhaps the most brilliant exponent of the old order, recognizes that there is, for the moment at least, an insoluble dilemma. "For centuries," he told the Institute of Strategic Studies in London on June 25, 1976, "it was axiomatic that increases in military power could be translated into almost immediate political advantage. It is now clear that in strategic weapons new increments of weapons or destructiveness do not automatically lead to either military or political gains. The destructiveness of strategic weapons has contributed to a nuclear stalemate." This is another way of saying that war between the United States and the Soviet Union is unwinnable, and the threat of such a war, politically valueless. Kissinger would not have admitted this fifteen or twenty years ago, when he was promoting the nostrum of *limited* nuclear war against the Soviets. Yet, having confirmed the point that military power no longer translates into political advantage, he finds his way out of the dilemma today by . . . bypassing it.

"The strategic balance," he advised a meeting of American ambassadors stationed in Europe, "provides increased opportunity for *regional* pressure" (emphasis added). Though a total war cannot be won or threatened, Kissinger still believes that America can apply military, economic, and other pressures to win partial victories on a regional basis—say in the Middle East or Africa.

This is the essence of the Kissinger-Nixon policy of "détente" and of the present strategy of selective response and limited nuclear war: whittle away at Soviet power until it becomes vulnerable to the final blow, or until the United States achieves a decisive technological breakthrough that may make total victory possible. The dreams of emperors, monarchial and republican, die hard.

Soviet leaders, too, seem to be motivated by "national security," waiting for economic crisis in the West and the decomposition of American influence overseas, to expand their own national power. The rhetoric of Leonid Brezhnev stresses the unwinnability of strategic war just as does that of American leaders. "The very idea of using nuclear weapons in the territory of Europe," he told a meeting of Communist parties in June 1976, "seems monstrous to the Soviet people. . . . Therefore we Communists . . . believe that it is now more important than ever before to pave the way for the relaxation of military tensions and to stop the arms race." But in practice the Soviet leader has hailed the Vladivostok agreement, between himself and Ford, which sets strategic arms targets two or three times higher than present ones. Soviet scientists pursue technological breakthrough with the same avidity as American ones. It is also significant that not since the late 1950's, when the Kremlin placed a temporary ban on its own nuclear testing, has the Kremlin taken a meaningful unilateral step towards disarmament. "Détente"—the relaxation of tensions—is for Moscow a waiting game, and while the Kremlin does not speak of exercising "regional pressures," it hopes that wars of national liberation and a turn to the left in developing countries, simultaneous with economic depression in the Western World, will undercut American power drastically. It has made no recent proposals for scrapping the nuclear stockpile or placing the atom under the control of an international authority. Like Washington, Moscow views the world from the prism of national interests.

Perhaps the most interesting approach to the current dilemma is that of the Chinese Communists. In an interview after a trip to China in early 1976, William Hinton, chairman of the U.S.-China Peoples Friendship Association and Peking's leading spokesman in the United States, reported that "the thinking in China is that short of revolution in the U.S. and the U.S.S.R., a third world war is inevitable." It is not likely to happen in the next three to five years, but is possible within ten and certain within thirty. Oddly enough the main enemy, in the Chinese view, is Russia, which in the Maoist lexicon is a "social imperialist" country. on the rise, while the United States is a "capital imperialist" country in decline. According to Hinton, the feeling in Peking "is that a major world war might well be fought with conventional arms. Even a nuclear war will not destroy mankind. 'Mankind will destroy the bomb, the bomb will not destroy mankind.' At least half the human race will survive." Hinton ends on the cheery note that "war will hasten revolution and revolution will solve problems that have long been unsolved." If the Chinese really think that World War III will be confined to conventional engagements between opposing planes and tanks, they are the only ones who do; not even the Pentagon would subscribe to that prognosis. And to look upon a war of the expected magnitude of World War III with such studied equanimity, because it will spark revolution, is startling to say the least.

It is highly doubtful that a war which kills off as many as two billion people (of a world population of four billion) will end in anything but the cries of the sick and the lash of a dictator demanding more work to bury the dead and speed "recovery." A salutary revolution that heals wounds and lays the groundwork for a better life is hardly a likely outcome from such a tragedy. What is instructive, however, about the Chinese analysis—assuming the Hinton account is accurate and that the policy is not changed now that Mao Tse-tung is dead—is that it offers no solutions to the dilemma of our times other than . . . "damage-limitation,"—save as many Chinese lives as possible so that after the "inevitable" war they may be able to reorganize the world along Marxist lines.

International revolution may be the answer to militarism, but if it is, it will have to take place before Doomsday, not afterwards. In any case, if the Communists—Soviet and Chinese both—were less dogmatic, they might realize that U Thant's "global partnership" is, in fact, itself a revolution, THE revolution. In the course of internationalizing the atom—and a half dozen other functions—the nations of the world will be forced to introduce worldwide economic planning, and various measures of an egalitarian nature. Among other things, the atom also dictates another type of revolutionary strategy, not necessarily outdating the national and social revolutions in developing countries, but adding to them an international dimension.

IV

Is there any hope for avoiding Doomsday?

The first prerequisite is to shed the illusion that war can be abolished so long as the war system and national war machineries continue to exist. Back in 1928, on the initiative of French Foreign Minister Aristide Briand and U.S. Secretary of State Frank Kellogg, fifteen leading nations (and sixty-three in all) signed the Pact of Paris, renouncing war as an instrument of policy. Many people felt this was a substantive move—the Boston *Herald* stated: "It is a thing to rejoice over, it is superb, it is magnificent. We should sing the *Te Deum Laudamus* . . ."—but in fact, as history proved a decade later, it was an empty and deceptive gesture. It would be a fatal mistake today to foster similar illusions, say by a declaration against "first use" of nuclear weapons. Such a declaration could only be of value if accompanied by meaningful acts towards controlling the atom and actual disarmament.

The obvious starting point for a reversal of the nuclear arms race is recognition that humankind generally and the United States specifically must replace the obsolete dogmas concerning war, military power, and national sovereignty, with new principles. If war and military power are no longer viable instruments for "national security" then a new set of institutions is required that will take the machinery of violence—nuclear violence in particular—out of the hands of the nation-state and put it into the hands of the international community.

The 1946 Baruch Plan for internationalizing nuclear energy (and ridding the world of atomic weapons) could have been a major step in that direction, if it had not been perverted into a ploy to assert the dominance of one nation, the United States. A genuine Baruch Plan is still the first order of business for human-kind. It would be far more difficult to implement today than in 1946, when there were no power reactors operating and only a small number of warheads at the disposal of the United States. But there are limited steps currently under way to curb the plutonium economy, and there is hope that these can be broadened. The present campaign by environmentalists to roll back the nuclear energy industry and concentrate on non-nuclear forms of energy production, such as solar energy, seems to be gaining momentum. An ever growing segment of the public, here and abroad, has become alarmed over the danger of accidents that can contaminate large areas with radioactivity and kill thousands of people in a single mishap. "The Paris-based Organization for Economic Cooperation and Development," reports the New York *Times* (August 12, 1976), "recently issued revised figures for atomic power plant capacity in its 23-nation developed-country membership, showing a cut of nearly 20 percent in plans for nuclear energy output by 1985." McKinley C. Olson, in his book, *Unacceptable Risk,* relates the story of the environmentalist protest, and concludes optimistically that "in the space of four short years, from 1972 to 1976, the tables had turned. And the powerful nuclear establishment which had once seemed omnipotent was beginning to run scared. Suddenly, in some circles, as if overnight, the word 'moratorium' . . . sounded almost passé. And one could hear the word 'phaseout' instead."

Blending with the environmentalist crusade is the disquiet expressed in Congress by such figures as Senator Ribicoff and ex-Senator Symington on the dangers of proliferation. These are flank attacks on the nuclear arms race, which have the effect—if successful—of denying plutonium to dozens of nations that might use them for atomic weapons production. What the situation calls for, beyond these limited activities, is a revival of the Ban The Bomb movement that will, among other things, revive the agitation for an authentic Baruch Plan. There is no such movement on the scene today, apart from the traditional pacifist groups—the War Resisters League, the American Friends Service Committee, the Fellowship of Reconciliation, and a few others who joined forces in 1976 to conduct a half-year-long "Continental Walk" to dramatize the need for nuclear disarmament. Whether there will be another surge of the anti-war movement, as in the 1960's, remains to be seen; but it should be noted that the largest anti-war protest in U.S. history, that against Vietnam, was preceded by many small actions like the Continental Walk, appealing to—and evidently affecting to an extent—the national conscience.

There is no end of transitional objectives—transitional towards full-scale disarmament—that a Ban The Bomb movement can promote with a fair chance of popular, even mainstream, support. High on such a list would be *unilateral* reduction of the U.S. nuclear stockpile from its present level of 30,000 warheads. An educational program that could convince Americans that the strategy of "deterrence" as now stated is a hoax, might also convince them that *stable* deterrence—the balance of terror stalemate—requires nothing more than a half dozen nuclear submarines capable of retaliating with a "second strike." Any single Poseidon submarine, and certainly any single Trident, can effectively devastate any nation on earth—and such submarines will remain invulnerable for at least another fifteen or twenty years. Even those who believe in a posture of deterrence should be able to see the wisdom of a drastic cutback in the nuclear arsenal. All that is needed is to create a climate for rational thinking on the subject.

There are hundreds of men and women, formerly part of the "defense" establishment and defenders of its policies, who have had a change of heart and can be enlisted in the drive for unilateral cutbacks. Clark Clifford, Secretary of Defense under Johnson, is one such man. Sitting in his posh law office within sight of the White House, he stated in 1976 that "you reach a point, as Churchill once said, where the bombs only make the rubble bounce." He was convinced that the number of nuclear warheads could be reduced to a very small fraction of the present number— "I know a scientist who says that fifty is enough and a military leader who puts the figure at four hundred"—without any harm to "national security."

A similar view is held by McGeorge Bundy, who served Kennedy and Johnson as Special Assistant for National Security Affairs. "Think-tank analysts," says Bundy, "can set levels of 'acceptable' damage well up in the tens of millions of lives. . . . They are in an unreal world. In the real world of real political leaders—whether here or in the Soviet Union—a decision that would bring even one hydrogen bomb on one city of one's own country would be recognized in advance as a catastrophic blunder; ten bombs on ten cities would be a disaster beyond history; and a hundred bombs on a hundred cities are unthinkable." The list of mainstream people who have come around to a position of this sort—or who have always held it—is long: Paul Warnke, a former Assistant Secretary of Defense; Admiral Gene LaRocque (ret.); Brigadier General Bertram Gorwitz (ret.); Herbert Scoville, once a top official at CIA and at Defense; Adrian Fisher, former deputy director of the arms control agency, and Herbert York, former director of Research and Engineering under Eisenhower and Kennedy, to mention only a few. But partial disarmament is not enough; as long as the military bureaucracy, including the research and development bureaucracy, remains in place, any international crisis can serve the Administration as a pretext for armament re-escalation. Nonetheless, any action that reverses the arms race can also provide momentum for the next steps, including the internationalization of the atom and multilateral disarmament. Additionally, it would certainly apply massive worldwide pressure on the Soviets to negotiate a genuine disarmament pact.

There are other transitional steps that make sense and hold the promise of success for a revived anti-war movement. During the 1976 presidential race, Democratic candidate Jimmy Carter called for a five-year moratorium on all nuclear testing, including underground testing no matter how small the device. Again, that is not enough, but if candidates and Presidents can be pressured to implement a full test ban, that would have further ramifications. Protest actions against the sale of arms to foreign countries and the training of foreign troops, or for closing of foreign bases, or for the dismantling of the National Security State, or for removal of tactical nuclear weapons—indeed any effort that weakens the Military-Industrial Complex and withdraws the American military presence from its present bastions, can have the salutary effect of stimulating further protest. At a certain point it will decisively reverse an arms race which never should have been permitted to begin.

The overall objective of a world without war requires a revolution in thinking and action more complex than the one for disarmament. But the starting point there, too, is to create counter-constituencies against the military-industrial establishment. Nothing can change on this planet unless and until the people themselves, here and abroad, take matters into their own hands. Shortly after his inauguration in 1961, Kennedy met with a group of Quakers who asked him to initiate programs for disarmament. Kennedy told them that if they could mobilize public opinion to shout itself hoarse for disarmament, he would lead their crusade. His advice is still appropriate. The political leaders of the world have failed to give leadership; only popular dissent can stir them to do what they should have been doing for decades.

Decision makers are enmeshed in their own follies, as attested to by the conclusions of a 1976 annual conference of the International Institute of Strategic Studies—made up of experts from Western Europe, the United States, Canada, Japan, and a few developing countries. Dr. Christoph Bertram, a West German defense expert and director of the Institute, told a news conference, as summarized by the New York *Times* (September 14, 1976), "that a new era is beginning, that many of the old rules of the world game are no longer workable but that nobody has yet figured out the new rules. . . . The people who spend their time studying the hard facts that lead to war no longer have even theoretical solutions for achieving what was once promised as a generation of peace."

The void left by a floundering leadership must be filled by a public passion for change—beginning with the recognition that we are at the day before Doomsday, and that no minor changes can be useful unless they are related to deeper changes in the way we —people and nations—relate to each other.

Every revolution begins as an idea. The twin concept of internationalizing the atom and disarming its errant children, the bombs, is an idea whose time has come. That revolution will ensue if the peoples of each country apply the requisite pressures on their governments to enter U Thant's "global partnership." This does not mean that workers will forgo their right to strike for a twenty-five-cent-an-hour wage increase, or that blacks, Chicanos, and native Americans will stop marching in the streets to end discrimination, or that Americans will call off picket lines in front of the South African embassy. On the contrary. But all of this must be packaged and focused into a single quest to disarm the world's nuclear armies and to forge simultaneously the institutions of global commonality.

The nuclear race is all but out of control! It is an impersonal lunacy in the process of fulfilling itself. Once we come to recognize that fact, impressive conclusions follow. The first is that neither Russia nor Communism can possibly threaten American or Western interests as much as the win syndrome and the nuclear technology with which it is linked. Assuming the worst, nothing that the Kremlin can do to the American people, short of committing suicide itself, can possibly hurt as much as continuation of the arms race. If that is understood, perhaps the cool air of reason can begin to be applied; and in their own *self*-interest the Soviet Union and the United States may strive to establish the "trust" that Henry Stimson urged on Harry Truman in 1945–46. The only way to win trust is to give it, by each side relinquishing something on its own—unilateral initiatives towards peace—until both feel comfortable enough with each other to multilaterally negotiate the destruction of nuclear explosives and the internationalization of nuclear energy. By acting on trust we (and the Russians) can achieve what the Baruch Plan was unable to achieve because it was a subterfuge for "winning" rather than a sincere effort towards "global partnership." *National* security today is impossible without *international* security, including the security of Russians, Chinese, Africans, Asians, Latin Americans, Americans.

A second conclusion is that present forms of capitalism and present forms of communism are doomed to extinction. They will die in a mushroom cloud if world war occurs, and they will be transformed into a type of society never seen before if humankind moves towards global commonality. What we are defending on both sides of the international equation is something that is indefensible; and the very fierceness with which we have been defending it attests to our lack of thinking about the new relations between our species and historical evolution. We have been—on both sides—defending a fantasy.

A third conclusion is that Americans need defense against their own leadership more urgently than defense against a foreign invasion. That is so not because the men in power are personally evil, but first because they have wandered so far from realism they can no longer be returned to it, and second because a win-oriented government in the nuclear age must necessarily suppress popular checks on its power. It was a lack of vigilance (the eternal price of liberty) that brought us to this pass; that vigilance must now be restored, for instance, by breathing life into Article 1 Section 8 of the Constitution, by demanding the right to vote on military engagements, by curbing and abolishing the CIA, by de-monarchizing the presidency.

It is difficult to think in new terms, difficult to overcome anti-Communist fears that have lasted nearly six decades; difficult to subordinate nationalistic pride—ingrained for two centuries—to an allegiance to humankind; difficult to disentangle ourselves from the clichés that have weakened our intelligence (e.g., "better dead than red"). It is difficult to convince "practical" people that a revolutionary departure from the past is not a "pipedream".

The nuclear age, however, gives us no choice. The human species has become victim to its own genius, and must therefore subdue its inner greeds and its outer ambitions, or perish.

Index

ABOUT THE AUTHOR

A leader in the labor movement for many years, Sidney Lens has been an editor of *Liberation* magazine and contributing editor to *The Progressive*. He has published articles in numerous other magazines and newspapers, and is the author of seventeen books on trade unionism, Communism, and the American Left.

Lens has devoted much energy to the effort toward world peace and nuclear disarmament, and co-chaired the New Mobilization Committee to End the War in Vietnam.

A resident of Northbrook, Illinois, he speaks at universities across the country, and on television and radio.